PAR4
GRAPH

SENTENCE

THE WORLD'S BEST
TYPOGRAPHY 2018
The 39th Annual of the Type Directors Club

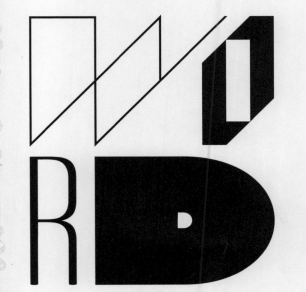

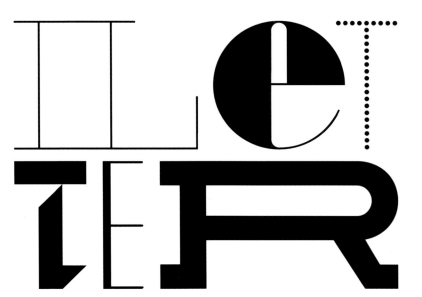

TABLE OF CONTENTS

TDC MEDAL GERARD UNGER

DUTCH MODERN STYLE
BY PAUL SHAW

Gerard Unger is a type designer's type designer. Although he has been designing typefaces for nearly half a century, he is not well known beyond his native Holland and the University of Reading Department of Typography and Graphic Communications, where he has taught since 1994. But in the formerly small world of type design Unger has long been regarded with great respect for his singular vision in creating typefaces marked by simplicity and clarity combined with grace. Unger is one of the rare type designers whose body of work, with a single exception, evinces a coherent aesthetic.

From Markeur (1972) to Sanserata (2016), Unger's career has been an ongoing quest to make supremely legible typefaces. However, he has not simply honed one design over and over again in pursuit of a Platonic ideal; instead he has applied what he has learned about legibility to both serif and sans serif types. In this respect, Unger's work has been part of the modernist quest. For a typeface, improved legibility leads to improved readability, which, in turn, means improved functionality.

The chief characteristics of Unger typefaces are large counters, lateral apertures, tall x-heights, simple joins, elegant curves, low stroke contrast, and strong serifs. In the digital era many of these features have become commonplace, adopted by other designers, but in combination they make

Centraal Station

Bijlmer HOayW
PRO AMWO
Hgx St
Qknx
unZu
MWA

Santa Croce in
Gerusalemme

Colosseo

Ponte Sisto

The archetypal Unger letter

a typeface unmistakably Ungerian. In fact, it can be argued that Unger's types have, consciously or not, been a primary influence on type design since the 1990s.

Unger was born in 1942, in the midst of World War II, in Arnhem in the Netherlands. He attended the famed Gerrit Rietveld Academie in Amsterdam and then went to work as an assistant to the modernist apostle Wim Crouwel at Total Design. It was there that Unger—in rebellion against the incessant use of Akzidenz Grotesk, Helvetica, and Univers—began to develop his deep interest in legibility. His break from the modernist sans serif triumvirate is already evident in the design of Markeur, his first typeface, distinguished by laterally open apertures. But it is with M.O.L. (1974), designed for signage on the Amsterdam metro system, that Unger first began experimenting with the counters of letters to improve legibility.

Unger's career as a type designer began at a moment of transition for the industry. Not only was photocomposition finally pushing out metal, but digital type was in its infancy. His first text typefaces were designed under contract with Dr.-Ing. Rudolf Hell GmbH for the Digiset, the first typesetting machine to assemble characters from bitmaps. The bitmaps were coarse and final output was still photographic, two factors that encouraged Unger to continue his experiments

with enlarged counters in the design of Demos (1976) and Praxis (1977). Both faces are also marked by a tall x-height, low stroke contrast, and sharp junctures. Although large x-height typefaces were the fashion in the 1970s, spurred by the theories promulgated by the International Typeface Corporation (ITC), in Unger's designs they were a direct outgrowth of his pursuit of larger counters. Demos and Praxis were designed, respectively, as a serif and sans serif pair—the first such combination to reach market, a decade before Lucida and ITC Stone.

Due to the limitations of early bitmapping methods, Demos, Unger's first serif typeface, has sturdy, minimally bracketed, and slightly stubby serifs. By 1983 when he designed Hollander, technology had improved. Instead of bitmaps built up by hand, characters were drawn in outline using the Ikarus program developed by Peter Karow, and then output with laser beams instead of cathode ray beams. That allowed Hollander, inspired by the seventeenth-century types of Christoffel van Dijck, to have longer, bracketed serifs. Swift (1985; redesigned 1995), his last typeface for Hell, also has long serifs, though they are more trapezoidal in form.

Swift is one of the signature typefaces of the digital era. It is an original design with features that are neither indebted to historical forms nor overly tied to a specific technology. It feels wholly modern

yet has a palpable, if undefinable, link to the past. It is the Unger typeface that has deservedly garnered the most praise and the widest use. Although designed for newspapers, like Times New Roman before it, Swift has found greater use in periodicals. Unger's preoccupation with legibility and the impact of large counters culminated in Gulliver (1993), another typeface designed for newspapers. In order to save space it also has short serifs and an extremely large x-height.

A majority of Unger's typefaces have been designed for either signage (Markeur, M.O.L., ANWB, Capitolium, and Vesta) or newspapers (Swift, Gulliver, Coranto, and Capitolium News), two areas where his interest in legibility has proven essential. Although only Sanserata has been designed specifically for screen use, virtually all of his types function well in that realm since the features that make them work for newspapers and signs transfer perfectly to the screen.

With the exception of the ANWB signage typeface (1997), Unger has been able to pursue his singular vision unhampered by the demands of clients for nearly fifty years. During that time he has maintained his aesthetic while working within the changing constraints of technology. He has also, on occasion, bent historic forms to meet that aesthetic. Four of his typefaces (Hollander, Capitolium, Paradox, and Alverata) have roots in the past, but none of them can be accurately called a revival. They remain stubbornly Ungerian.

Early in his career Unger was fascinated by the late nineteenth-century American gothics he found in *Types of the De Vinne Press* (1907). A sample phrase in the showing of Gothic Condensed No. 240 in that book anticipated Unger's philosophy of type design: "Simplicity is desirable / But legibility is even more important." For his lifelong dedication to that spirit, the Type Directors Club is pleased to award its 30th TDC Medal of Excellence to Gerard Unger.

CHRONOLOGICAL LIST OF GERARD UNGER'S TYPE DESIGNS

1972	Markeur (Joh. Enschedé & Zonen)
1974	M.O.L. (Amsterdam Metro)
1976	Demos (Dr.-Ing. Rudolf Hell GmbH)
1977	Praxis (Dr.-Ing. Rudolf Hell GmbH)
1983	Hollander (Dr.-Ing. Rudolf Hell GmbH)
1984	ITC Flora (International Typeface Corporation)
1985	Swift (Dr.-Ing. Rudolf Hell GmbH)
1986	Amerigo (Bitstream)
1987	Oranda (Bitstream; originally designed for Océ)
1991	Argo (Dutch Type Library)
1991	Delftse Poort (Nationale Nederlanden)
1992	Decoder (FontShop)
1993	Gulliver
1995	Swift 2.0
1997	ANWB fonts
1998	Capitolium (commissioned by n | p | k design firm)
1999	Paradox (Dutch Type Library)
2000	Coranto
2001	Vesta
2003	Big Vesta
2005	Allianz (in collaboration with Veronika Burian; commissioned by Claus Koch)
2006	Capitolium News
2008	Leiden Letters (Academiegebouw of Leiden University)
2013	Alverata (TypeTogether)
2016	Sanserata

COMMUNICATION DESIGN

CHAIRMEN'S STATEMENT

The world-renowned competition of the Type Directors Club is now in its 64th year and our printed annual showcasing the winners has been published continuously for almost 40 years. Keeping with the sequential numbering of the annual, the book you're holding should be titled *Typography 39*. But last year, for the first time ever, the TDC annual also included a subtitle: *The World's Best Typography*. When we became co-chairs for this year's competition, the new subtitle got us thinking, *What does it mean to be the World's Best?*

To identify the world's best typography you must first cast a world-wide net. This year we attracted 1835 entries from 55 different countries, featuring work in dozens of different languages.

Once you have breadth, via an amazing pool of entries, you need a jury that has the expertise and acuity to dive deep and identify the best of the best. We chose each of our seven judges not just for their incredible work or critical eye, but also because they energize our community as mentors, innovators, and thought leaders.

At the end of each year's competition, the winning work is showcased in an exhibition that starts in New York City and then travels the world—it visited over 50 cities last year. Even as co-chairs who had shepherded the entire competition from beginning to end, we didn't fully realize the impact that the final collection of winning work had until we attended the opening in New York. It was—and is—awe-inspiring.

So this year, we are making it official. For the first time in almost 40 years, we've changed the title of the annual. The World's Best Typography is now collected in a book called just that. We hope you are as inspired as we are by this incredible picture of the future of typography. Thank you to our judges and to everyone who entered, and congratulations to all of the winners!

**CATHERINE CASALINO &
CHRISTOPHER SERGIO**

CATHERINE CASALINO

CO-CHAIR / COMMUNICATION DESIGN

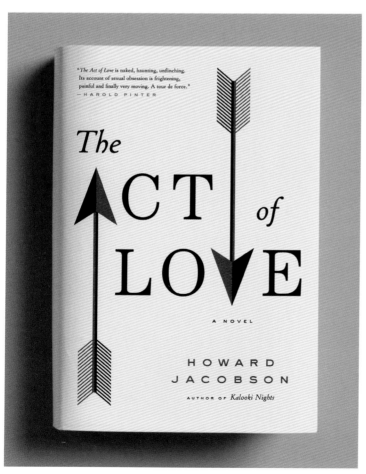

Catherine Casalino is the principal and Creative Director of Casalino Design Inc, an independent design company in New York City focusing on print, book design, and branding. Casalino Design Inc's clients include Penguin Random House, A&E Television, Simon & Schuster, IBM, HarperCollins, Hachette Book Group, Epic Media, and *The New York Times*. Casalino has worked in-house at Grand Central Publishing, Random House, and Simon & Schuster as an Art Director and Designer, and began her career at Rodrigo Corral Design. Her work has been recognized by the Type Directors Club, AIGA, *Print* magazine, *Communication Arts*, *Eye* magazine, and the New York Book Show.

website: catherinecasalino.com
instagram: @cat.casalino
twitter: @c_casalino

CHRISTOPHER SERGIO

CO-CHAIR / COMMUNICATION DESIGN

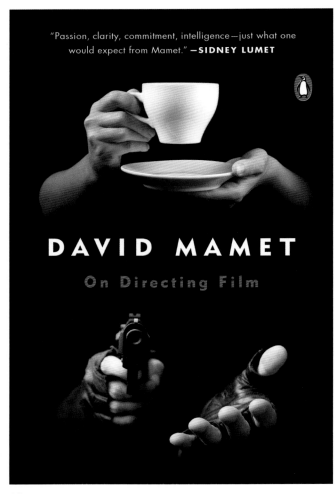

Christopher Sergio is a VP Art Director at Penguin Random House and also runs Christopher Sergio Design, a freelance design studio that focuses on design for print, book covers, and film. Previously, he has worked in-house at Simon & Schuster and Random House as an Art Director and Designer, as well as in the arts, with theater artist Robert Wilson. Chris is an executive board member of the Type Directors Club, a frequent lecturer and design jurist, and has won numerous awards in recognition of his work, including from AIGA, *Print* magazine, *Communication Arts,* and the Type Directors Club. He is an alumnus of the Rhode Island School of Design and LaGuardia High School of Music and Art and Performing Arts, and is a New York City native.

website: csergiodesign.com
instagram: @csergiodesign

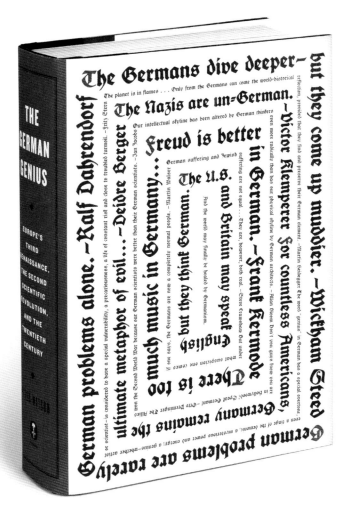

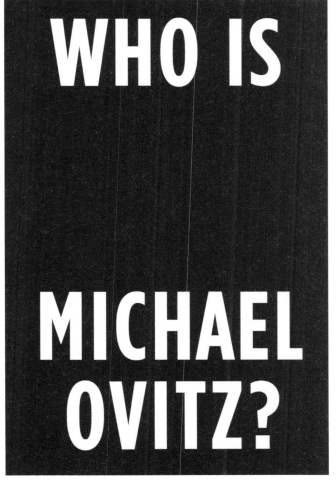

MEET THE JUDGES

NICHOLAS BLECHMAN

Nicholas Blechman is a New York–based art director and illustrator. Since 2015, he has been the Creative Director of *The New Yorker*. Blechman is the former Art Director of *The New York Times Book Review* and *The New York Times* Op-Ed page. Since 1990 he has published, edited, and designed the political underground magazine *NOZONE*, featured in the Smithsonian Institution's National Design Triennial. His illustrations have appeared in *GQ*, *Travel + Leisure*, and *Wired*. In 2012, Blechman won the Rome Prize in Design at The American Academy in Rome, where he created a *Food Chains*, an illustrated blog for *The New York Times*. He co-authors "One Hundred Percent,"a series of limited-edition illustrated books, with Christoph Niemann. The latest in this series, "Conversations," was published in 2017. His work was included in an exhibit at The Met museum titled "Talking Pictures."

website: nicholasblechman.com
instagram: @nblechman
twitter: @nblechman

Mike Essl is a graphic designer, educator, and Mr. T memorabilia collector. With over twenty years in the field, Essl's bold approach has earned him equal acclaim for his elevation of comic books with DC Comics and Rizzoli as for websites with Wikipedia and San Francisco Opera. At The Chopping Block (co-founded 1996) and on his own, Essl led projects that were featured by the AIGA, ComicCon, the Cooper Hewitt, and MoMA. Essl's illustrations have been included in the *New York Times, New York Magazine,* and the Yale University Art Gallery, and his outspoken commentary has been featured on Design Matters with Debbie Millman, The Howard Stern Show, and VH1's Totally Obsessed. Essl is presently the Acting Dean of the Cooper Union School of Art, where he has been an Associate Professor of graphic design since 2002.

website: mike.essl.com
instagram: @EsslMike
twitter: @Essl

21

BRYONY GOMEZ-PALACIO

Born and raised in Mexico City, Bryony Gomez-Palacio is a graphic designer and writer now living in Bloomington, Indiana. She is co-founder of UnderConsideration—a graphic design firm and publishing enterprise all rolled into one—where she manages the behind-the-scenes of the online network comprising Brand New, FPO, Quipsologies, and The Art of the Menu. Bryony has co-authored five books with her husband and partner, Armin Vit—their most popular titles being *Graphic Design, Referenced* and the self-published *Flaunt*. Most recently, they conceived and presented the Brand New Conference, the Brand New Awards, the FPO Awards, and the recently launched lecture series by The Austin Initiative for Graphic Awesomeness. Bryony enjoys conducting workshops and lecturing when not tending to her two young daughters and their crazy schedules.

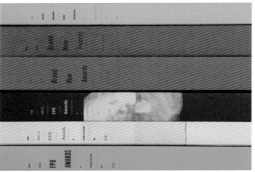

UNDERCONSIDERATION
website: underconsideration.com
instagram: @ucllc
twitter: @ucllc

BRAND NEW CONFERENCE
website: underconsideration.com/
brandnewconference
instagram: @bnconf
twitter: @bnconf

twitter: @bryonygp

NATASHA JEN

Natasha Jen is a graphic designer, educator, and partner at Pentagram New York. Born in Taipei, Taiwan, her work is recognized for its innovative use of graphic, digital, and spatial interventions that challenge the critical bounding assumptions surrounding media and culture. In 2015, Natasha was named one of the "World's Nine Leading Designers" by *Wired* magazine. She teaches at the School of Visual Arts and and has been a guest critic at Yale University, School of Art, Rhode Island School of Design, and Maryland Institute College of Art. She serves on the Board of Directors for Storefront for Art and Architecture and previously AIGA New York.

website: pentagram.com / njenworks.com
instagram: @njenworks
twitter: @njenworks

JONATHAN KEY

Jon(athan) Key is an art director, designer, and writer. His collaborations have led him to work with a diverse set of clients and institutions as designer, educator, and artist, including HBO, Nickelodeon, IDEO, Grey Advertising, The Public Theater, MICA, American University in Beirut, Parsons, and the Whitney Museum. His creative pursuits have allowed his work to be featured internationally in galleries, museums, and collections in Boston, Toronto, New York, London, and Ljubljana, Slovenia. He currently serves as a contributing art director to *The Tenth* magazine, a black, queer arts, and culture magazine, and he just launched Morcos Key, a design studio, with his partner Wael Morcos. Jon is a co-founder and the design director of Codify Art, a Brooklyn-based multidisciplinary artist collective whose mission is to create, produce, and showcase work that foregrounds the voices of people of color, highlighting women and queer people of color. He is a graduate of the Rhode Island School of Design, where he received a Bachelor of Fine Arts in Graphic Design.

website: MorcosKey.com
JonKey.co
instagram: @Jkey13
@morcoskey
twitter: @JonKey13
@morcoskey

GEMMa O'BRiEN

Over the past ten years, Australian designer and artist Gemma O'Brien has taken her passion for typography and built a flourishing career around drawing letters. Her bold type, expressive calligraphy, and detailed illustration can be seen in advertising campaigns, editorial publications, and large-scale murals in galleries and interiors around the world. A number of her projects have received the Award of Typographic Excellence from the Type Directors Club. In 2015, she was recognized as an ADC Young Gun, and in 2016 she was named one of *Print* magazine's New Visual Artists: 15 under 30. She has collaborated with numerous global brands and publications, including Apple, Adobe, Westfield, Volcom Stone, Oreo, QANTAS, L'Oréal, *Entertainment Weekly*, *Playboy*, and *The New York Times*. Beyond her commercial work, Gemma O'Brien is a regular speaker at international conferences and also hosts hand-lettering workshops at design schools, agencies, and events.

website:	gemmaobrien.com
instagram:	@mrseaves101
twitter:	@mrseaves

SUSAN SELLERS

Susan Sellers is a Founding Partner and Executive Creative Director at 2x4, a design firm that focuses on strategy, design, and brand development for forward-thinking creative brands and organizations globally. Sellers views design as an inquiry into the ideas and values implicit in the built environment, an elaborated journalism that unpacks and retells the world in evocative, informative, immersive experiences. Her work spans the urban, cultural, and commercial—integrating print, screen, and architecture. From 2012 to 2016, Sellers served as Head of Design at the Metropolitan Museum of Art, leading design for the opening of the landmark Marcel Breuer Building, The Met Breuer, exhibition and the museum's new brand identity. Sellers is Senior Critic in Graphic Design at Yale School of Art in New Haven, Connecticut. Sellers received a B.F.A. in Graphic Design from the Rhode Island School of Design in 1989 and an M.A. in American Studies from Yale University in 1994.

website: 2x4.org
twitter: @2x4

JUDGES' CHOICES

BEST OF THE 20

STUDENT AWARDS

Bryony Gomez-Palacio

The proportion and thickness of this book caught my attention from across the room. I was drawn by the overly simplistic cover that revealed nothing about what I was about to encounter on the inside—pages upon pages of beautiful typography and exquisite production. Even though I was unable to read the text due to the language barrier, I found myself perusing each spread, touching the paper, interacting with the folds, admiring the depth of details that kept on giving. This is a book that serves as an example of what is possible when design and production come together for a common goal— a visual representation of careful planning, consideration, and, above all, an understanding of positive and negative space within a page. This book is a true delight to the senses.

BEST IN SHOW + JUDGE'S CHOICE

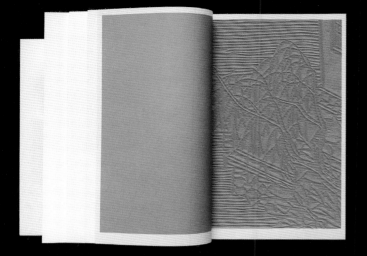

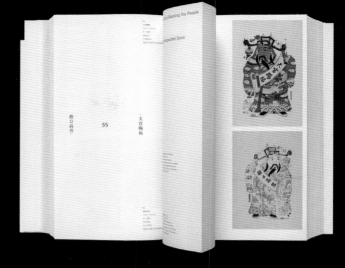

**THE RECORD OF SUZHOU'S
PROSPERITY: COLLECTED
WORKS OF SUZHOU TAOHUAWU
WOODBLOCK NEW YEAR
PAINTING EXHIBITION**

Books

DESIGN
Qingting Guo
Yu Zhang,
Beijing

ART DIRECTION
Xiaoxiang Liu

STUDIO
XXL Studio

PRINCIPAL TYPE
FZSongYi
FZShuSong
Adobe Jenson Pro

DIMENSIONS
8.6 x 13.3 in.
(21.9 × 33.8 cm)

CONCEPT
The special binding of this book was designed in accordance with the
content, which has complex hierarchies. It improves on the traditional
Chinese wrapped ridge binding. After appropriate page arrangement,
the extra thickness of accordion folding pages is balanced, so the
book can still keep flat. To simplify production, the short French
folding pages and accordion folding pages were folded by one paper,
and therefore measure less than 1 meter—the maximum size of the
printing machine. The two carving sharp shapes on the Swiss-style
cut-flush binding cover also match the theme.

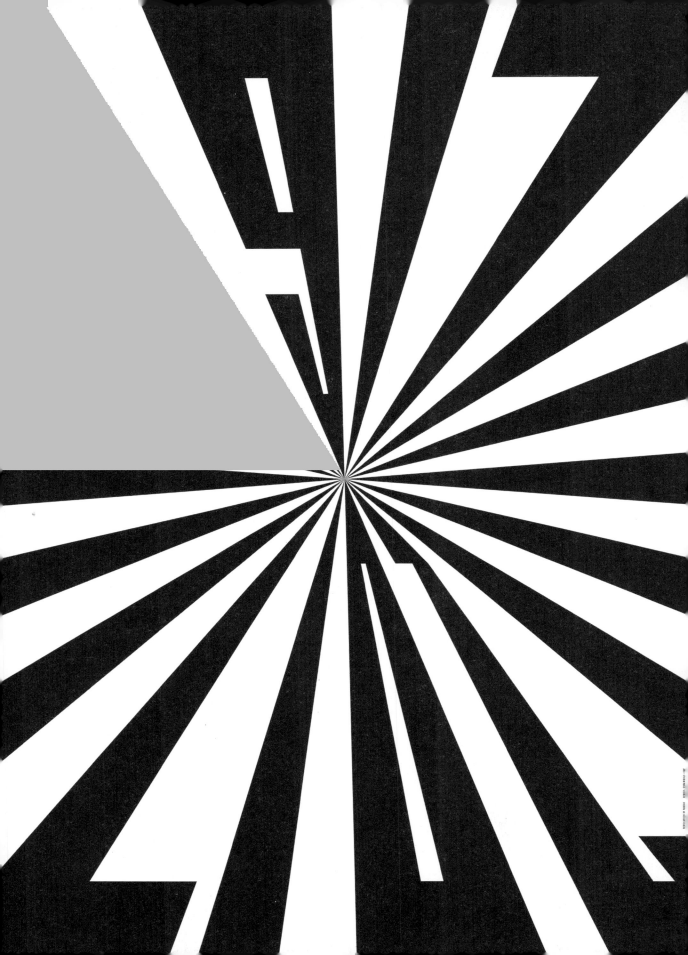

Nicholas Blechman

In an era of visual clutter and popup ads, this poster cuts through the surrounding noise with a graphic clarity and strength that is rare. The 1917–2017 poster is both retro and contemporary. It bridges the gap between past and present, echoing Russian Constructivist design on the one hand, and modern minimalism on the other. To fully appreciate this poster is to see it in person. After a weary two days of judging everything from zines to animation, this poster stood out. This is partly due to its size, a massive 35.2 x 50.4 inches. Its tactility is even more impressive when you realize it is silkscreened. This nod to craft and physicality, in a period of impermanence and Instagram, speaks to the integrity of the designer. I've been following Cybu Richli's work for some time and was particularly pleased to discover that he and his firm, C2F, were behind this poster.

RUSSIAN REVOLUTION
1917–2017

Posters

DESIGN DIRECTION
Cybu Richli,
Luzern

URL
c2f.ch

STUDIO
C2F

CLIENT
Serge Serov,
Moscow

PRINCIPAL TYPE
Custom

DIMENSIONS
35.2 x 50.4 in.
(89.5 x 128 cm)

CONCEPT
The Golden Bee Global Biennale of Graphic Design, led by Serge Serov, invited Cybu Richli from C2F to design a poster for the hundredth anniversary of the Russian Revolution. Out of five hundred posters, this one was chosen for the world tour exhibition. The information on the poster is reduced to the essentials; it shows only the two years 1917 and 2017. The design refers to the Russian propaganda posters and is printed in cinnabar red using silkscreen printing.

Mike Essl

This poster made me stop and laugh. Not because it's particularly funny, but because it's incredibly clever. There is a beautiful concreteness in using the movement of the press to promote a show about movement. This simple idea is delivered so efficiently and effectively that the viewer learns simultaneously about the subject matter of the exhibition and the process by which the poster was made. It's a deceptively simple marriage of form and content that rewards a closer look. I wish I had thought of it.

CONTRIBUTORS
Philipp Koller
Lukas Küng
Giulia Schelm,
Berlin

URL
im-burrow.de

DESIGN FIRM
Burrow, Berlin

CLIENT
Francisco Regalado
and Benjamin Skop

PRINCIPAL TYPE
Burrow.otf
Custom

DIMENSIONS
19.7 x 13.8 in.
(35 x 50 cm)

CONCEPT
This is a series of silkscreen-printed announcement posters for the exhibition *On Movement No. 1* by Francisco Regalado and Benjamin Skop. For the first exhibition of the series the two artists present the viewer with interpretations of the deconstruction of movement. (De)construction of the word "movement" is visualized through constantly shifting and tilting the silkscreen while printing different layers on paper. Therefore, the actual process of printing a poster has become the main design element. We worked with four different rotation angles, two screens and four print runs each, generating a total of four poster variations. The blue information layer remained static while the customized black type was placed systematically, each overlapping the previous layer, creating the illusion of moving sideways.

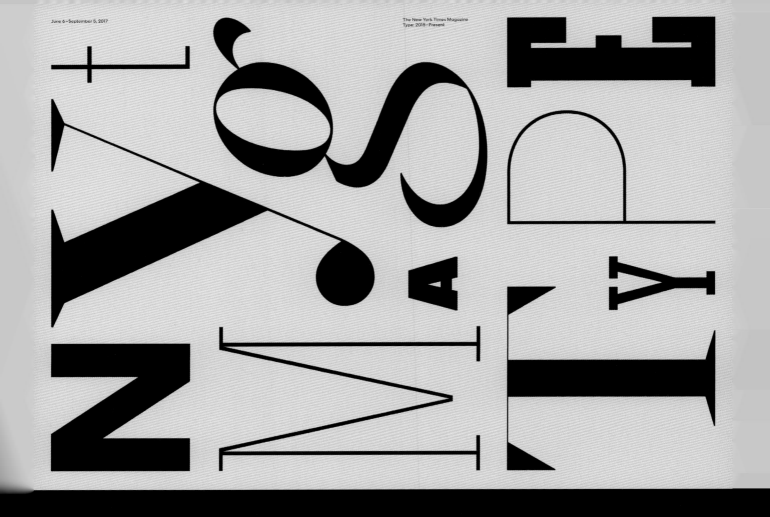

Gemma O'Brien

To me, this type specimen represents bespoke typography at its
finest: bold, restrained, and beautiful. The design of the letterforms
is contemporary yet classic, and the layout is flawless. The crisp black
characters on the soft pink newsprint make this a tangible design
object that is refreshing to behold in our digitally saturated age.

JUDGE'S CHOICE

abcdefghijklmn
opqrstuvwxyz

ABCDEFGHIJKLMN
OPQRSTUVWXYZ

1234567890.,::!?&*a*

ABCDEFGHIJKLMN
OPQRSTUVWXYZ

1234567890.,::!?&@

8

TYPE: 2015—PRESENT

Type Specimen

DESIGN
New York Times Magazine Team, New York

URL
nytimes.com/ section/magazine

PUBLICATION
The New York Times Magazine

PRINCIPAL TYPE
NYT Mag Sans
NYT Mag Serif
NYT Mag Slab

DIMENSIONS
10.25 x 7 in.
(26 x 17.8 cm)

CONCEPT
To accompany an exhibition of typographic highlights from *The New York Times Magazine*, we designed a forty-page type specimen as a giveaway for visitors. It showcases the suite of custom typefaces designed by Henrik Kubel for use in the magazine as well as bespoke typography created by the magazine's art department. We wanted to emphasize the rigor, versatility, and beauty of our brand fonts and the range of typographic experimentation that characterizes the design. It is printed on newsprint, of course.

The New York Times Magazine

December 17, 2017

SHE SAID.

ON POWER AND SEX IN THE WORKPLACE.

Susan Sellers

Competitions tend to be riddled with typographic flourish, demonstrations of visual prowess ultimately finessed to impress designers themselves. All that style and beauty can be blinding; not much stands out in a field of hundreds of entries. It begs the question: Why? What's all this for?

This design gets straight to the point. It demonstrates that design has a role to play in the urgent and critical debates of our time. The power of typography here is less about labor and craft and more about the careful selection of words, a specific phrase with a specific history, represented through a spare yet striking typographic gesture.

The phrase "He said/she said" was highly politicized in the '90s, the era of the Anita Hill/Clarence Thomas hearings and later the Monica Lewinsky testimony. Originally potent with the debate and the implications of gender difference and bias, its excessive use (along with status quo court decisions, an aborted impeachment, and public complacency) exhausted its pique. Dulled down and docile, it was left to stand in for "irreconcilable dispute."

Now, in this raw typographic collision, the designer reinvests the phrase with tension, difference, and debate. And frustration. And anger. It's no longer neutral. This typography doesn't aspire to innovation or newness. Rather, it takes on the most basic yet critical potential of the discipline: to call out, to question, and reach every-one fast. It is efficiency, responsiveness, and urgency that is important here. Here we see design's essential ability to reconnect words with truth and to prompt action.

vers

DESIGN DIRECTION
Gail Bichler

ART DIRECTION
Matt Willey

ILLUSTRATION
Jessica Walsh

URL
nytimes.com/
section/magazine

PUBLICATION
The New York Times Magazine

PRINCIPAL TYPE
Handlettering

DIMENSIONS
10.9 in. x 9 in.
(27.6 x 22.9 cm)

CONCEPT
For the cover of our issue on power and sex in the workplace, we played off a phrase that is often used to discredit a woman's side of the story: "He said/she said." Jessica Walsh tried many versions of the lettering. We wanted the "S" to feel urgent and angry. The blood-red scrawl stood out in stark contrast to the formality of the type, and you could feel the hand of the writer viscerally. Adding the period at the end gave women the last word. It's simple, graphic, and you get it right away.

As someone who doesn't speak any of the four languages, I can't judge the linguistic or the semiotic aspects of the experiment, but utility seems the least important thing. What's most interesting to me is the multilayered ambition. This is not a simple typographic form exercise. This is also a linguistic exercise that challenges how we understand languages. How is meaning created? What's the relationship between the meaning and the words? How does a character work in human cognition? Can it serve the same meaning and purpose once its form is radically changed? If culture plays a role in the representation of an alphabet, can we tinker with the latter to test cultural proximity?

So many questions. There's a level of novelty here that's extremely creative, yet there's real complexity and scholarship that makes the project one-of-a-kind. What's genius about the typographic drawings is how this project meticulously breaks down the formal and semantic essences of each language, layer by layer, or stroke by stroke, then some of the relational elements get combined and hybridized. This taxonomical approach in a way transcends the foreignness of the languages, in a surreally yet universally communicative way, and that ties it all back to the very nature of typography: to communicate.

I salute Yuliana Gorkorov for the ingenuity she has demonstrated in this project. It's a masterpiece.

Natasha Jen

Unrecognizable yet familiar. Seemingly ancient yet contemporary. Exact yet wildly imaginative. Centered yet expansive. The *Global Alphabet* book stood out for its almost-alien beauty, as it wasn't anything that could be easily categorized by conventional typographic standards.
The project attempted to look at possible ways to unite Latin, Cyrillic, Hebrew, and Arabic: writing systems that share the same root of the Phoenician alphabet. The results were five different fonts, each a blended experiment of two languages.

JUDGE'S CHOICE + 1ST PLACE STUDENT

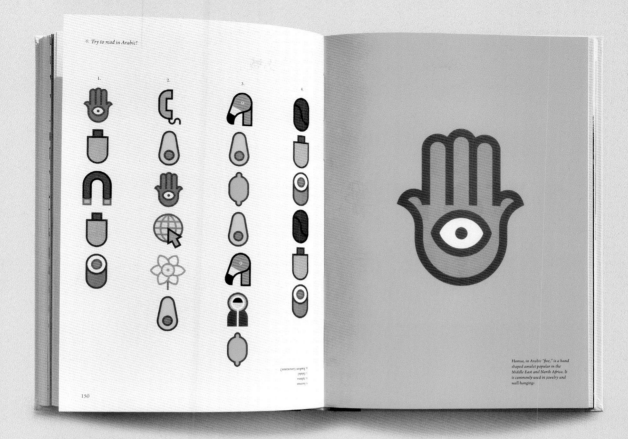

Hansa, in Arabic "five," is a hand shaped amulet popular in the Middle East and North Africa. It is commonly used in jewelry and wall hangings.

GLOBAL ALPHABET

Student Work

DESIGN
Yuliana Gorkorov°,
Essen, Germany

URL
mutualphabets.com

PROFESSORS
Book:
Ralf de Jong
Christin Heinze
Fonts:
Ralf de Jong
Natascha Dell
Christin Heinze

SCHOOL
Folkwang University
of the Arts

PRINCIPAL TYPE
Abjad Lino
Akrofont
ApocalypsA
Arno Pro
BABEL2014
LATAR

DIMENSIONS
6.7 x 9.4 in.
(17 x 24 cm)

CONCEPT
In our globalized, digitized world, people from different cultures communicate with one another daily. Although we speak different languages, many words can be understood by all of us. But such words are unrecognizable when written in a foreign alphabet. The Latin, Cyrillic, Hebrew, and Arabic alphabets look unrelated despite their shared historical origin. For five years I looked for the best way to reunite them in a new alphabet that would be readable to people from different cultures. The results are five fonts presented in *Global Alphabet*. This book shows how such fonts can be integrated in our daily life. To extend the scope of the book and to make it interactive, I used foldout pages and augmented reality.

Jonathan Key

With a background in both theater and graphic design, I am constantly looking to merge these two forms into a context that elevates the source material and lends new meaning to the work. Unsurprisingly, I was immediately drawn to this bright orange book with "Othello" spaced in blackletter down the spine.

In *To Live and Die in Venice*, the designer dismisses conventions for play and script typesetting, presenting instead exploding typography that travels across the page. The Shakespearean play is adapted to create parallels between the studied lyricism of the past and the contemporary energy and urgency of hip-hop. The setting of the words animates the players' lines while shifting faces express the personalities of individual characters. *To Live and Die in Venice* is a beautiful display of confidence, control of language, complex grid structures, and movement with type, and a design object that expansively reimagines Othello's world as a Shakespeare for today's generation.

We were even more impressed upon discovering that *To Live and Die in Venice* was a student's work. As you flip through the volume, each page demonstrates unexpected refinement in execution and illuminates new interpretations of the text, all the while radiating the simple joy of designing. Fearless and bold, the gestures in the work assert a unique edge to this designer voice, and I am eager to continue listening.

JUDGE'S CHOICE + 2ND PLACE STUDENT

EMILIA:

I mean you might as well change your last name to Lopez. Cause when you find him its at least a. Bullet that was left in his eye however you want it. The black or the coon got him on his block, like where Cortez. Is it the earn got him, I'm like yeah. Gonna get earn, clap, no coffin.

You better armor all, maybe a shot gun, I gotta chart off.

OTHELLO:

They put earn in the uh and he earned that. Let him run I got a scope and a red dot. Let him think he really got away then let that lead pop. Now should I kill a game and show him an aim. And give him a headshot. I'm aimin' for his calves. I figure fourI make his legs lock, this nigga beat me, not at all. You can take this chain but you gon' die when you got it on. And that, when you playin' in the sky. Like Monsterball, I kill his whole entire team. You better armor all maybe a shot gun I gotta chart off. Gage in his shoulder blade his arm will look sword off. And it came with a knife in the front. I took the sword off, his head was laying right in the street. You saw it off my niggas 'bout that action. Fuck that small talk. My killas who around without a leash like a dog park. Most of these niggas suckasI get them hold off. Find them laying in the junkyard.

Gage in his shoulder blade his arm will look sword off.

Whoa, whoa, okay, You did a good job, Lil' Bitch. I mean, Lil' Othello. My bad.

Yo, try to cross reference my epic preference

EMILIA:

Grown men bras something you gotta deal with. Cause no matter how big these man boobs get racks. They ain't gon equal up to no real tits. Come on now you know me. Finally I got you and I'm packing shit that's silver nigga. But I'm snappin' off the block kickin' shit. Like silver nigga hold on. You the type to rap for the bread to eat. Well that's why you better roll T. But just know there's 40 hours, so don't owe T. Matter fact bar for bar I'm killin' this shit. Honestly bar for bar I'm killin' this shit. That's how I feel T. I just open doors and let y'all live, that's real T. Come on all this preachin' stuff gon' lead to preachin' blood. Yo Math, How does remains in the blood in the tub. I go bleach the tub, matter fact, you come through. All this preachin' stuff gon' mean you a stand up nigga. And since you snitchin' you gon' need the crutch.

GRATIANO:

Matter fac... ...ldiers Rome in. I get ...ease ...get to squeeze and ...ck on... ...Nigga you ain't deep ...t like I said. Fuck ...reac... ...is preacher blood. I staffe... ...ns, come through ...squeeze the b... ...Matter fact hold on. ...amn I fucked that up all the way I can't ...ave that shi. I ain't gon choke though, ...t I need... shit. Honestly you ...sed and sa... And the sad you ...Winslow, get it, I

...VE AND DIE IN VENICE

...ent Work

DESIGN
İdil Gücüyener
Anna Kabanina,
Barcelona

INSTRUCTOR
Pol Pérez

TYPOGRAPHY TUTOR
Laura Meseguer

SCHOOL
ELISAVA Barcelona
School of Design and
Engineering

PRINCIPAL TYPE
Akzidenz-Grotesk
Extended
Akzidenz-Grotesk
Medium Extended
Pitch Regular
William Regular
William Regular Italic

DIMENSIONS
5.8 x 9 in.
(14.7 x 23 cm)

CONCEPT
Shakespeare and hip-hop may seem contradictory at first glance. But there are parallels between these two elements of culture. In terms of artistic expression, the use of wordplay, lyricism, and rhythm are akin. Love, jealousy, violence, and betrayal are common subject matters in both. Influenced by hip-hop and Shakespearean theatrical performances, *To Live and Die in Venice* is an interpretation of *Othello* set in hip-hop's golden age.

The atmosphere of a play is present with serif typefaces, tabulations, and navigation elements commonly found in scripts. Hip-hop is introduced with rap-battle lyrics when characters face arguments. As the story heats up, highlights, violated text blocks, and images reflect the offensive and blitz of the rap-battle environment.

RANK & FILE

"Racism is the lynchpin that holds American capitalism together despite all its inequality and misery."
ANDREW TILLETT-SAKS

00:02:54
An image like an expression, which can be suited to many statements.

OUR POWER LIES IN ORGANIZATION
I WW
BUILD MILITANT UNIONISM

Independently of the liberal, integrationist civil rights leadership, radicals took "Black Power" into American industry, helping to trigger a national strike wave that involved a significant minority of both Black and white workers.

The strike activity demonstrated that a united struggle of Black and white workers against their employers was possible even in a highly polarized racial climate that saw liberal Democrats—both Black and white—join the chorus of racists who condemned the Black Power movement. ...

Continued on p. 47

"Employed workers who are union members declined to about 11% in 2014, the lowest share in a century."
CHARLIE POST

"DON'T MOURN, ORGANIZE!"

PEOPLE HEAR US SINGING, BREAD AND ROSES, BREAD AND ROSES   LYRICS FROM BREAD AND ROSES BY JAMES OPPENHEIM

3RD PLACE STUDENT

backs her), Sanders has promised to direct societal resources away from the banks to rebuild inner cities, create jobs, and provide free college education.

Applying his vision to trade unionism means rejecting the idea that capital has an inherent right to do what it wishes to our jobs and our communities.

In the periods of labor's greatest growth, big ideas have fueled trade union activity—ideas like "human labor is not a commodity," "labor creates all wealth," and "human rights are superior to property rights."

The Communications Workers of America (CWA) voted to endorse U.S. Senator Bernie Sanders for president in the 2016 election. With 700,000 members, CWA is one of the largest unions in the U.S. The CWA's endorsement is the third and biggest Mr. Sanders has received from a national labor union.

Law professor James Pope has written perhaps more than any other historian on the role of these ideas in the 1930s labor movement. He argues that unions cannot uphold the right to strike without an awareness of human labor's role in the economy:

The treatment of labor as a commodity subject to the rules of the marketplace is a defining feature of capitalism. The claim of a constitutional right to strike—a right to interdict the free competition of individuals in the buying and selling of labor power—obviously imperiled the ideology and practice of commodity labor.

The right to strike could not be justified without addressing the question of labor liberty per se.

Bringing the labor movement back to life will involve borrowing strike tactics from the 1930s—like mass picketing and workplace solidarity—that are illegal under the existing order.

To engage in such tactics, the labor movement must recognize

that the government and the NLRB are not ineffective protectors of labor, but rather part of the political establishment Sanders rails against.

The success of the Sanders campaign—despite the efforts of the corporate elite, establishment politicians, and the mainstream media—demonstrates that this kind of left-wing, anti-establishment unionism can find a base of support within the contemporary working class.

CLASS-STRUGGLE UNIONISM
Reintroducing class struggle into trade unionism also necessitates

having a serious discussion about the state of labor's reform-minded wing. Supportive of diffuse activism, this broad coalition includes true reformers and those who, in the past, would have been considered collaborationist hacks.

Many in labor embrace what could be called "labor pragmatism"—initiatives that try to fight smart within the existing system, like the inside strategy, the corporate campaign, and the one-day strike.

All of these are sensible strategies for workers forced to struggle within an unjust framework of labor control. But because they do not challenge the underlying paradigm, they cannot revive the labor movement.

Many in labor's progressive wing favor the phrase "social movement unionism" to describe a form of unionism that emphasizes community ties and rejects narrow unionism. This is particularly true in public-sector unions, which live or die based on public support.

Social movement unionism is a broad concept that can encompass a wide range of activities, from the class-struggle approach of the Chicago Teachers Union to staff-driven models more akin to business unionism.

It's time to move beyond these concepts and toward a more Sanders-inspired vision of labor organizing, which puts our fight in the context of the struggle between the 1 percent and the rest of the population.

Class-struggle unionism incorporates the broad demands of social movement unionism into a workplace-centered struggle against management.

POLITICAL REVOLUTION, LABOR REVOLUTION Labor's most recent upsurge was the 1960s wave of illegal public-sector strikes, which pitted public employee unions against union officials, the media, the courts, and pro-corporate politicians from both parties. Labor's next upsurge will contend with the same forces and require a similar anti-establishment bent.

Without a strong left wing to hold them accountable, national labor leaders are largely given a pass. While they may adopt progressive positions and embrace new forms of organizing, they rarely discuss breaking free from repressive labor laws or engaging in a Sanders-style political revolution against the establishment.

Indeed, substantial blocks of the labor movement lined up behind Hillary Clinton. (To see which unions truly constitute the Left of the labor movement, you only need to look at which endorsed Bernie.)

Now is the time for labor activists to inject a class-focused perspective into union circles.

Millions have responded to Bernie Sanders's demands to end insider politics, to take on the financial elite that impoverishes American workers, and to create a better future. For a labor movement on life support after decades of business unionism, a similar call represents our best and only hope. Begging for crumbs from a rigged system of labor control is no future—we need a labor revolution.

HARUN FAROCKI'S 1995 VIDEO CHARTS THE HISTORY OF WORKERS APPEARING IN FILM ACROSS THE DECADES. STARTING WITH THE FIRST FILM EVER SHOT, THE VIDEO ESSAY BECOMES A TACIT EXPOSE OF A HISTORY OF EMPLOYER/EMPLOYEE RELATIONS.

DURATION: 42 MIN. 26 SEC

RANK AND FILE

Student Work

DESIGN
Anna Feng°,
Brooklyn, New York

URL
anna-feng.com

TWITTER
@_annafeng

INSTRUCTOR
Andrew LeClair

SCHOOL
Parsons School
of Design,
The New School

PRINCIPAL TYPE
Platform
Portrait

DIMENSIONS
13.5 x 19.25 in.
(34.4 x 48.9 cm)

CONCEPT
Rank & File commits to centering radical voices of the labor movement and highlighting workers' personal experiences in the workplace. As a platform for union members of every level, it creates a network of workers, union leaders, and political activists that allows them to engage in discussion through various perspectives. *Rank & File* also provides direct interaction between the publication and its readers as a means to promote nonviolent direct action. For example, posters and petitions are included in the newspaper to help workers organize and spread their messages.

TDC
64
WINNERS

LET'S GO

START A STANDING OVATION

THEATRE

CATEGORIES/GENRE

LARGE CUSTOM HEADLINE

....

"LET'S GO!"

Advertisements

DESIGN
Tristan Dubin
Joe Haddad,
New York

SENIOR DESIGNER
Lauren King

CREATIVE DIRECTION
Ang Church
Eric Collins
Joey Ellis
Larry Pipitone

URL
grandarmy.com

TWITTER
@grandarmy

DESIGN STUDIO
GrandArmy

CLIENT
SeatGeek

PRINCIPAL TYPE
Encore Sans

CONCEPT
SeatGeek is a digital ticket-selling platform with a call to action that connects fans to the experiences they crave. "Let's Go!" populates the entire campaign, reskinning itself to reflect every genre, field, and subculture for which SeatGeek sells tickets. A robust suite of lettering pieces adapts to context, applying itself on lines of different lengths. Punk show tickets are collaged like a Sex Pistols cover, while basketball tickets are always accompanied by Jumbotron bitmap typography. In essence, SeatGeek becomes the biggest fan, with the deepest knowledge of whatever world it's representing.

BOSCH MEGATREND REPORT M7

Annual Reports

DESIGN AND CONCEPT DEVELOPER
Katharina Bergmann,
Stuttgart

CREATIVE DIRECTION
Jochen Theurer

DIRECTOR PROJECT MANAGEMENT
Jeannette Kohnle

PROJECT MANAGER
Julius Ulrich

DTP
Thomas Langanki

POSTPRODUCTION
Schlossberg-Medien

PRINT
raff media group

PHOTOGRAPHY
monotoomono.com
Dr. Jörg Kirchhoff
depositphotos

ILLUSTRATIONS
Bernd Schifferdecker
The Noun Project
Strichpunkt

URL
sp.design

TWITTER
@STRICHPUNKT

AGENCY
Strichpunkt Design

CLIENT
Robert Bosch GmbH
Dr. Andrej Heinke,
Future Research and
Technology Strategy

PRINCIPAL TYPE
Bosch Sans

DIMENSIONS
9.7 x 13.4 in.
(24.5 x 34 cm)

CONCEPT
"The time is out of joint." This Shakespeare quote from *Hamlet* is the motto of the seventh *Megatrend Report*, by which Bosch gives deep insight into the political, economic, and social future. How will we live and work tomorrow? And to what extent do agile, disruptive, and collaborative life and work models change us? The world of tomorrow unfolds in a striking atlas format. Image portraits and illustrative fact sheets design a plastic image of the future. A compact management summary links to future markets of the global technology and mobility group.

JAHRESBERICHT 2015–2016

Annual Reports

DESIGN
Anna Cairns
Sascia Reibel
Lino Santo,
Karlsruhe,
Germany

URL
hfg-karlsruhe.de

CLIENT
University of Art and
Design Karlsruhe

PRINCIPAL TYPE
Adobe Caslon Pro
Gothic 720

DIMENSIONS
6.3 x 9 in.
(16 x 23 cm)

CONCEPT
This annual report was inspired by the idea of "(ex-)change." The arrival of a new rector had triggered debate and set old structures in motion. This presented an opportunity to initiate conversations among all departments to discuss academically and institutionally relevant topics. The book cover—white, with one of eight sticker sheets enclosed—is a playful invitation to overcome the dreaded "blank sheet of paper," to exchange words like stickers, and to thereby participate in shaping ideas and artifacts in the way this is lived and taught at the university.

MISSION

The National Bonsai Foundation is a section 501(c)(3) nonprofit organization established in 1982 to sustain the National Bonsai & Penjing Museum. It cooperates with the U.S. National Arboretum by offering financial support and advice to the Museum.

This private/public collaboration between the Foundation and the Arboretum enables the Museum to promote the art of bonsai and penjing to visitors through masterpiece displays and educational programs while also fostering intercultural friendship and understanding.

THE NATIONAL BONSAI FOUNDATION ANNUAL REPORT 2016

Annual Reports

DESIGN
Leslie Krivo-Kaufman, Washington, D.C.

CREATIVE DIRECTION
Gavin Wade

PRINCIPALS
Jason Mannix
Lindsay Mannix
Gavin Wade

PRINTING
Mosaic

URL
polygraphcreative.com

TWITTER
@PolygraphDC

DESIGN FIRM
Polygraph

CLIENT
National Bonsai Foundation

PRINCIPAL TYPE
Chronicle

DIMENSIONS
5.75 x 9.25 in.
(14.6 x 23.5 cm)

CONCEPT
The National Bonsai Foundation's first annual report was an opportunity to share the mission of the foundation to a larger audience and to celebrate the beauty and restraint of this traditional Japanese art form. We kept the reporting information to a sophisticated monotone navy on beautifully flecked uncoated French paper, while the middle section, celebrating the year's new bonsai trees, is presented in full color and rich black on coated stock. The cover uses a Cordtone stock to emphasize the natural textures in the art form and to give the reader a pleasant feel in hand.

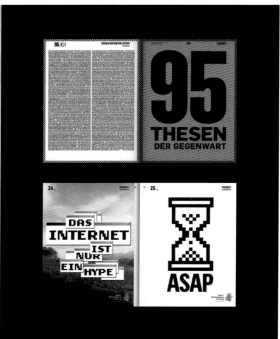

BADEN-WÜRTTEMBERG STIFTUNG
FREEDOM! ANNUAL REPORT 2016

Annual Reports

SENIOR DESIGNER
Bianca Bunsas,
Stuttgart

CREATIVE DIRECTION
Jochen Theurer

CONCEPT DEVELOPER
Katharina Bergmann

DIRECTOR PROJECT
MANAGEMENT
Jeannette Kohnle

PROJECT MANAGER
Annkathrin
Schwämmle

DTP
Thomas Langanki

ILLUSTRATIONS
Bernd Schifferdecker

POSTPRODUCTION
Schlossberg-Medien

MANAGING DIRECTOR
Christoph Dahl

HEAD OF COMMUNICATIONS
Julia Kovar-
Mühlhausen

PRINT
raff media group
GmbH

URL
sp.design

TWITTER
@STRICHPUNKT

AGENCY
Strichpunkt Design

CLIENT
Baden-Württemberg
Stiftung GmbH

PRINCIPAL TYPE
Flama

DIMENSIONS
6.3 x 9.1 in.
(16 x 23 cm)

CONCEPT
What do we believe in? What do we stand
for? And what does freedom mean to us? In
the Luther year 2017, ninety-five new theses
provided new answers, raised questions, and
provoked confrontation and discussion. On
ninety-five leaflets and with a public poster
campaign, the Baden-Württemberg Stiftung
foundation demonstrated its attitude and
expressly communicated what encourages
and motivates it. This extensive report draws
a sculptural picture of the foundation's
work—individually designed, illustrative, and
with striking accents in powerful neon.

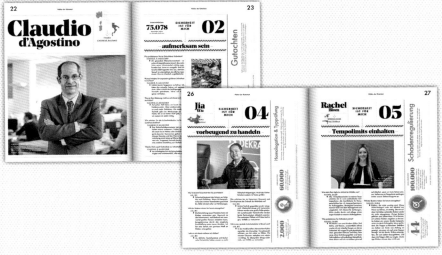

**HEROES OF SAFETY—
DEKRA ANNUAL REPORT
2016/17**

Annual Reports

**DESIGN AND
ART DIRECTION**
Ulla Oberdörffer,
Stuttgart

CREATIVE DIRECTION
Jochen Theurer

**DIRECTOR PROJECT
MANAGEMENT**
Jeannette Kohnle

PROJECT MANAGER
Raphael Knolmayer

**DIRECTOR MARKETING
AND COMMUNICATIONS**
Stephan Heigl

COMMUNICATIONS
Dr. Torsten Knödler

DTP
Thomas Langanki

URL
sp.design

TWITTER
@STRICHPUNKT

AGENCY
Strichpunkt Design

CLIENT
DEKRA e.V.

PRINCIPAL TYPE
Futura
Minion
Noe Display

DIMENSIONS
8.7 x 11.2 in.
(22 x 28.5 cm)

CONCEPT
DEKRA has been taking care of safety since its foundation in 1925. More than 39,000 employees in 50 countries around the globe fulfill this basic need for a safe world. Twelve heroes of safety from different regions, the board of directors, and the management board tell what safety means for them personally and at work. The reports are linked to the twelve service lines of DEKRA and thus cover the entire performance portfolio. Large-format images, bold illustrations, and individual infographics visualize the respective content. The typography and the individual design elements form a visual bracket across all chapters.

HELLO FUTURE
OTTO GROUP
ANNUAL REPORT 2016/17

Annual Reports

DESIGN
Johanna Schuhmacher,
Berlin and Stuttgart

CREATIVE DIRECTION
Tobias Nusser

JUNIOR ART DIRECTOR
Svetlana Visnakova

DIRECTOR PROJECT MANAGEMENT
Antje Grieshaber

HEAD OF CORPORATE COMMUNICATIONS FINANCE, OTTO GROUP
Robert Hegel

VICE PRESIDENT CORPORATE COMMUNICATIONS
Thomas Voigt

SENIOR COMMUNICATIONS CONSULTANT
Jennifer Buchholz

CORPORATE COMMUNICATIONS CONSULTANT
Kristina Drews

URL
sp.design

TWITTER
@STRICHPUNKT

AGENCY
Strichpunkt Design

CLIENT
Otto GmbH & Co KG

PRINCIPAL TYPE
The Sans
The Sans Mono

DIMENSIONS
8.8 x 11.7 in.
(21 x 29.7 cm)

CONCEPT
Hello future, future of work! Together with external experts we have investigated why strict hierarchies are becoming obsolete and what focusing on customer needs means for the Otto Group's daily business. We asked what kinds of tools are needed to promote this cultural change and how robots and artificial intelligence will fundamentally change our practices. As a symbol of dialogue, powerful typography is being used extensively and playfully. Broad imageries and unusual perspectives provide insight into a range of topics. Concrete examples show how the future of work is shaped at Otto.

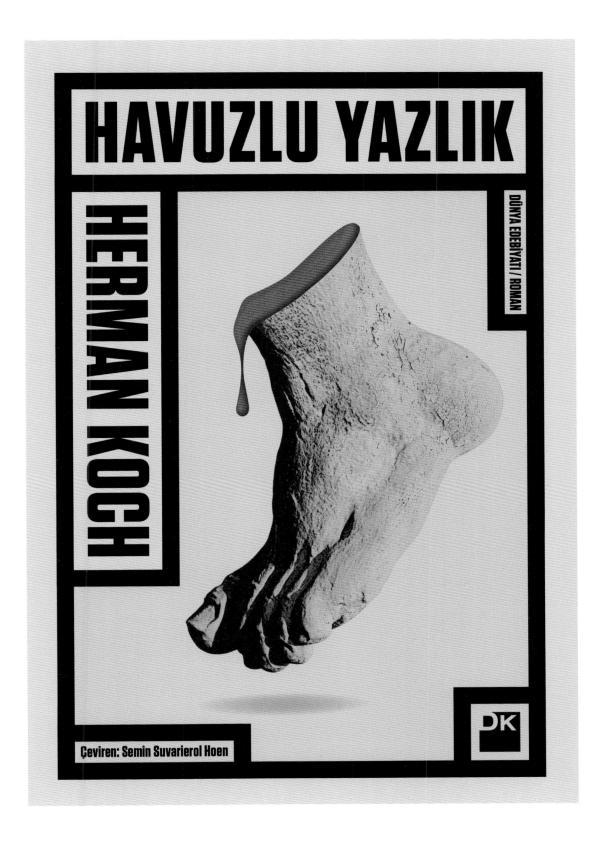

SUMMER HOUSE
WITH SWIMMING POOL

Book Jackets

DESIGN
Geray Gencer,
Istanbul

DESIGN FIRM
Studio Geray Gencer

CLIENT
Dogan Egmont
Publishing

PRINCIPAL TYPE
Tungsten

DIMENSIONS
5.3 x 7.7 in.
(13.5 x 19.5 cm)

CONCEPT
Our main goal was to create a visually
powerful image in which crime, self-
destruction, and a summer atmosphere
are revealed.

FUKT MAGAZINE #16:
DIRTY DRAWINGS: THE SEX ISSUE

Book Covers

DESIGN
Ariane Spanier,
Berlin

URL
arianespanier.com

DESIGN FIRM
Ariane Spanier
Design

CLIENT
Fukt Magazine

PRINCIPAL TYPE
Grouch BT
and handlettering

DIMENSIONS
6.5 x 9.1 in.
(16.5 x 23 cm)

CONCEPT
A mask hides the first page of *Fukt*'s Sex Issue.

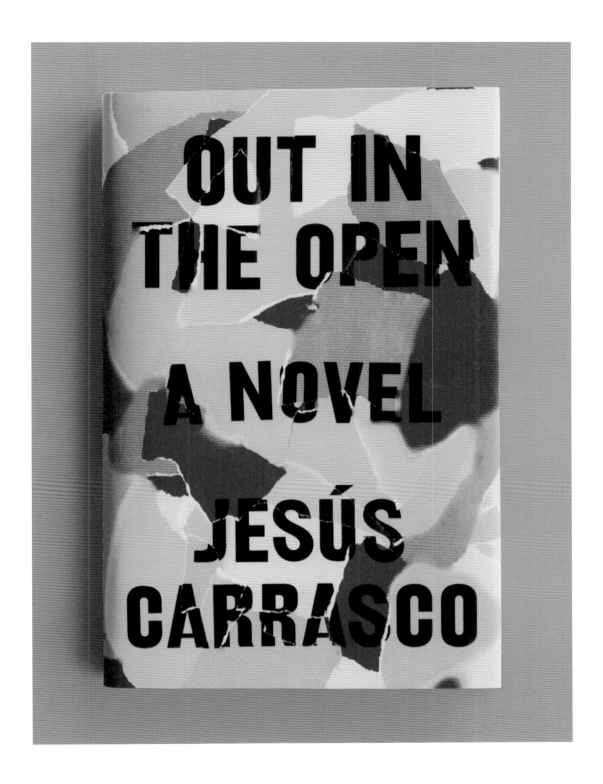

OUT IN THE OPEN

Book Jackets

DESIGN
Ben Denzer
New York

ART DIRECTION
Helen Yentus

URL
bendenzer.com

PUBLISHER
Riverhead Books,
Penguin Random
House

PRINCIPAL TYPE
Railroad Gothic
Com Regular

DIMENSIONS
5.5 x 8.25 in.
(13.5 x 21 cm)

CONCEPT
Jesús Carrasco's *Out in the Open* is a searing
dystopian vision of a young boy's flight
through an unnamed, savaged country. The
novel is not fixed in time, belonging equally to
the distant past and the far future. The jacket
aims to be stark but beautiful, both ripped
apart and blended together to confuse any
single understanding of process.

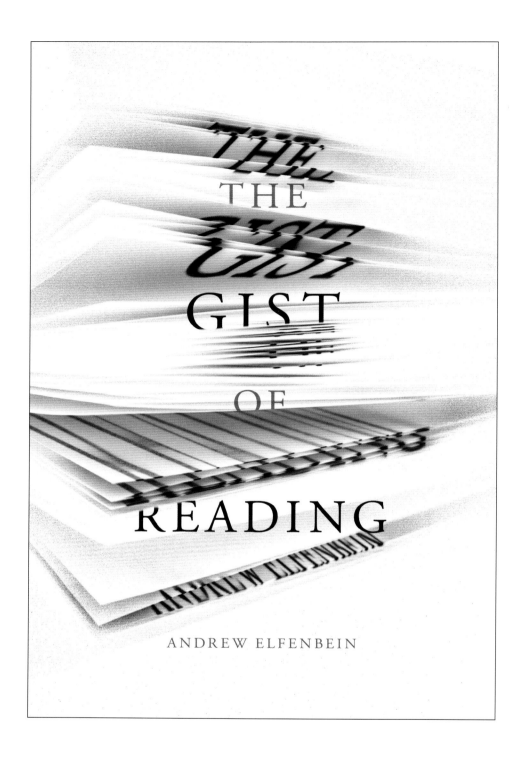

THE GIST OF READING

Book Jackets

DESIGN AND PHOTOGRAPHY
Mitch Goldstein
Anne Jordan,
Rochester, New York

ART DIRECTION
Rob Ehle

URL
annatype.com

TWITTER
@annatype
@mgoldst

STUDIO
Anne Jordan
Mitch Goldstein

CLIENT
Stanford
University Press

PRINCIPAL TYPE
Adobe Garamond Pro

DIMENSIONS
6 x 9 in.
(15.2 x 22.9 cm)

CONCEPT
This is the cover for a book about the constant interplay between automatic and controlled processes in the brain during the act of reading. We wanted to make a book—the iconic symbol for reading—come alive, as if we were opening up the book and seeing the process of reading going on within the pages. We projected typography onto blank pages of a book and photographed the setup in our studio. The final book cover captures the feeling of reading bursting out of the pages.

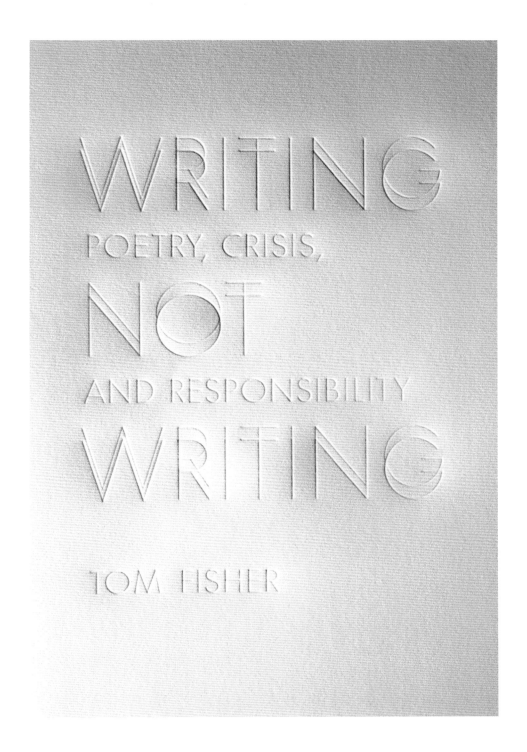

**WRITING NOT WRITING: POETRY,
CRISIS, AND RESPONSIBILITY**

Book Jackets

DESIGN AND PHOTOGRAPHY
Mitch Goldstein
Anne Jordan,
Rochester, New York

ART DIRECTION
Karen Copp

URL
annatype.com

TWITTER
@annatype
@mgoldst

STUDIO
Anne Jordan
Mitch Goldstein

CLIENT
University of
Iowa Press

PRINCIPAL TYPE
Futura

DIMENSIONS
6 x 9 in.
(15.2 x 22.9 cm)

CONCEPT
This is the cover for a literary criticism book about the role of poetry
during crisis, told through the lens of several poets who renounced
poetry. During war, for example, writers question how poetry can be of
service in a world that is falling apart. Silence, refusal, and disavowal
are often alternative modes of response during continuous crisis.
Our goal was to create a bare, silent, minimal cover. We embossed the
text into a blank piece of creamy paper. The text is made visible by
the embossing and lighting in our photo studio. The result is type that
is strong yet silent.

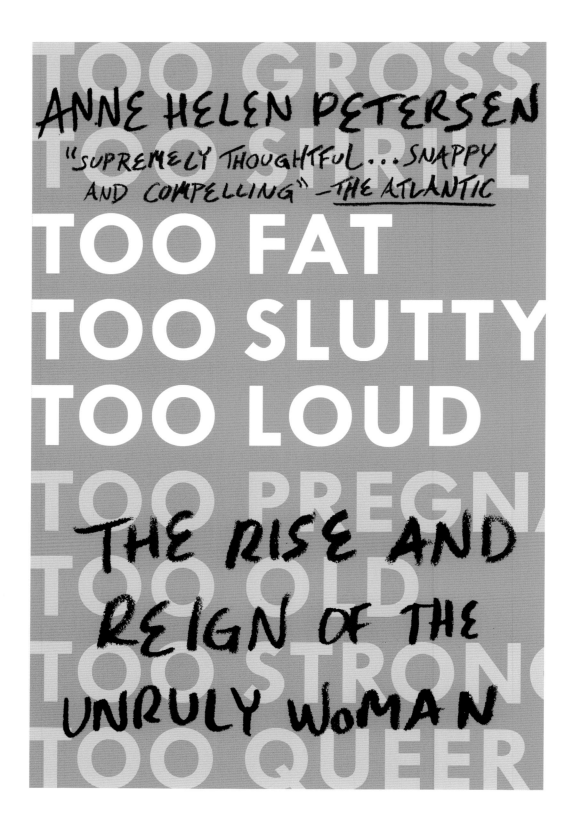

TOO FAT, TOO SLUTTY, TOO LOUD

Book Jackets

DESIGN
Spencer Kimble,
New York

ART DIRECTION
Jason Booher

URL
blueriderpressart.
tumblr.com

PUBLISHER
Plume

PRINCIPAL TYPE
Twentieth Century
Bold and handlettering

DIMENSIONS
5.3 x 8.5 in.
(14.25 x 21.5 cm)

CONCEPT
The repeated lines "Too ... Too ... Too ..." set up the visual rhythm that fills the composition. The black lettering sits against the vibration of the acid yellow type on the pink with just enough visual conflict to fight against easy legibility.

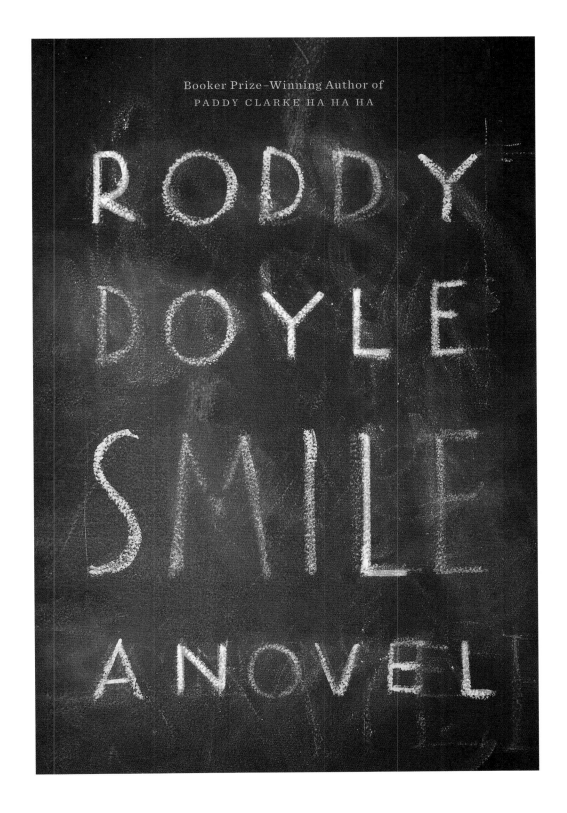

SMILE

Book Jackets

DESIGN
Nick Misani,
New York

ART DIRECTION
Jason Ramirez°

URL
misani.com

TWITTER
@nickmisani

INSTAGRAM
@nickmisani

PUBLISHER
Viking Books

PRINCIPAL TYPE
Handlettering

DIMENSIONS
5.6 x 8.5 in.
(14.3 x 21.6 cm)

CONCEPT
This is a novel about memory and how one contends with the past. Brother Murphy's class. Young Victor's smile. Weekend homework erased from a chalkboard. In telling his life story, a middle-aged man dredges up disturbing memories of the years he spent being taught by the Christian Brothers in secondary school.

UMBERTO ECO
SOMON BALIĞIYLA YOLCULUK
Çeviri: İLKNUR ÖZDEMİR
♥can deneme

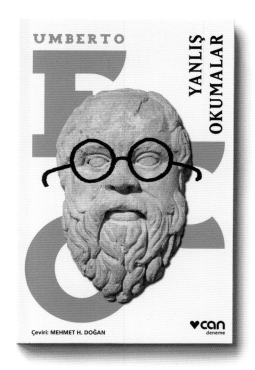

UMBERTO ECO
YANLIŞ OKUMALAR
Çeviri: MEHMET H. DOĞAN
♥can deneme

UMBERTO ECO
ANLATI ORMAN-LARINDA ALTI GEZİNTİ
Çeviri: KEMAL ATAKAY
♥can deneme

UMBERTO ECO
AÇIK YAPIT
Çeviri: TOLGA ESMER
♥can deneme

UMBERTO ECO SERIES

Book Jackets

DESIGN
Utku Lomlu,
Istanbul

URL
utkulomlu.com

TWITTER
@utkulomlu

DESIGN STUDIO
Lom Creative

CLIENT
Can Publishing

PRINCIPAL TYPE
Fela
Matrix

DIMENSIONS
4.9 x 7.6 in.
(12.5 x 19.5 cm)

CONCEPT
With his studies on semiotics, Italian scholar Umberto Eco was one of the most important novelists of postmodernist literature. In his lively writing style, language is not a structure that represents reality but establishes it. To create coherence in the covers of the Eco series, a typographic structure was created with his name, and then a fictional solution using both images and drawings was integrated with the typography. The covers aim to reflect Eco's outstanding imagination, sense of humor, and literary plain style—and they seek not to represent one reality but to reach a multiple meaning instead.

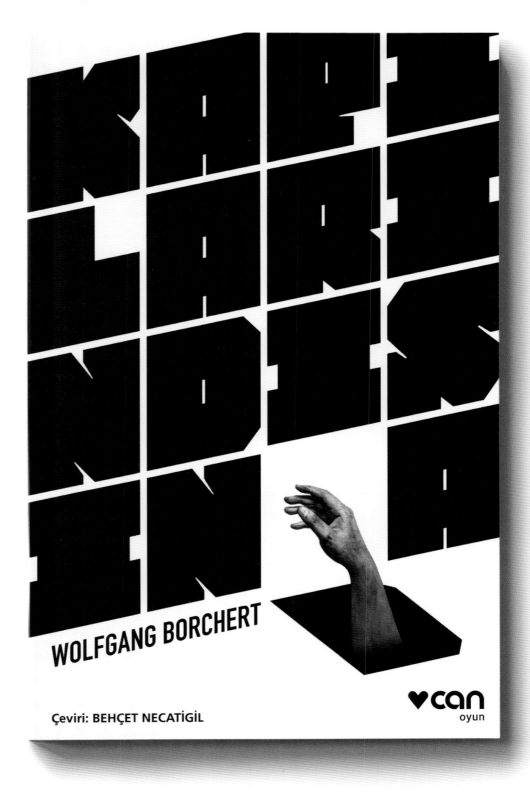

**THE MAN OUTSIDE
(KAPILARIN DIŞINDA)**

Book Jackets

DESIGN
Utku Lomlu,
Istanbul

URL
utkulomlu.com

TWITTER
@utkulomlu

DESIGN STUDIO
Lom Creative

CLIENT
Can Publishing

PRINCIPAL TYPE
DIN Condensed
Custom

DIMENSIONS
4.9 x 7.6 in.
(12.5 x 19.5 cm)

CONCEPT
Wolfgang Borchert's only play, *The Man Outside*, tells the story of a postwar soldier. He witnessed the destruction and pain of war and returns home to find that he has lost his wife, his home, and his beliefs. Every door closes to him. Now he belongs to the outside. Captured by a strong nihilism, the protagonist desires only his death. The cover of Borchert's play is treated as a theater poster for strong impact. The typography structure represents all the constructions this man made for himself in life. Destruction is necessary for passage to the underworld.

RIVOLUZIONE LANGOSTERIA

Book Jackets

DESIGN
Leonardo Traina,
Milan

DESIGN DIRECTION
Pasquale Di Meglio

CREATIVE DIRECTION
Giacomo Cesana

URL
cba-design.it

TWITTER
@CBAItaly

AGENCY
CBA Italy

CLIENT
Langosteria Holding

PRINCIPAL TYPE
Custom version
of Bauer Bodoni

DIMENSIONS
7.8 x 10.6 in.
(20 x 27 cm)

CONCEPT
This book tells the entrepreneurial story of Enrico Buonocore and of Langosteria, the best seafood restaurant in Milan, with a rhythm that is upbeat but introspective, dreamlike and at the same time very down-to-earth. The result is a blend of biography and business guide. The title is powerful and speaks of revolution, translated graphically in the rhythm and balance of a classic typeface that spreads harmoniously over the cover, overturned to underline the meaning of the word "revolution."

THE WEIGHT OF THINGS

Book Jackets

DESIGN
Erik Carter,
Oakland, California

ART DIRECTION
Andy Pressman,
Portland, Oregon

URL
erikcarter.net

TWITTER
@erikinternet

CLIENT
Verso Books

PRINCIPAL TYPE
Canela
Sharp Grotesk

DIMENSIONS
7.8 x 5.1 in.
(19.8 x 12.9 cm)

CONCEPT
The Weight of Things was Marianne Fritz's debut novel, a story about how we can't control the burden of circumstances that are beyond our control. The cover design is a play on the title, with the letters slowly distorting and becoming crushed by their own weight.

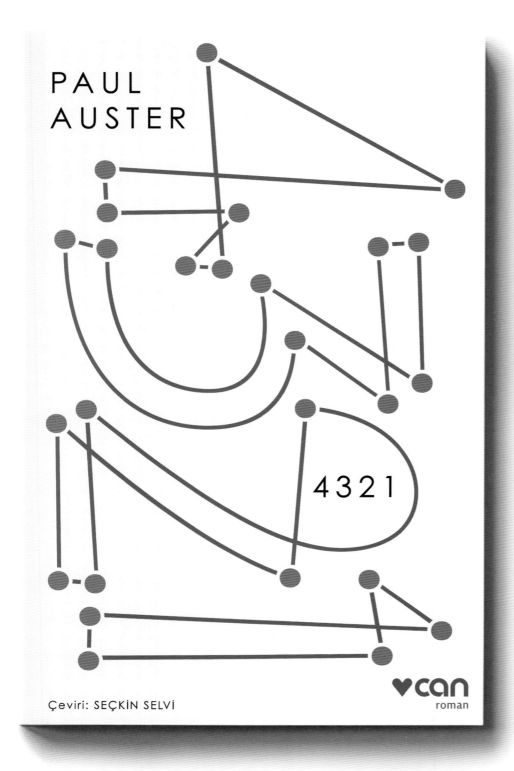

PAUL
AUSTER

4 3 2 1

Çeviri: SEÇKİN SELVİ

♥can
roman

4 3 2 1

Book Jackets

DESIGN
Utku Lomlu°,
Istanbul

URL
utkulomlu.com

TWITTER
@utkulomlu

DESIGN STUDIO
Lom Creative

CLIENT
Can Publishing

PRINCIPAL TYPE
Century Gothic
Eames Numerals
customized

DIMENSIONS
4.9 x 7.6 in.
(12.5 x 19.5 cm)

CONCEPT
Paul Auster's novel *4 3 2 1* presents four parallel lives of the
protagonist. These four versions of his life are told simultaneously.
There are some moments when these four versions become parallel
and other moments when these versions fall far from one another,
touching only slightly. The typography represents these versions by
becoming parallel, then separate. At the crossroads in the life of the
protagonist we see stops and turns. The cover tries not to intervene
in the simplicity of the name of the book and avoids standing between
the book and the reader.

FREISTIL 6—THE BOOK OF ILLUSTRATORS

Book Jackets

DESIGN
Sarah Schnurbus,
Bielefeld, Germany

EDITOR
Raban Ruddigkeit

URL
sarahschnurbus.de

PUBLISHER
Verlag Hermann
Schmidt

PRINCIPAL TYPE
Maison Neue
Numero

DIMENSIONS
6.8 x 9.4 in.
(17.3 x 24 cm)

CONCEPT
Freistil 6—The Book of Illustrators presents a selection of 150
illustrators, three interviews, and information on new trends and
developments. The book cover picks up on a striking pixel font based
on a grid system. The word "FREISTIL" is gradually assembled from
pixels and dissected to visualize a creative process. To highlight single
elements, some were isolated and colored in a sequence of rainbow
colors. The book title and the name of the publisher were placed like
all the other headlines and illustrators' names in the book to create
continuity and tranquility.

NISSE, 400 ESZETT-SCHNITTE

Books

DESIGN
Maximilian Borchert
Hannah Häußer,
Stuttgart

URL
hum-co.de

STUDIO
HuM Collective

CLIENT
Verlag Hermann
Schmidt

PRINCIPAL TYPE
Droid Sans
Droid Serif
PT Sans
Google Fonts

DIMENSIONS
4.7 x 6.3 in.
(12 x 16 cm)

CONCEPT
This is a printed collection of 400 Google
Fonts, categorized and listed in font families.
We used the lower case ß, a curious glyph
mainly used in the German language and
known as "the German B," as a sample for
showing the differences among the fonts and
celebrating the birth of its capital letter on
June 29, 2017.

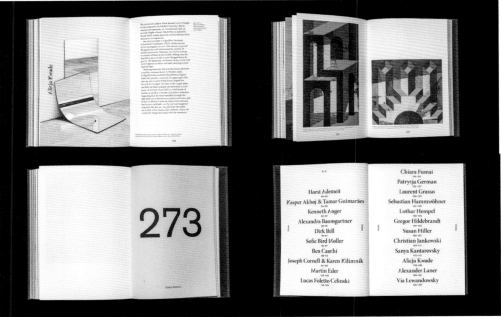

ASTRAL BODIES

Books

DESIGN
Jenny Hasselbach
Franziska Morlok,
Berlin

URL
rimini-berlin.de

INSTAGRAM
@riminiberlin

DEISGN STUDIO
Rimini Berlin

CLIENT
Künstlerhaus
Bethanien, Berlin

PRINCIPAL TYPE
Akzidenz Grotesk
Minion

DIMENSIONS
6.7 x 9.5 in.
(17 x 24 cm)

CONCEPT
Künstlerhaus Bethanien is an international cultural center dedicated to supporting contemporary visual arts. This catalog examines the influence of esoteric practices in art, showing work by artists such as Alicia Kwade, Christian Jankowksi, and Claudia Wieser, as well as accompanying texts by Thomas Macho and Shubigi Rao. The design of the book refers to the topic in a clear yet subtle way with altered typography, a dark blue metallic book cover, and black edge finishing.

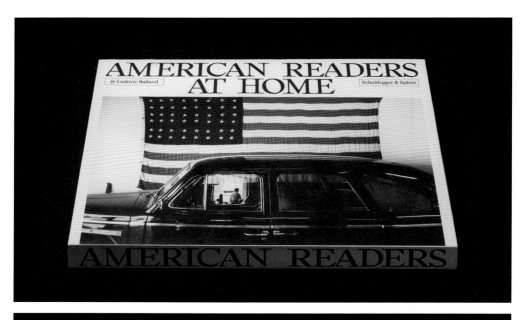

AMERICAN READERS AT HOME

Books

DESIGN
Ludovic Balland
Rahel Oberhummer,
Basel

CO-EDITORS
Jonathan Blower
Benjamin Olschner,
London and New York

AUTHOR AND EDITOR
Ludovic Balland

TYPESETTING
Ludovic Balland
Rahel Oberhummer

LITHOGRAPHY
Christian Brosche
Jennifer Niederhauser
Schlup,
Altenburg, Germany,
and Lausanne,
Switzerland

PHOTOGRAPHY
Ludovic Balland

URL
ludovic-balland.com

PRODUCTION AND PRINTING
DZA Druckerei
zu Altenburg,
Altenburg, Germany

TWITTER
@ludovicBalland

STUDIO
Ludovic Balland
Typography Cabinet

PUBLISHER
Verlag Scheidegger
& Spiess, Zürich

PRINCIPAL TYPE
Stanley Family

DIMENSIONS
13 x 9.5 in.
(33 x 24 cm)

CONCEPT

This unconventional book by Ludovic Balland is a road trip in photographs and interviews. It sets the spotlight on the readers, collecting personal snapshots of daily consumption of the news. *American Readers at Home* is a document of the months before and after the American presidential election of 2016, a vast book project in an innovative editorial format. Interview journalism and documentary photography together capture the diversity and the desire for change in American society—though without coming down on either side of the political divide. The fifty-five interviews and four hundred pictures contained in this book focus on American readers and their milieus. They look at media consumption habits and the perception of the media, providing stark insights into its increasingly tyrannical role in society.

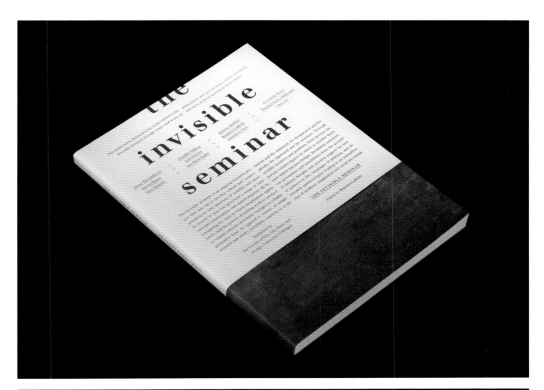

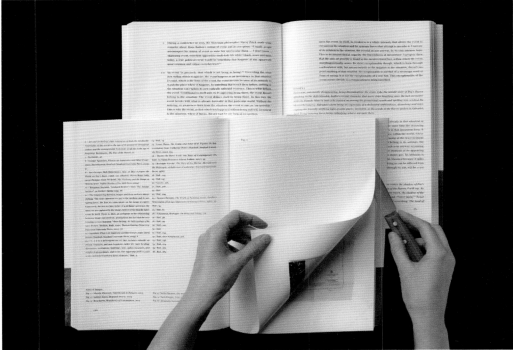

THE INVISIBLE SEMINAR

Books

DESIGN
André Heers
Annette le Fort,
Berlin

CREATIVE DIRECTION
Cesar Finamori
Kara Goodwich

DESIGN FIRM
fliegende Teilchen

CLIENT
Faculty of Fine Art,
Music and Design,
University of Bergen,
Norway

PRINCIPAL TYPE
Walbaum

DIMENSIONS
8.7 x 11.7 in.
(22.2 x 29.7 cm)

CONCEPT
This book for a research project plays with the theme of invisibility. Using the coated and uncoated sides of one paper and a Japanese binding, the book presents all the text on the outside while hiding the image content in the secret rooms of the folded pages. Photographic works and documentation appear behind the scenes and are accessed by readers cutting open the pages. The title on the cover is printed on the backside of an oversized dust jacket and only partially folded over to the front, leaving some of the information to be discovered.

ATTICA: USA, 1971

Books

ART DIRECTION
Susanna Shannon°,
Paris and Marseilles,
France

AUTHOR
Philippe Artières

CLIENT
Béatrice Didier with
David Benassayag and
David Barriet, Le Point
du Jour Editeur

PRINCIPAL TYPE
Franklin Gothic Extra
Condensed
ATNewNumber Two

DIMENSIONS
8.25 x 11 in.
(21 x 28 cm)

CONCEPT
We wanted the book to look respectful, powerful, and peaceful in response to the tragedy and the violence of the event that took place at Attica in 1971. From a strict design point of view, we didn't want the book to look like a superficial imitation of an old militant publication from the '70s; we wanted it to have an authentic paste-up feel. (Late designer David King in London spoke of "paste-up" as an art.)

WINTER

Books

DESIGN AND LETTERPRESS PRINTING
Jamie Murphy,
Dublin

ILLUSTRATION
David Rooney

EDITING
Lisa Griffith

TYPESETTING
Ruairi Conaty
Jordan Huysmans
Michael Simpson

BOOKBINDING
Tom Duffy

DESIGN FIRM
The Salvage Press

URL
thesalvagepress.com

TWITTER
@thesalvagepress

CLIENT
The Salvage Press

PRINCIPAL TYPE
Monotype Caslon
Woodtype

DIMENSIONS
8.5 x 13 x 3 in.
(22 x 34 cm)

CONCEPT
The challenge was to bring the voices of fourteen very different war poets together in a cohesive manner. The project focused on producing a finely printed book while evolving an experimental secondary element that would enhance the experience for the reader. Great effort was made to push the book in new and interesting directions. The codex itself is linear and easy to navigate and digest. The accompanying portfolio of typographic prints relies on a strict grid system while seeming free from constraint. There are essentially just three colors employed: process black, jewel silver (mixed by hand), and process blue. The metal and wooden types are contemporary to the Great War. The project was typeset, letterpressed, and finished by hand.

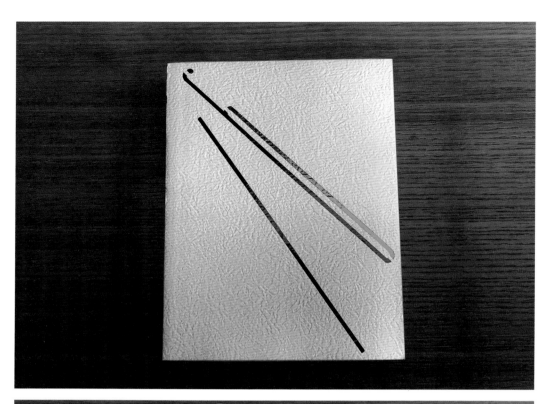

**THE 2ND SHENZHEN
INTERNATIONAL POSTER
FESTIVAL WORKS COLLECTION**

Books

DESIGN
Pingbo Chen°,
Shenzhen,
Guangdong, China

DESIGN FIRM
Chen Pingbo Graphic
Design Consulting

PRINCIPAL TYPE
FZ Hei
Helvetica

DIMENSIONS
7.7 x 10.3 in.
(19.5 x 26 cm)

CONCEPT
This poster festival collection included 386 shortlisted and award-winning entries. The book design used the main portion of the symbol of the festival. The outer cover was designed in a unique way to let the reader personally rip up the adhesive paper in the outer box. This matched up well with the core aim of the festival: opening and blending. In addition, for the internal cover of the book, 20 and 16 were designed to form the year 2016.

SEASON 2017/2018

Books

DESIGN
Lukas Betzler
Simon Bork
Armin Roth,
Stuttgart

URL
studiopanorama.de

STUDIO
studio panorama

CLIENT
Theater Konstanz

PRINCIPAL TYPE
Basis Grotesque
ITC Weidemann

DIMENSIONS
5.9 x 9.5 in.
(15 x 24 cm)

CONCEPT
Theater Konstanz commissioned us to create a new visual concept
for their next season. With computer-simulated fabric we tried
to illustrate "Faith," the season's topic. The resulting graphics are
impermanent and always changing—they show only a brief moment of
a motion in flow. The fabric morphs, distorts, disguises, and sometimes
makes the invisible visible. Equipped with text, it transforms into
protest banners. The typography mixes features of bible design with
a modern grotesk font.

»Sensing the Ocean« basiert auf der Zusammenarbeit des Kieler Meeresforschungsclusters *The Future Ocean* und der Muthesius Kunsthochschule. Das Buch zeigt, wie sich Künstler, Designer und Wissenschaftler kreativ ergänzen, was künstlerische und wissenschaftliche Forschung unterscheidet und veranschaulicht, wie aus dem Zusammenspiel der Kompetenzen neue Erkenntnisse erwachsen.

»Sensing the Ocean« is based on the collaboration between the Kiel Marine Research Cluster of Excellence *The Future Ocean* and the Muthesius University of Fine Arts and Design. The book shows how artists, designers and scientists can complement each other creatively, what differentiates artistic and scientific research, and illustrates how the interplay of competences gives rise to new insights.

ISBN: 978-3-95763-389-0

Sensing the Ocean

A Collaboration between Art, Design and Science

Hrsg.
Tom Duscher
Stephan Sachs
Manfred Schulz

SENSING THE OCEAN

Books

DESIGN
Teresa Döge
Björn Schmidt,
Kiel, Germany

EDITORS
Tom Duscher
Stephan Sachs
Manfred Schulz

COVER PHOTOGRAPH
Jolan Kieschke

URLS
bjoernschmidt.info
teresadoege.com

CLIENT
Muthesius University
of Fine Arts and
Design, Kiel
(Muthesius
Kunsthochschule,
Kiel)

PRINCIPAL TYPE
Frederick
GT Walsheim

DIMENSIONS
9.5 x 12.5 in.
(24 x 3.5 cm)

CONCEPT
Sensing the Ocean, released after ten years of cooperation between the Muthesius University of Fine Arts and Design and the Cluster of Excellence The Future Ocean, presents various texts on the relationship between art, design, and science and three practical projects. This publication uses the medium of the book to create new views on the projects through reflection and analysis. These illustrations of space, interactivity, and time form a core element of the publication.

ANDREAS MÜHE
PATHOS AS DISTANCE

Books

DESIGN
Anna Bühler
Nina Odzinieks
Pit Stenkhoff, Berlin

URL
neuegestaltung.de

CLIENT
Andreas Mühe

DESIGN FIRM
Neue Gestaltung
GmbH

PRINCIPAL TYPE
Burgess Italic
Burgess Regular
Courier New Regular
Courier New
Regular Italic

DIMENSIONS
9.1 x 11.3 in.
(23 x 28.8 cm)

CONCEPT
Accompanying photographer Andreas Mühe's retrospective *Pathos als Distanz*, Kehrer is releasing the exhibition catalog that purposefully uses only a few subtle design elements. By juxtaposing Mühe's works with extracts from Florian Illies' book *1913*, the catalog creates an edgy visual composition that draws on the interplay between imagery and text. In order for this impressive contextualization to come to full effect, the compact information section is placed at the end of the book.

XXL
Studio
出品

诗

文爱艺爱情诗集

广西美术出版社

WEN AIYI'S LOVE POEMS

Books

ART DIRECTION
Xiaoxiang Liu,
Beijing

STUDIO
XXL Studio

CLIENT
Guangxi Fine Arts
Publishing House

PRINCIPAL TYPE
Century
FZYaSong-D
FZLanTingHei-M

DIMENSIONS
5.1 x 8.4 in.
(12.9 x 21.5 cm)

CONCEPT
This is a concept book about poetry and love, a handmade publication.
Besides its unique binding, the book also features embossed French-
folding thick pages screen-printed inside pages bearing poems and
week calendars. Any careless move may cause those pages separated
from the book to fall like autumn leaves, implying that only tender care
can make love last long.

**OUR DAILY LIVES HAVE
TO BE A SATISFACTION IN
THEMSELVES**

Books

**DESIGN, EDITOR, PRINTER,
BINDER, AND PUBLISHER**

Emily Larned,
Bridgeport,
Connecticut

PHOTOGRAPHY
Noel Furie

URL
emilylarned.com

INSTAGRAM
@emilylarned

PRINCIPAL TYPE
Eskorte and
handlettering

DIMENSIONS
5.25 x 8 in.
(13 x 20 cm)

CONCEPT
This book documents forty years of Bloodroot, a feminist vegetarian
restaurant and bookstore in Bridgeport, Connecticut. The pages are
designed to allow ample space for the copious footnotes of Bloodroot's
founders, who are avid readers. The book is set in the diverse family
of Eskorte, the debut typeface of designer Elena Schneider. A very
readable and serviceable textface in its regular version, the lively
italics of its heavier weights recall 1970s typography. Studious yet
spirited, reminiscent of the '70s yet also thoroughly contemporary,
designed by a woman: Eskorte seems to me the perfect typeface for
a book on Bloodroot.

**WALKING THE PATH
TO ETERNAL FRAGRANCE**

Books

DESIGN
Hui Shi
Qing Zhao,
Nanjing, China

DESIGN FIRM
Nanjing Han Qing
Tang Design Co., Ltd.

CLIENT
Phoenix Science
Press

DIMENSIONS
9.3 x 11.8 in.
(23.5 x 30 cm)

CONCEPT
This is a book about the art of plants. There are two major parts
of the book, each divided into several chapters. Every chapter adopts
a different kind of paper according to the content, such as retro
beige paper for ancient painters' works and smooth white paper for
the contemporary works. We also put a square blank in the middle
of the English and Chinese texts, so as to constitute a "frame," echoing
the paintings. With the linen cover, inside papers, layout, and so on,
all of the designs took hand painting as the core concept in order
to highlight the painters' original and rustic craftsmanship.

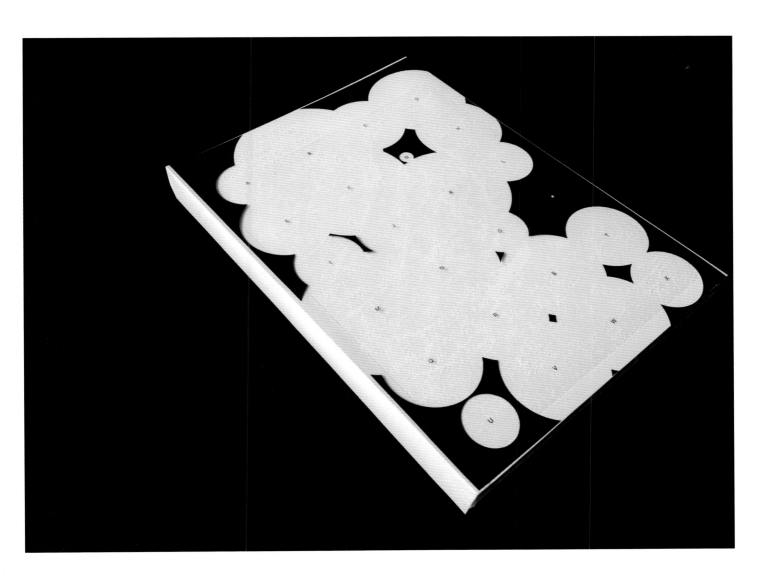

**THE MOST BEAUTIFUL
SWISS BOOKS**

Books

CREATIVE DIRECTION
Jonas Voegeli
Kerstin Landis
Zurich

DESIGN
Romy Strasser
Hoang Nguyen
Scott Vander Zee
Matthias Michel

URL
hubertus-design.ch

DESIGN FIRM
Hubertus Design

CLIENT
Federal Office
of Culture,
Bern, Switzerland

PRINCIPAL TYPE
Devanagari Sangam
MN modified into
Default Sans

DIMENSIONS
8.7 x 11.8 in.
(22 x 30 cm)

CONCEPT
How do you judge beauty? On the level of execution of one's design skills, the printing and binding quality, or the relationship between content and form? Through our design of the catalog we've tried to raise such questions, and scrutinize them. We would like to share the fascination of purely formal, obsessive, and technological details—letting a reader look through the eyes of the jury in an extensive/magnified way. Thus, we allow the books, and their details, to almost become obsolete or parodies of themselves (perhaps similar to the format of the competition itself?).

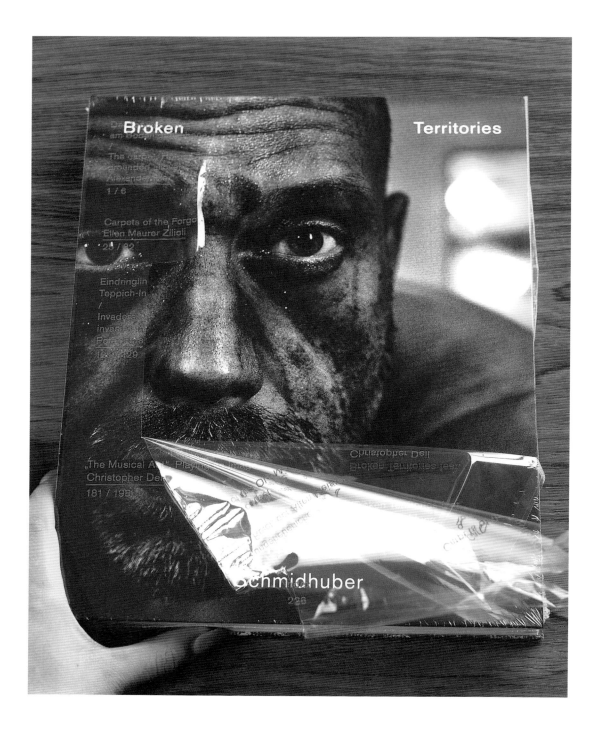

BROKEN TERRITORIES

Books

ART DIRECTION
Chris Steurer
Fuenfwerken Design
AG,
Wiesbaden, Germany

EDITORS
Sammlung Teunen
Museum Wiesbaden

AUTHORS
Dr. Christopher Dell
Dr. Peter Forster
Dr. Alexander Klar
Dr. Ellen Maurer-
Zilioli

TRANSLATIONS
Dr. Jeremy Gaines

PHOTOGRAPHY
Carsten Beier
Marcus Michaelis
Holger Schmidhuber°

URL
dreizeichenverlag.com

DESIGN FIRM
Fuenfwerken Design
AG

CLIENT
dreizeichen Verlag,
Berlin

PRINCIPAL TYPE
Berthold Akzidenz
Grotesk and Courier

DIMENSIONS
9.1 x 1.4 in.
(23 x 29 cm)

CONCEPT
In *Broken Territories*, Holger Schmidhuber
presents contemporary painting evolved
from Oriental carpets up to a century old in
an unusual historical context. Presented as
walk-on paintings among the Old Masters
in a solo exhibition at Landesmuseum
Wiesbaden, Schmidhuber's disruptive avant-
garde approach has drawn the crowds
and for months dominated media coverage
of the museum. The book continues the
striking journey that the exhibition started.
A thoughtful editorial design frames
Schmidhuber's work, illustrating his art in
photography and text.

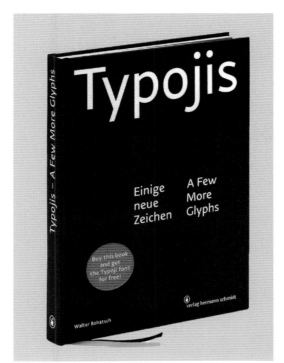

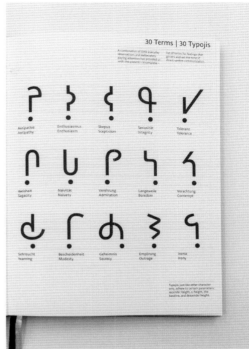

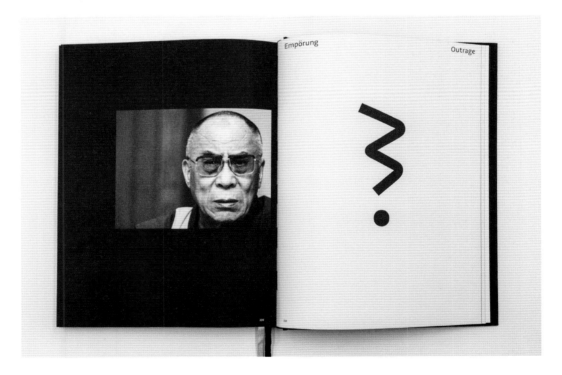

TYPOJIS

Books

DESIGN AND CREATIVE DIRECTION
Walter Bohatsch, Vienna

ASSISTANCE
Igor Labudovic

URL
typojis.com

DESIGN FIRM
Bohatsch und Partner GmbH

PRINCIPAL TYPE
Typoji

DIMENSIONS
48.3 x 64.8 in.
(19 x 25.5 cm)

CONCEPT
Bring more clarity to your written communication! Avoid misunderstandings by letting undertones and shades of meaning resound in the mind's ear. The book illustrates the typojis' semantic meanings by juxtaposing them with symbolic photographs, and subsequent initial glimpses into how typojis are actually used come in the form of personal contributions by forty-nine individuals hailing from a wide range of disciplines. Each entry includes exercise pages that invite you to try writing these new characters for the first time—making your copy a unique exemplar. Included are texts by Walter Bohatsch, Gabriele Reiterer, and Ernst Strouhal.

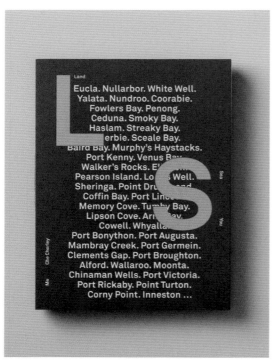

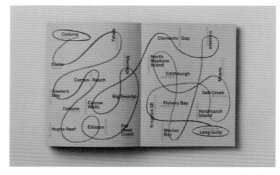

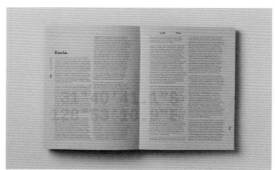

LAND SEA YOU ME

Books

DESIGN AND CREATIVE DIRECTION

Anthony De Leo, Adelaide, Australia

URL

voicedesign.net

TWITTER

@voice_of_design

DESIGN FIRM

Voice

PRINCIPAL TYPE

Akkurat Pro
Milieu Grotesque
GT Pressura Mono

CONCEPT

Land Sea You Me is difficult to define. In photographer Che Chorley's words, "Is this a photo essay? Not really. A surf magazine? No. A visual history of South Australia? Yes and no. An adventure novel? Kinda, but not really." To convey this abstract, wandering concept, the book was compiled into three distinctive sections, creating a conceptual narrative. The first begins with a snapshot of the trials and tribulations Che endured using journal-like illustrations, which are given context later in the book. The middle presents the photographic journal that was documented—"LAND SEA" and its people ("YOU") are presented with little intervention. The last section presents "ME"—a 40,000-word journal detailing the relationship between Che, the bike, and the road. The naive hand typography and illustrations complement Che's raw, earthy, tough, and personal journey.

**RAKAMLAR VE HAYVANLAR
(NUMBERS AND ANIMALS),
RAKAMLAR VE BUYUK TASITLAR
(NUMBERS AND BIG MACHINES)**

Books

**DESIGN AND CREATIVE
DIRECTION**

Murat Celep,
Istanbul

URLS
muratcelep.com
deney.com.tr

TWITTER
@MMuratCelep

DESIGN STUDIO
Deney Design Studio

CLIENT
Iletisim Publishing

PRINCIPAL TYPE
Brandon
Grotesque Black
and Bryant Medium

DIMENSIONS
8.3 x 8.3 in.
(21 x 21 cm)

CONCEPT
These numbers whisper to children. There is so much they want
to say! On each page they play among themselves, shoving and
grabbing, crouching down and jumping up, changing their hue and
creating a surprise. Often, they whisper about animals and vehicles,
giving clues about what they've made. When a page is turned, the
shoving and laughter stop. The numbers have done their task. They
remain as they were, hiding their colors—until the next page opens.
Unique and engaging, these Numbers Art activity books introduce
young readers to the joy of numbers and mathematics.

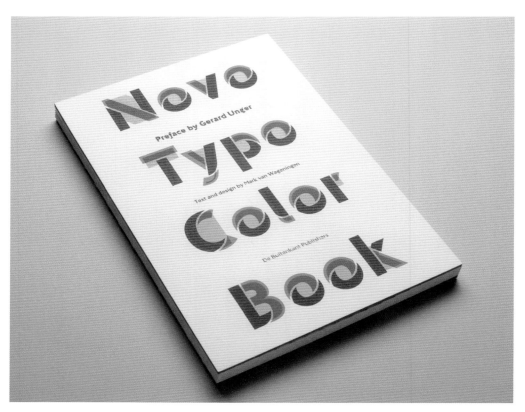

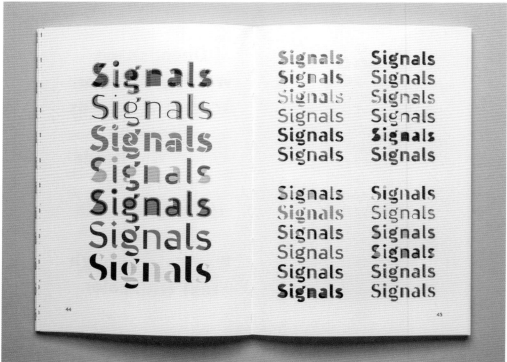

NOVO TYPO COLOR BOOK

Books

DESIGN
Mark van Wageningen,
Amsterdam

URL
novotypo.nl

TWITTER
@NovoTypo

DESIGN FIRM
Novo Typo

PRINCIPAL TYPE
NT Ziza Color

DIMENSIONS
9.4 x 6.5 in.
(24 x 16.5 cm)

CONCEPT
Are typographers and type designers really black-and-white thinkers?
Are they so conservative as to think that the text you see everywhere,
even on your laptop, tablet, or mobile phone, should always be
black? Traditionally, texts in manuscripts were written in black, but
this is probably because of the technical limitations of Gutenberg's
groundbreaking invention. Mark van Wageningen is pushing to change
this accepted norm, celebrating the functionality and decoration
of letters.

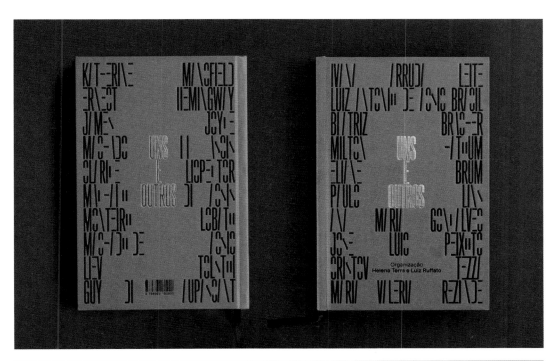

UNS E OUTROS—
CONTOS ESPELHADOS

Books

DESIGN AND
ART DIRECTION
Gabriela Castro
Paulo André Chaga
Gustavo Marchetti,
São Paulo, Brazil

EDITORS (ORGANIZATION)
Helena Terra
Luiz Ruffato

PUBLISHER
Dublinense

PRINTING AND
IMAGE PROCESSING
Geográfica

URL
blocografico.com.br

INSTAGRAM
@blocografico

STUDIO
Bloco Gráfico

CLIENT
Tag Livros

PRINCIPAL TYPE
Various

DIMENSIONS
5.4 x 8.3 in.
(13.8 x 21 cm)

CONCEPT
The challenge of the design was to graphically explore the
book's concept of mirroring classical and contemporary authors.
The cover consists of deconstructed lettering with the names of all
eighteen authors, forming an almost abstract typographical drawing
that would be fully revealed only on the title pages. A different font
family was used for each pair of authors—as if there were ten
books within one. The hot stamping, embossing, gray paper, lack
of lamination, metallic end paper, and silver ribbon were all elements
used to establish a dialogue between the reading structure of the
book and its form.

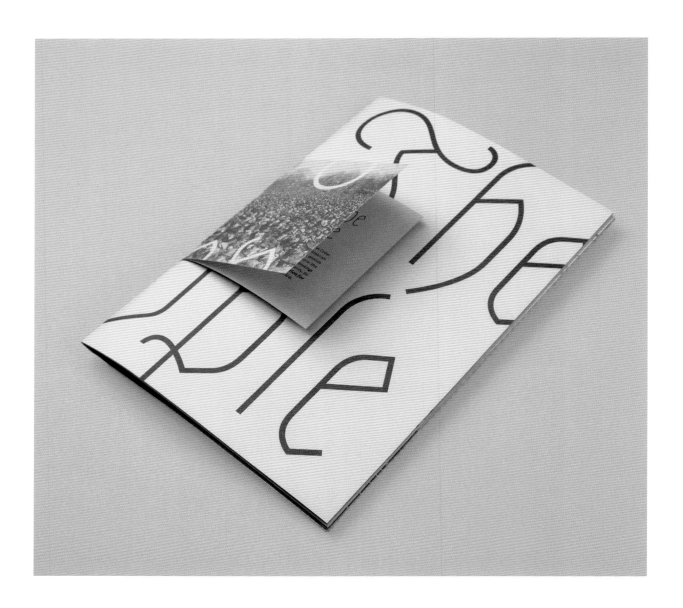

**REBRANDING THE
U.S. CONSTITUTION**

Books

DESIGN
Wednesday Krus
Jee-Eun Lee,
New York

CREATIVE DIRECTION
Anna Milivojevich

URL
thoughtmatter.com

DESIGN FIRM
ThoughtMatter

PRINCIPAL TYPE
Astloch
HK Grotesk
GT Sectra Fine

DIMENSIONS
7 x 10 in.
(17.9 x 25.4 cm)

CONCEPT
In 2017, we redesigned the U.S. Constitution, approaching the historical document with the design principles we would apply to any brand. Because we believe great design can elevate messages both simple and complex, we made sure to create a system that delivers the Constitution's content in a more accessible, visually exciting, and easy-to-read format than typical versions. We did so during a divisive time in American history, when the document is being constantly referenced, interpreted, and debated—in hopes it would spark new conversations about what the document means to every U.S. citizen.

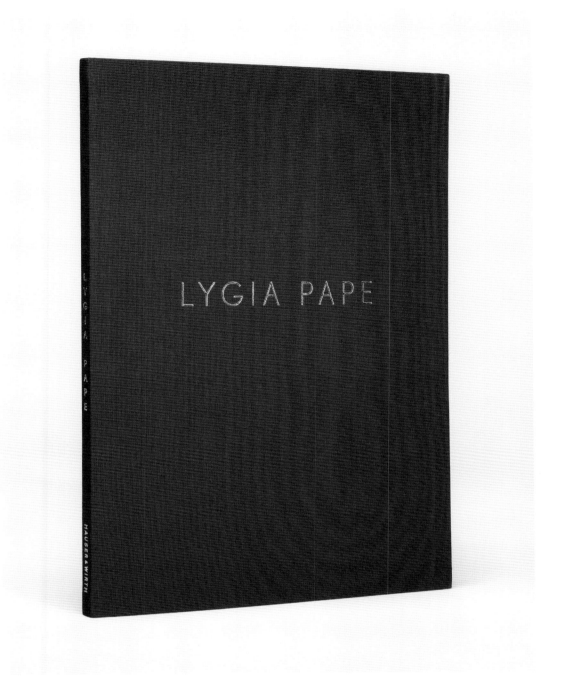

LYGIA PAPE

Books

**DESIGN AND
ART DIRECTION**
Damien Saatdjian,
Brooklyn, New York

CONCEPT
Oliver Renaud-
Clément

EDITOR
Michaela Unterdörfer

ESSAYS
Daniel Birnbaum
Briony Fer

PROJECT COORDINATION
Ricardo Fortes
António Leal
Emily Rothrum
Astrid Suzano

ASSISTANCE
Suzanne Gerber
Stefan Zebrowski-
Rubin

URLS
damiensaatdjian.com
hauserwirth.com/
publications

DESIGN FIRM
Damien Saatdjian

CLIENT
Hauser & Wirth

PRINCIPAL TYPE
Plain

DIMENSIONS
9.5 x 12.7 in.
(32.8 x 24.7 cm)

CONCEPT
Lygia Pape was a Brazilian artist central to
the Neo-Concrete movement who pioneered
a unique approach to geometric abstraction.
This catalog is an extension of an exhibition
that focused on Pape's works on paper,
installations, and a film. Designed in
collaboration with the curator and the artist's
estate, the publication employed a strong
modernist grid system inspired by Brazilian
Neo-Concrete graphic design. The book's deep
blue cover, as well as the translucent blue
pages bound in throughout, pays homage to
her *Ttéia no. 7*, an installation consisting of
two small blue pyramids illuminated by a blue
light from above.

SKRIVANDETS FÖRHANDLINGAR

Books

DESIGN, ART DIRECTION,
AND ILLUSTRATION
Jiri Adamik-Novak,
Stockholm

PRINTING AND BINDING
Hana Böhmova,
Protisk,
Czech Republic

URL
jiriadamiknovak.com

CLIENT
Konstfack Collection,
Stockholm, Sweden

PRINCIPAL TYPE
GT Sectra

DIMENSIONS
4.7 x 8 in.
(11.9 x 20.3 cm)

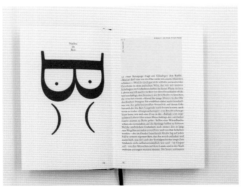

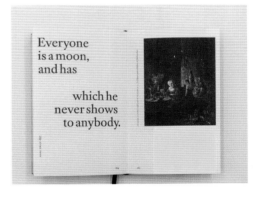

DAS BUCH DER NÄCHTE

Books

DESIGN
Isabel Bach
Patrick Bittner
Daniel Hahn,
Saarbrücken,
Germany

ART DIRECTION
Isabel Bach
Daniel Hahn

CREATIVE DIRECTION
Patrick Bittner

URL
hdw1.de

AGENCY
HDW Neue
Kommunikation

CLIENT
Klaus Beyrer,
Museum für
Kommunikation
Frankfurt

PRINCIPAL TYPE
Kis Antiqua Now

DIMENSIONS
5.5 x 8.7 in.
(14 x 22 cm)

CONCEPT
With its fifty-two weekly calendars, *Das Buch der Nächte* (The Book of Nights) is a diary of the night. It contains lots of inspiring essays and thoughts concerning the night character and individually designed night logs. Actually, the book is a wonderful poetry album in which dozens of lyrical and visual authors perpetuate themselves. They invite the reader to explore the night. Every page differs in its design, and typefaces alternate constantly. With drawings, collages, and photography, followed by poems, quotes, essays, and the recurrent campaign promoting the night, there is always a dash of mystery and inscrutability resonating in this homage to the darkness.

**SCHOOL OF VISUAL ARTS
SENIOR LIBRARY**

Books

DESIGN
Jen Marchese,
New York

ART DIRECTION
Regina Puno

CREATIVE DIRECTION
Scott Buschkuhl

URL
hinterlandstudio.com

TWITTER
@HinterlandNY

DESIGN FIRM
Hinterland

CLIENT
School of Visual Arts,
New York

PRINCIPAL TYPE
Akkurat
Custom

DIMENSIONS
7.5 x 11 in.
(19.1 x 27.9 cm)

CONCEPT
This is a portrait of the design and advertising students at SVA
as they are just about to embark on their careers. The design
conceptually expands on the Choose Your Own Adventure children's
book series. There are a few ways to navigate the book. The jacket
doubles as a poster with a visual index of the students on one side
and an alphabetical index on the other (with faculty/majors noted).
If you prefer to just flip through the pages, information in the gutter
will lead you to additional work from each student.

MATERIAL

Books

ART DIRECTION
Yanik Hauschild
Andreas Uebele°,
Stuttgart

DESIGN FIRM
büro uebele visuelle
kommunikation

URL
uebele.com

PRINCIPAL TYPE
Adapted version of
Maison Neue Book
Maison Neue Italic/
Medium/Bold;
Antwerp Regular/
Semibold/Bold
Massimo Bold

DIMENSIONS
7.3 x 9.4 in.
(18.5 x 24 cm)

CONCEPT
What is beautiful? What is functional? What works and what doesn't?
Where does it feel wrong and why? This is a sketchbook, a project
catalog, a collection of interviews, and a volume of essays. It explains
and describes with and through pictures. It's a book for reading and
for using. It presents eighty-five projects along with the materials
from which they emerged, interspersed with material by people
who've accompanied us along the way.

NUOVO DEVOTO-OLI

Books

DESIGN STUDIO
Leftloft,
Milan

URL
leftloft.com

TWITTER
@leftloft

CLIENT
Mondadori Education

PRINCIPAL TYPE
LFT Iro Sans Symbols
Nitti Grotesk
Sole Serif

DIMENSIONS
6.7 x 9.4 in.
(17 x 24 cm)

CONCEPT
Devoto-Oli was one of the most important dictionaries of the Italian language, published by Le Monnier. The aim of this project was to make *Nuovo Devoto-Oli*, an enjoyable and easy-to-use tool to improve the mastery of a language. A careful information hierarchy and some graphic elements have been designed to enable quicker research, as well as the understanding and the correct use of the words in different contexts. The typography has been completely redesigned along with the color use and icons system. Sections and boxes have been added to point out the most used words and common mistakes.

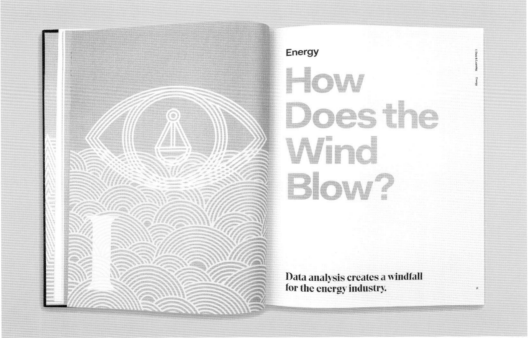

UPTAKE

Books

DESIGN
Brankica Harvey
Pedro Mende,
New York

DESIGN ASSISTANTS
Shannon Jager
Jonathan Rinker
Rebecca Sylvers

ART DIRECTION
Eddie Opara

URL
pentagram.com

DESIGN FIRM
Pentagram°

CLIENT
Uptake

PRINCIPAL TYPE
Eksell
Fakt Pro

DIMENSIONS
9.5 x 12.25 in.
(24.1 x 31.1 cm)

CONCEPT
Uptake wanted to showcase data in an exciting new way, demystify the subject of predictive analytics, and demonstrate its know-how in the field. The team developed almost a hundred new charts, diagrams, and other infographics for the book, as well as a set of custom icons used throughout.

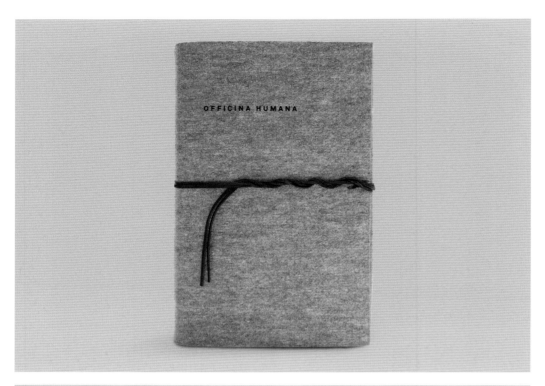

OFFICINA HUMANA

Books

DESIGN
Tatjana Brenner,
Stuttgart

**CONCEPT AND
CREATIVE DIRECTION**
Danijela Djokic
Martin Grothmaak
Jürgen Späth

AUTHORS
Andreas Kulick
Christoph Quarch
Jan Teunen

URL
projekttriangle.com

DESIGN STUDIO
Projekttriangle
Design Studio

CLIENT
ASB Landesverband
Hessen e.V.

DIMENSIONS
7.9 x 11.8 in.
(20 x 30 cm)

CONCEPT
How can the office help to inspire us? The ASB Landesverband Hessen asked itself this question and consequently founded a consulting company, as well as created the book *Officina Humana*, which we designed and implemented visually. Every refinement in its design follows the aim of bringing to life the essence of the office. The dust jacket made of felt embodies the origin of the term "office." The white hardcover, with its imprinted title, opens up a space for thought. Four different papers symbolize the multifaceted nature of the theme, and chapter separators in the form of tabs combine the vision with tradition.

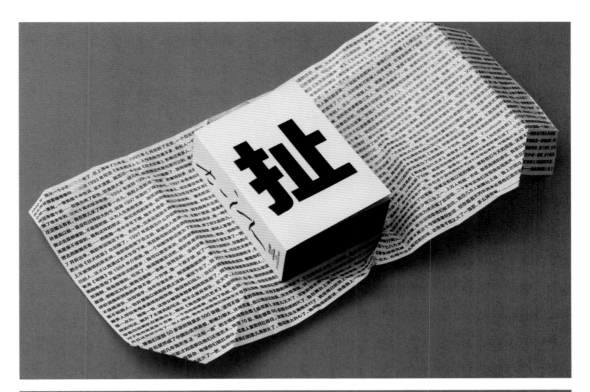

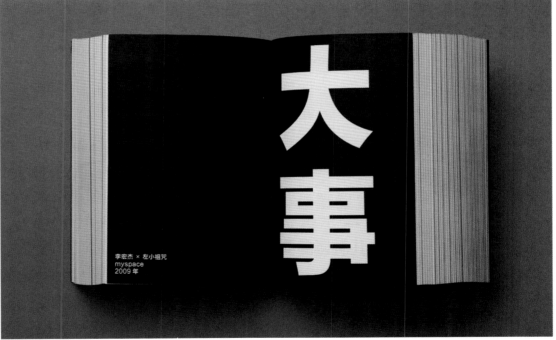

**CHE PI: INTERVIEW
WITH ZUOXIAOZUZHOU**

Books

DESIGN
Sun Xiaoxi,
Beijing

DESIGN FIRM
PAY2PLAY

CLIENT
Zuoxiaozuzhou Studio

PRINCIPAL TYPE
HYQiHei
STZhongsong

CONCEPT
Che Pi is a ten-year interview of the Chinese rock star Zuoxiaozuzhou. The book is pocket sized yet contains 1,028 pages. One page shows a question, and the opposite page shows the answer. But the text of the answers is not always the same size; it varies from page to page, which visually represents the changes in speech. Therefore, the questions and answers build up new relationships, demonstrating the strong power of Chinese characters, as well as a sense of humor. The book is wrapped in a paper full of text—the book's preface. The reader must tear off this paper, which corresponds to the title, "Che Pi," which means not only "tear off" in Chinese but also "chatter." The preface can then be thrown away, further reinforcing the rock star's rebellious nature.

KREATUR

Books

DESIGN
Daniel Wiesmann,
Berlin

PHOTOGRAPHY
Ute Zscharnt
Luna Zscharnt

URL
danielwiesmann.de

DESIGN STUDIO
Daniel Wiesmann
Büro für Gestaltung

CLIENT
Sasha Waltz
and guests

PRINCIPAL TYPE
Akzidenz-Grotesk

DIMENSIONS
12 x 19 in.
(4.7 x 7.5 cm)

CONCEPT
This is a program for the dance piece "Kreatur" by choreographer Sasha Waltz. The first and last sections are produced with cold foil overprinted by offset color, creating mirror-like pages, which are then followed by rehearsal photographs that themselves portray mirrors. The text in the center section is set in black and silver ink printed on thin, opaque paper. This opacity allows text printed on the reverse side of the pages to be readable through the front. The cover material is gray cardboard, with hot foil for the motif and blind blocking for the type.

GALAXY OF HANGEUL

Books

GRAPHIC DESIGN
Son Byung-Kook,
Seoul

URL
yoondesigngroup.com

STUDIO
Yoondesign

PRINCIPAL TYPE
Yoon-Gothic modified

DIMENSIONS
16.5 x 23.4 in.
(42 x 59.4 cm)

CONCEPT
This design visually expresses information about the history of change in Hangeul, the Korean alphabet. The dots are gathered and become the lines, lines become planes, planes become space, and a lot of space becomes the world.

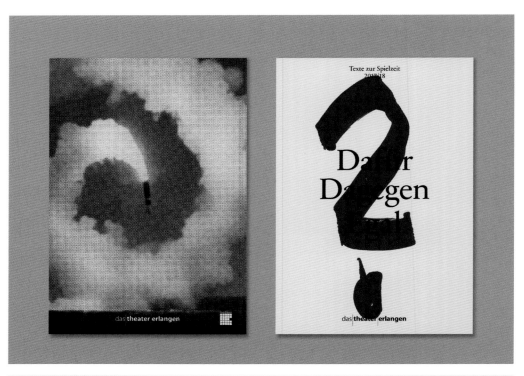

THEATER ERLANGEN SEASON PROGRAM 2017–18

Brochures

DESIGN FIRM
Neue Gestaltung GmbH

URL
neuegestaltung.de

DESIGN
Anna Bühler
Nina Odzinieks
Pit Stenkhoff
Katerina Trakakis,
Berlin

CLIENT
Theater Erlangen

PRINCIPAL TYPE
Avenir, Courier New,
SabonNextLTPro,
and handwritten
fonts by Neue
Gestaltung

DIMENSIONS
6.5 x 9.4 in.
(16.5 x 24 cm)

CONCEPT
There is no motto for Theater Erlangen's 2017–18 season. Accordingly, the season program's cover and first page are dominated by a large question mark and exclamation mark—a call for analysis and debate. The program further reflects the theater's role as an arena of free political discourse by supplementing the clearly laid-out information section with copious accompanying material aimed at encouraging critical thinking, with protest movement serving as the overall theme in content and design.

**RISD SCHOLARSHIP
REPORTS**

Brochures

DESIGN
Sarah Verity,
Providence,
Rhode Island

CREATIVE DIRECTION
Sarah Rainwater

PHOTOGRAPHER
Christopher Garrison

URL
studiorainwater.com

DESIGN FIRM
Studio Rainwater

CLIENT
Rhode Island School
of Design (RISD)

PRINCIPAL TYPE
GT Sectra

DIMENSIONS
7.5 x 10 in.
(19 x 25.5 cm)
5.5 x 8.5 in.
(14 x 21.5 cm)

CONCEPT
RISD Development sought a style to use for
internal projects and publications, ranging
from donor reports to financial reports. GT
Sectra's unusual but refined style holds
down the text-driven booklets and keeps the
past-meets-future sensibility of RISD without
looking overly branded.

ART ET LIBERTÉ

Brochures

DESIGN
Simon Brenner
Sascha Lobe°,
Stuttgart

URL
l2m3.com

STUDIO
L2M3
Kommunikationsdesign
GmbH

CLIENT
Stiftung
Kunstsammlung
Nordrhein-Westfalen

PRINCIPAL TYPE
Berthold Akzidenz
Grotesk Custom

DIMENSIONS
Various

MARCEL BROODTHAERS

Brochures

DESIGN
Simon Brenner
Sascha Lobe°,
Stuttgart

URL
l2m3.com

STUDIO
L2M3
Kommunikationsdesign
GmbH

CLIENT
Stiftung
Kunstsammlung
Nordrhein-Westfalen

PRINCIPAL TYPE
Berthold Akzidenz
Grotesk

DIMENSIONS
Various

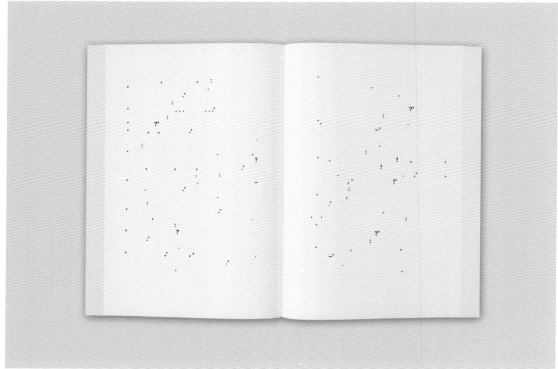

THE REMAINED STRUCTURE

Brochures

ART DIRECTION
Choong Ho Lee

DESIGN
Choong Ho Lee,
Ulsan, Korea

CLIENT
BY T9

PRINCIPAL TYPE
Times New Roman

DIMENSIONS
4.3 x 6.9 in.
(11.1 x 17.6 cm)

CONCEPT
This work explores the structure of specific text through punctuation marks rather than text itself. It also explores the author's writing habits and characteristics through repeated use of punctuation marks.

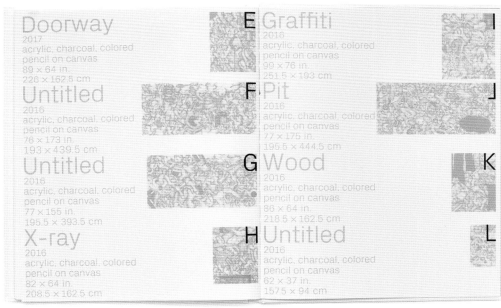

AHMED ALSOUDANI

Catalogs

DESIGN
Ingo Ferdinand
Offermanns, Hamburg

URL
ingooffermanns.com

DESIGN FIRM
Studio Ingo
Offermanns

CLIENT
Marlborough
Contemporary

PRINCIPAL TYPE
PX Grotesk Light, PX
Grotesk Light Italic

DIMENSIONS
11.5 x 14.25 in.
(29.3 x 36 cm)

CONCEPT
"Reducing to the max" is a hackneyed phrase, but in this case it's appropriate. The curators of the exhibition went for a concise choice of sixteen works, so that the artist's massive and detailed paintings could unfold their full impact. An adequate way to translate this approach into a publication seemed to me to turn the material into something like a portfolio for prints. The reader should have the impression of opening up a box with large-scale prints that you can unfold and dive into—image sizes go up to 30.5 x 13.75 inches (77.5 x 35 cm).

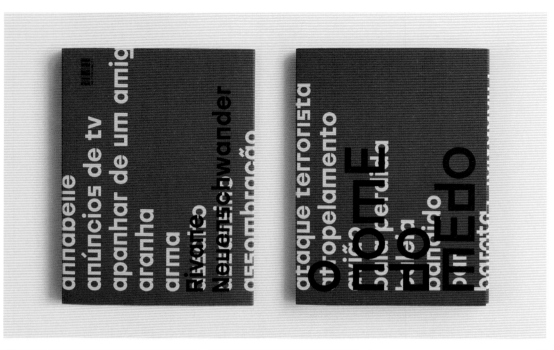

**O NOME DO MEDO
(THE NAME OF FEAR)
BY RIVANE NEUENSCHWANDER**

Catalogs

**DESIGN AND
ART DIRECTION**
Gabriela Castro
Paulo André Chagas
Gustavo Marchetti,
São Paulo, Brazil

ARTIST AND AUTHOR
Rivane
Neuenschwander

**AUTHOR AND EDITOR
(ORGANIZATION)**
Lisette Lagnado

GRAPHIC PRODUCTION
Lilia Góes

**PRINTING AND
IMAGE PROCESSING**
Ipsis Gráfica e
Editora

INSTAGRAM
@blocografico

URL
muratcelep.com
deney.com.tr

TWITTER
Bloco Gráfico

PUBLISHER
Iletisim Publishing

CLIENT
Museu de Arte do
Rio and Escola de
Artes Visuais do
Parque Lage

PRINCIPAL TYPE
Newzald
Stolzl Display

DIMENSIONS
6.9 x 9.6 in.
(17.6 x 24.5 cm)

CONCEPT
The catalog is for Rivane Neuenschwander's
exhibition *The Name of Fear*. The artist
conducted workshops with children on the
theme of fear, where they were asked to
create capes that represented and protected
them from their own fears. The catalog shows
the creative process, combining rich visual
material with critical texts. It consists of
two volumes protected by a single cover,
emulating the effect of the capes worn by
the children. The list of fears was written
in a large and geometric font (named after
Bauhaus's only female master), which
became a graphic element for the project's
visual identity.

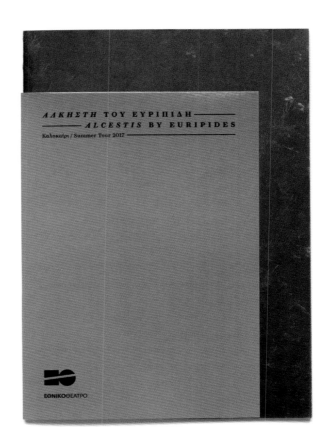

πόλεμος πάντων μὲν πατήρ
ἐστι, πάντων δὲ βασιλεύς, καὶ
τοὺς μὲν θεοὺς ἔδειξε τοὺς δὲ
ἀνθρώπους, τοὺς μὲν δούλους
ἐποίησε τοὺς δὲ ἐλευθέρους.

Ἡράκλειτος, Περὶ φύσεως.

**NATIONAL THEATRE OF
GREECE SUMMER TOUR 2017**

Catalogs

ART DIRECTION
Maria Kefala
Vicky Nitsopoulou,
Athens

CREATIVE DIRECTION
Dimitris Gkazis

ACCOUNT DIRECTOR
Gina Mavrommati

URL
busybuilding.com

**BRANDING AND
DESIGN AGENCY**
busybuilding

CLIENT
National Theatre
of Greece

PRINCIPAL TYPE
Farnham Display
GFS Orpheus Classic

DIMENSIONS
6.7 x 9.5 in.
(17 x 24 cm)

CONCEPT
We were commissioned to create a complete communications campaign for Greece's largest cultural organization, the National Theatre, for its 2017 summer tour. The campaign included everything from outdoor and digital communications to booklets and posters for two plays: Euripides' *Alcestis* and Aristophanes' *Irene* (a drama and a comedy, respectively). For the booklets, we applied the unusual layout and asymmetrical binding we had introduced for the theater's previous season, but we also experimented with the combination of photography and typography. The visual elements thus develop as a semiotic metanarrative inspired by the theme and content of each play.

**EDDIE MARTINEZ:
ANTS AT A PICKNIC**

Catalogs

DESIGN
Katherine Hughes,
Boston

CREATIVE DIRECTION
Clif Stoltze°

MUSEUM DIRECTOR
Lisa Fischman

AUTHORS
Lisa Fischman
Jim Lewis

URL
stoltze.com

TWITTER
@stoltzedesign

AGENCY
Stoltze Design

CLIENT
Davis Museum at
Wellesley College

PRINCIPAL TYPE
Big Ed
Pitch
Post Grotesk

DIMENSIONS
11 x 12.5 in.
(30.7 x 31.75 cm)

CONCEPT
This oversized catalog showcases seven monumental paintings and
seventeen sculptures included in the exhibition at the Davis Museum
at Wellesley College. To reflect the scale, technique, and materiality
of the work, each painting is shown in its entirety, followed by two
full-bleed, close-cropped details. The black-on-black foil-stamped
cover is wrapped with a folded poster of the exhibition's eponymous
painting. For headlines we used Big Ed, a typeface that was appropriately
loose and off-kilter. To the same end, the body text was set in columns
of varying heights to accommodate supporting images.

Her skin is
perpetually on fire.
He can't even feel
a bone break.

Together they
might hold the key
to ending America's
opioid epidemic.

BY
Erika Hayasaki

ART BY
Sean Freeman

PAIN

Magazine Spreads

DESIGN
Eve Steben,
London

ART DIRECTION
Mike Ley

CREATIVE DIRECTION
David Moretti

TYPOGRAPHER
Sean Freeman

URL
thereis.co.uk

DESIGN FIRM
THERE IS Studio

CLIENT
Wired

PRINCIPAL TYPE
Futura Medium

CONCEPT
This design was created to illustrate a story about the physiology
of pain through contrasting freak experiences: People either never or
constantly feel it. The idea was to develop type that evokes the feeling
of pain in a scientific and emotional mood, based on the metaphorical
use of pins and needles.

The battle for Westeros

may be won or lost on the back of a lime green mechanical bull. That's what it looks like on a January Monday in Belfast, as *Game of Thrones* films its seventh season here. Certainly no one believes the dragons that have thrilled viewers of HBO's hit series exist in any real sense. And yet it's still somewhat surprising to see the British actor Emilia Clarke, who plays exiled Queen Daenerys, straddling the "buck" on a soundstage at Titanic Studios, a film complex named after this city's other famously massive export.

◆◆◆

Photographs by Miles Aldridge for TIME

The machine under Clarke looks like a big pommel horse and moves in sync with a computer animation of what will become a dragon. Clarke doesn't talk much between takes. Over and over, a wind gun blasts her with just enough force to make me worry about the integrity of her ash blond wig. (Its particular color is the result of 2½ months' worth of testing and seven prototypes, according to the show's hair designer.) Over and over, Clarke stares down at a masking-tape mark on the floor the instant episode director Alan Taylor shouts, "Now!" Nearby, several visual-effects supervisors watch on monitors.

Clarke and I talk in her trailer before she heads to the soundstage, at the beginning of what is to be a long week inhabiting a now iconic character. Behind the scenes it's more toil than triumph, though. The show's first season ended with Daenerys' hatching three baby dragons, each the size of a Pomeranian. They've since grown to the size of a 747. "I'm 5-ft.-nothing, I'm a little girl," she says. "They're like, 'Emilia, climb those stairs, get on that huge thing, we'll harness you in, and then you'll go crazy.' And you're like, 'Hey, everybody! Now who's shorty?!'"

She has reason to feel powerful. On July 16, Clarke and the rest of the cast will begin bringing *Thrones* in for a landing with the first of its final 13 episodes (seven to air this summer, six to come later). *Thrones*, a scrappy upstart launched by two TV novices in 2011, will finish its run as the biggest and most popular show in the world. An average of more than 23 million Americans watched each episode last season when platforms like streaming and video on demand are accounted for. And since it's the most pirated show ever, millions more watch in ways unaccounted for. *Thrones*, which holds the record for most Emmys ever won by a prime-time series, airs in more than 170 countries. It's the farthest-reaching show out there—not to mention the most obsessed-about.

People talk about living in a golden age of TV ushered in by hit dramas like *The Sopranos*, *Mad Men* and *Breaking Bad*. All had precisely honed insights about the nature of humanity and of evil that remade expectations of what TV could do. But that period ended around the time *Breaking Bad* went off the air in 2013. We're in what came next: an unprecedented glut of programming, with streaming services like Netflix, Amazon and Hulu jumping into an ever-more-crowded fray. Now, there's a prestige show for every conceivable viewer, which means smaller audiences and fewer truly original stories.

Except for *Thrones*, which merges the psychological complexity of the best TV with old-school Hollywood grandeur. You liked shows with one antihero? Well, *Thrones* has five Tony Sopranos building their empires on blood, five Walter Whites discovering just how far they'll go to win, five Don Drapers unapologetic in their narcissism. Oh, and they're all living out their drama against the most

emilia
clarke
*daenerys
targaryen*

hero as possible as Season 7 begins, has outgrown the box he originally came in. Snow, an illegitimate child never embraced by his father's wife, is a James Dean daydream of Sir Walter Scott. "I made mistakes and felt that he wasn't interesting enough," says Kit Harington of the way he's played Snow. We're in a Belfast hotel bar, and Harington is squeezing in a coffee before he makes an evening showing of *Manchester by the Sea*. "That sounds weird, but I've never been quite content with him. Maybe that's what makes him him. That angst." His character has been slowly absorbing lessons about duty and power—and "this year there is this huge seismic shift where all of what he's learned over the years, suddenly ..." Harington trails off. "He's still the same Jon, but he grows up."

Dinklage, too, found in Tyrion a character who surpassed his expectations. The actor says he'd never read fantasy beyond *The Lord of the Rings*. "That's the part of the bookstore I don't really gravitate toward," he says. "This was the first time in this genre that somebody my size was an actually multidimensional being, flesh and blood without the really long beard, without the pointy shoes, without the asexuality."

Thrones catapulted Dinklage, the only American in the main cast, from a well-regarded film and

A Season 7 teaser shows the long-awaited moment Daenerys and her dragons finally arrive in Westeros after years of exile

theater actor to among the most-recognized actors on earth in part because the asexuality is quite absent. Tyrion thirsts for wine, sex and, crucially, love and respect. As the offspring of a wealthy and powerful family, the first two are easy to come by. The latter not so much. "He covers it up with alcohol, he covers it up with humor, he does his best to maintain a modicum of sanity and he perseveres," says Dinklage. "He's still alive. Anyone who's still alive on our show is pretty smart."

Indeed, with just 13 episodes left, everything is possible—alliance, demise or coronation. "Every season I go to the last page of the last episode and go backward," says Dinklage. "I don't do that with books, but I can't crack open page one of Episode 1 not knowing if I'm dead or not."

the drama

The size of *Thrones*' controversies have, at times, been as large as its following. Its reliance on female nudity, especially Daenerys', was an early flash point. "I don't have any qualms saying to anyone it was not the most enjoyable experience. How could it be?" says Clarke. "I don't know how many actresses enjoy doing that part of it." That aspect of the role has faded as Daenerys found paths to power beyond her sexuality. This evolution from a passive naïf into a holy terror who rules by the fealty of her subjects is what has earned Daenerys, according to Clarke, the audience's loyalty. "People wouldn't give two sh-ts about Daenerys if you didn't see her suffer," she says.

More controversy still has been the prevalence of sexual violence. Many of the major female characters have been assaulted onscreen. In a 2015 sequence, Sansa, the Stark daughter played by Sophie Turner, was raped by her husband. According to the logic of the show, the plot gave her character a reason to seek revenge and power of her own. It nonetheless generated substantial blowback online and clearly turned some fans away from the series for good. "This was the trending topic on Twitter, and it makes you wonder, when it happens in real life, why isn't it a trending topic every time?" says Turner, who is 21. "This was a fictional character, and I got to walk away from it unscathed ... Let's take that discussion and that dialogue and use it to help people who are going

maisie
williams
*arya
stark*

**GAME OF THRONES:
HOW THEY MAKE
THE GREATEST SHOW ON EARTH**

Magazine Spreads

**SENIOR ART DIRECTOR
AND ILLUSTRATOR**

Martin Gee,
New York

URLS
time.com
ohmgee.com

TWITTER
@ohmgee

PUBLICATION
Time

PRINCIPAL TYPE
Isotype30

DIMENSIONS
15.75 x 10.5 in.
(40 x 26.7 cm)

CONCEPT
I drew this typeface as a personal project years ago and finally had the right assignment to use it. My goal was to draw something techy and somewhat minimal based on my love for blackletter and isometric hexagons and cubes. Three versions of Isotype30 exist: a horizontal version used here, as well as 30° and -30° baseline versions.

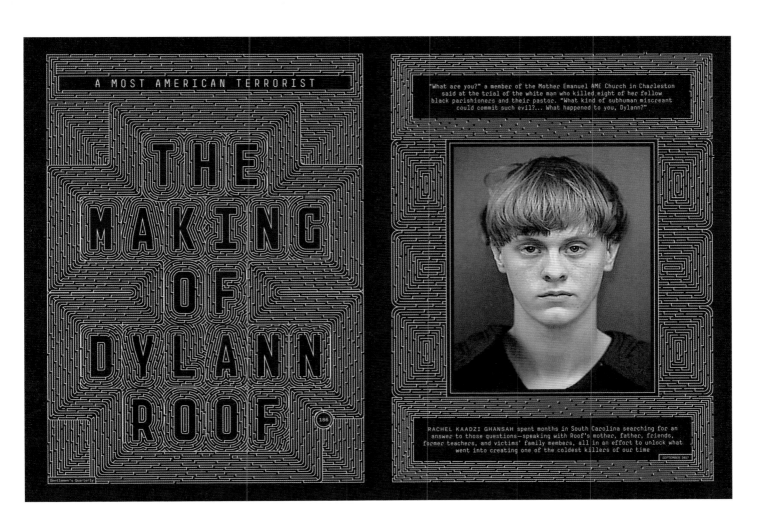

A MOST AMERICAN TERRORIST

THE MAKING OF DYLANN ROOF

"What are you?" a member of the Mother Emanuel AME Church in Charleston said at the trial of the white man who killed eight of her fellow black parishioners and their pastor. "What kind of subhuman miscreant could commit such evil?... What happened to you, Dylann?"

RACHEL KAADZI GHANSAH spent months in South Carolina searching for an answer to those questions—speaking with Roof's mother, father, friends, former teachers, and victims' family members, all in an effort to unlock what went into creating one of the coldest killers of our time

SEPTEMBER 2017

Gentlemen's Quarterly

THE MAKING OF DYLANN ROOF

Magazine Spreads

DESIGN
Kristie Bailey,
New York

DESIGN DIRECTION
Fred Woodward

PHOTO DIRECTOR
Krista Prestek

PUBLICATION
GQ

PRINCIPAL TYPE
Hand-drawn based
on Arete Mono

DIMENSIONS
15 x 11 in.
(38.1 x 27.9 cm)

The Outsiders

PHOTOGRAPHS BY
Peter Hapak

They steal scenes from stars. They're dangerous even when they don't play bad guys. And they definitely aren't doing this for an invite to the Oscars. (Although you'll probably see some of them there.) These charismatic Hollywood misfits are the most unpredictable actors in the game

76 *Gentlemen's Quarterly* 01. 2017

CRISPIN
GLOVER

THE OUTSIDERS

Magazine Spreads

DESIGN
Andre Jointé,
New York

DESIGN DIRECTION
Fred Woodward

PHOTO DIRECTOR
Krista Prestek

PUBLICATION
GQ

PRINCIPAL TYPE
Optimum Condensed

DIMENSIONS
15 x 11 in.
(38.1 x 27.9 cm)

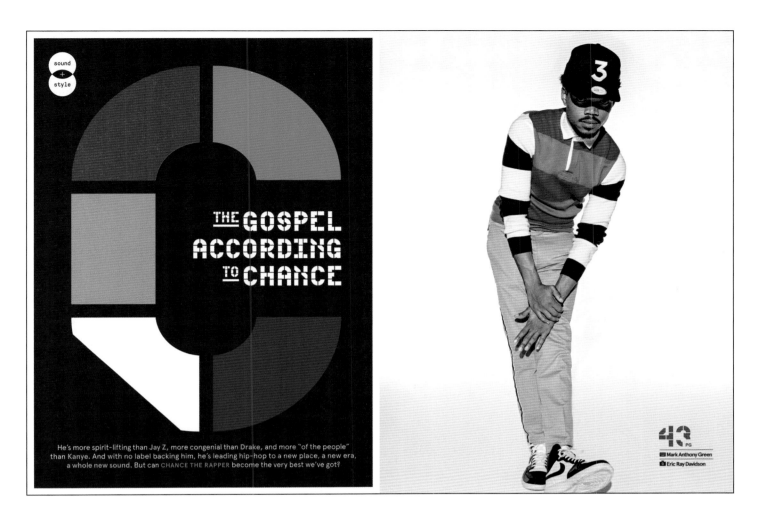

THE GOSPEL
ACCORDING TO CHANCE

Magazine Spreads

DESIGN
Kristie Bailey,
New York

DESIGN DIRECTION
Fred Woodward

PHOTO DIRECTOR
Krista Prestek

PUBLICATION
GQ

PRINCIPAL TYPE
Letterboxes

DIMENSIONS
15 x 11 in.
(38.1 x 27.9 cm)

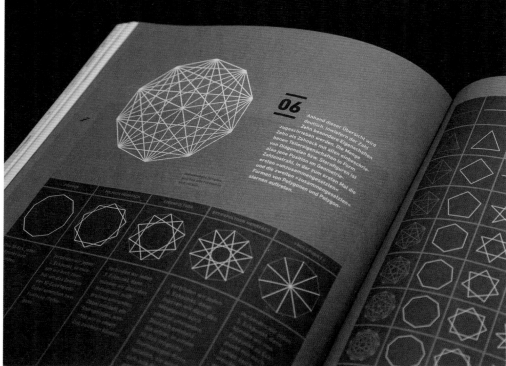

KWER—
MAGAZIN DER ABSTRAKTION N°3

Magazines

ART DIRECTION
Hartmut Friedrich,
Berlin

EDITOR-IN-CHIEF
Dave Großmann

URL
kwer-magazin.de

DESIGN FIRM
Großmann &
Friedrich GbR

PRINCIPAL TYPE
DIN Next LT Pro
DIN Next Slab Pro
Tiempos Text
Headline

DIMENSIONS
9 x 11 in.
(23 x 28 cm)

CONCEPT
How do we interpret abstraction? The term is ubiquitous and can
be found in any form of expression and creation. Be it in the arts,
philosophy, or the natural sciences, we explore the topic of abstraction
from each and every angle. Each edition of this magazine is dedicated
to the number of publications, ranging from the numbers 1 to 9 and
finally completing the series with edition 0. Moving from point 1 to line
2 to triangle 3 over to square 4 and closing with the shape of the circle
(0) in its last edition, each publication examines one geometrical shape
visually as well as in regard to its content. Here are ten titles that shall
be characterized by both their diversity as well as their timelessness.

ÉTAGE MAGAZINE

Magazines

DESIGN
Vyacheslav Kirilenko,
Almaty, Kazakhstan

DESIGN DIRECTION
Zhanar Serikpayeva

DIGITAL DESIGN
Darina Baimukhanova

ART DIRECTION
Karina Iskakova

ILLUSTRATION
Olga Khvan

COLLAGES
Almaz Shadyrkulo

PHOTOGRAPHY
Can Dagarslani
Damir Otegen
Eugene Shishkin
Yuji Watanabe

EDITORS
Fariza Abdraimova
Assel Abilkhamit

URL
etagegroup.kz

**DESIGN STUDIO/
PUBLISHER**
Étage Group

PRINCIPAL TYPE
Various

DIMENSIONS
11.7 x 9 in.
(29.7 x 23 cm)

CONCEPT
Étage Magazine is a publication created by
Étage Group, a design studio based in Almaty,
Kazakhstan. It is an independent magazine
that talks about processes in design,
art, architecture, fashion, and business,
phenomena both structural and chaotic,
temporary and eternal. Rotated ninety
degrees, *Étage VI* enters a new level
of dialogue with the reader. The main goal is
to retrieve the genre of extended interviews
and tell stories of inspiring people whose
opinions truly matter, whose belief systems
inspire discourse.

25 SONGS THAT TELL US
WHERE MUSIC IS GOING

Magazine Spreads

DESIGN
Jason Sfetko,
New York

DESIGN DIRECTION
Gail Bichler

ART DIRECTION
Matt Willey

URL
nytimes.com/
section/magazine

PUBLICATION
*The New York
Times Magazine*

PRINCIPAL TYPE
Custom

DIMENSIONS
10.9 x 9 in.
(27.6 x 22.9 cm)

THE MYSTERIES OF AN EVERYTHING MAN

FOLLOWING THE DEPARTURE OF HIS SUPERSTAR TEAMMATE, RUSSELL WESTBROOK WAS LEFT TO LEAD THE OKLAHOMA CITY THUNDER ALL BY HIMSELF. THAT'S WHEN SOMETHING SPECIAL HAPPENED.

BY SAM ANDERSON
PHOTOGRAPH BY SOLVE SUNDSBO

**THE MYSTERIES OF
AN EVERYTHING MAN**

Magazine Spreads

DESIGN
Ben Grandgenett,
New York

DESIGN DIRECTION
Gail Bichler

ART DIRECTION
Matt Willey

URL
nytimes.com/
section/magazine

PUBLICATION
*The New York
Times Magazine*

PRINCIPAL TYPE
Custom

DIMENSIONS
10.9 x 9 in.
(27.6 x 22.9 cm)

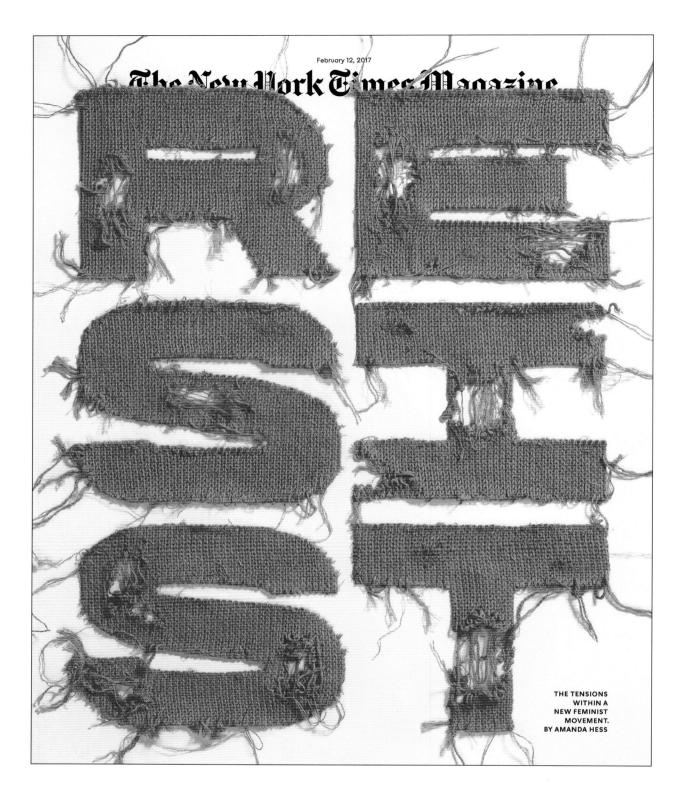

February 12, 2017

The New York Times Magazine

THE TENSIONS
WITHIN A
NEW FEMINIST
MOVEMENT.
BY AMANDA HESS

RESIST

Magazine Covers

DESIGN
Daniel Brokstad
Felipe Rocha,
New York

**CREATIVE AND
ART DIRECTION**
Jessica Walsh

**NEW YORK TIMES
MAGAZINE DESIGN
DIRECTOR**
Gail Bichler

**NEW YORK TIMES
MAGAZINE ART DIRECTOR**
Matt Willey

DEPUTY ART DIRECTOR
Jason Sfetko

PHOTOGRAPHY
Aron Filkey

PRODUCER
Molly Brunk

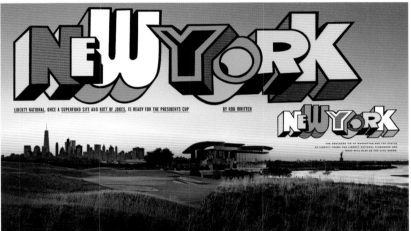

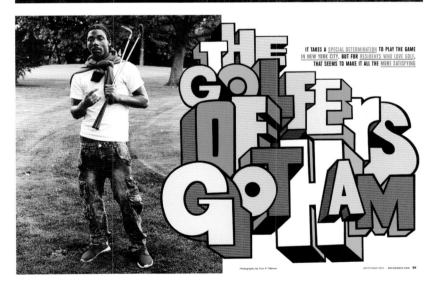

NEW YORK, NEW YORK

Magazine-Themed Stories

DESIGN
Ken De Lago,
New York

PUBLICATION
Golf Digest

PRINCIPAL TYPE
Custom lettering
by Greg Lamarche

DIMENSIONS
16 x 8.5 in.
(40.6 x 21.6 cm)

CONCEPT
When you're tackling a typographic solution for golf in New York,
the only logical answer is to use graffiti.

FONT MAGAZINE

Magazine Cover

DESIGN AND CREATIVE DIRECTION
Jan Šabach,
Northampton,
Massachusetts

URL
codeswitchdesign.com

TWITTER
@codeswitchtweet

DESIGN FIRM
Code Switch

CLIENT
Font Magazine

PRINCIPAL TYPE
Futura Bold
Futura Bold Italic

DIMENSIONS
8.3 x 11.7 in.
(21 x 29.7 cm)

CONCEPT
This issue of Font Magazine is all about
chewing gum, so a visually deconstructed gum
felt like an appropriate design solution.

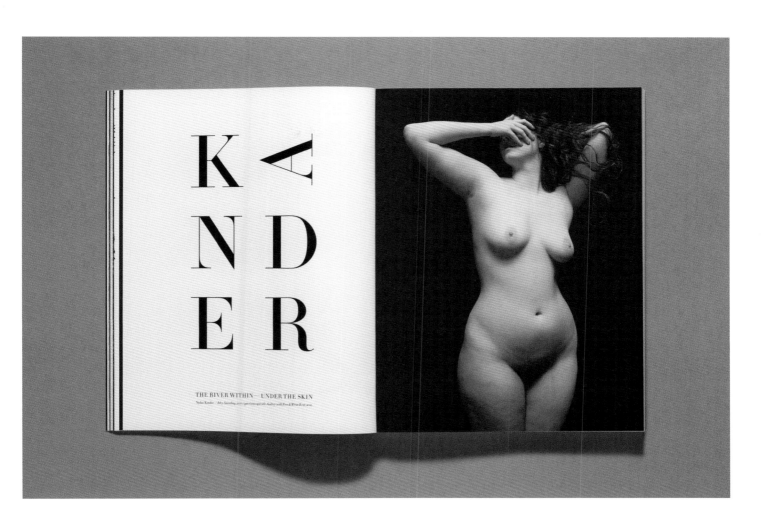

PAN & THE DREAM
MAGAZINE ISSUE 1:
"THE EMPEROR'S NEW CLOTHES"

Magazines

DESIGN
Paul Belford,
London

URL
paulbelford.com

TWITTER
@Belford_Paul

DESIGN FIRM
Paul Belford Ltd

CLIENT
Pan & The Dream
Magazine

PRINCIPAL TYPE
HTF Didot
Didot Elder
Futura ND

DIMENSIONS
11 x 14.5 in.
(28 x 37.9 cm)

CONCEPT
Pan & The Dream's first volume concerns itself with the naked form. It is not nudity in and of itself that is interesting, but rather the context and the message that the image carries. Each artist portrays the nude differently; however, they all respond to the question of nudity in art and its suppression in the mediatized world. The issue is a coming together of new and archival work from esteemed artists and young creatives alike. It is a statement that defies the current wave of commercial puritanism and the mishandling of censorship in social media.

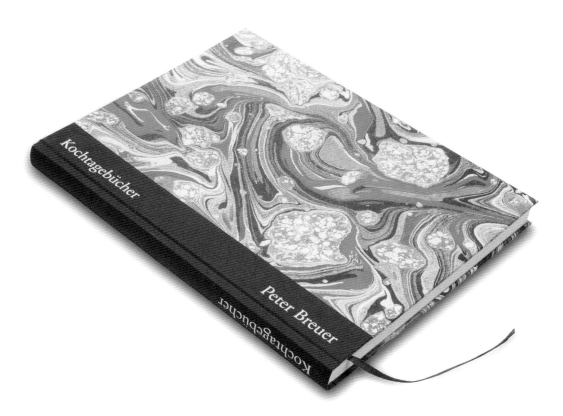

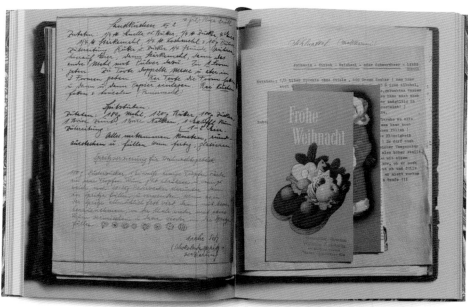

KOCHTAGEBÜCHER

Magazines

DESIGN
Fons Hickmann
Miriam Rech,
Berlin

PHOTOGRAPHY
Hans Hansen

LITHOGRAPHY
Sador Weinsċlucker

WRITER
Peter Breuer

EDITOR
Kerstin Leesch

URL
fonshickmann.com

TWITTER
@fonshickmannm23

DESIGN FIRM
Fons Hickmann m23,
Berlin

CLIENT
Greenpeace Media,
Hamburg

PRINCIPAL TYPE
Sabon Next
(Regular, Bold,
and Italic)

DIMENSIONS
8.9 x 11.8 in.
(22.5 x 30 cm)

CONCEPT
Kochtagebücher (Cooking Diaries) draws from
Peter Breuer's collection of handwritten,
personal cookbooks from the late eighteenth
to early twentieth centuries, which he has
been assembling for over a decade. The
spreads were printed in their original size
to give the reader an authentic impression
of these antique treasures. The cover is an
interpretation of the handmade marbled paper
that many of the cookbooks were bound in.
The book was set in Sabon Next in a classic
layout based on the golden ratio.

The New York Times Magazine

AUGUST 27, 2017

THE U.S. OPEN ISSUE

W O N D E R

YEAR

Roger Federer hadn't won a Grand Slam in almost half a decade. Then he made a crucial change to his game.

By Peter de Jonge

WONDER YEAR

Magazine Spreads

DESIGN
Deb Bishop,
New York

DESIGN DIRECTION
Gail Bichler

ART DIRECTION
Matt Willey

URL
nytimes.com/
section/magazine

PUBLICATION
*The New York
Times Magazine*

PRINCIPAL TYPE
A2 Beckett

DIMENSIONS
10.9 x 9 in.
(27.6 x 22.9 cm)

Photograph by Maurizio Cattelan and Pierpaolo Ferrari

FALL FASHION—2017

Magazine Spreads

DESIGN
Thomas Alberty
Christopher Cristiano
Aaron Garza
Randy Minor,
New York

PUBLICATION
New York Magazine

PRINCIPAL TYPE
Louis NYM Condensed

DIMENSIONS
10 x 15.75 in.
(25.4 x 40 cm)

CONCEPT
Some fonts just want to be used big, and Louis NYM Condensed is one of them. The unique letterforms of this typeface by Nicolas Franck Pauly have the qualities of a classic condensed sans without the strict uniformity of stroke thickness, and have just enough flair in some of the curvatures. In layouts, we used the typeface as large as we could, going for that monumentality that condensed type allows. Doing so showed off the face's unique characteristics, which ultimately paired well with the art.

Spring Fashion

New York | BY AMY LAROCCA

IT'S A SLIGHTLY uncomfortable time to be thinking about fashion; at this juncture in world history, does it really matter that yellow had a moment in Milan? Probably not, but the world does keep turning, for the moment, anyway, and here we are, faced with that sunshine yellow, a new crop of floral prints, and an exciting group of films (and stars) vying for Oscars at the end of the month. It certainly won't save the world to think about these matters, but they might, for a minute, provide a humanizing diversion, a glimpse of beauty or fantasy, before we dive back into the maw. Another thing to think about: the ways in which fashion can change perceptions and attitudes. Consider the launch of *Vogue Arabia* and the high-powered Saudi woman who's running that show, or the icons to whom actress Jessica Lange pays tribute in a photographic portfolio (Gloria Steinem among them). For politics to change, politics must change. But an iconic picture can, sometimes, become its own galvanizing rallying cry.

Boots by Marc Jacobs, at marcjacobs.com.

SPRING FASHION—2017

Magazine Spreads

DESIGN
Thomas Alberty
Christopher Cristiano
Aaron Garza
Randy Minor
Jamie Prokell,
New York

PUBLICATION
New York Magazine

PRINCIPAL TYPE
Elster
Ogg

DIMENSIONS
10 x 15.75 in.
(25.4 x 40 cm)

CONCEPT
Because this was a fashion issue, we looked for typography with strong thick and thin strokes—but we wanted something atypical. We found the beginning of a typeface by Bobby Tannam that embodied these qualities and worked with him to develop a full alphabet. The letterforms are condensed with an extremely high x-height, and the serifs flare out, almost as in blackletter type, creating a truly unique typeface. We then established a loose system of breaking the baseline in headlines to carve out positive and negative areas. Pairing Elster with the wider, delicate Ogg created another layer of texture and contrast.

BRECHTFESTIVAL AUGSBURG 2017

Magazines

ART DIRECTION
Mara Weyel,
Augsburg, Germany

CREATIVE DIRECTION
Artur Gulbicki

CALLIGRAPHY
Iris Schmitt
Mara Weyel

URL
kw-neun.de

FIRM
KW NEUN
Grafikagentur

CLIENT
Kulturamt der Stadt

PRINCIPAL TYPE
Aperçu
Rough Typewriter
Handlettering

DIMENSIONS
10.1 x 13.8 in.
(25.7 x 35 cm)

CONCEPT
The topic of Brechtfestival Augsburg 2017 was "Change the World—It Needs It." This quote from Bertolt Brecht was reassigned to communication. There's changing, crossing out, underlining, emphasizing, and correcting. This design was a tribute to Brecht, who was hardly out and about without his typewriter.

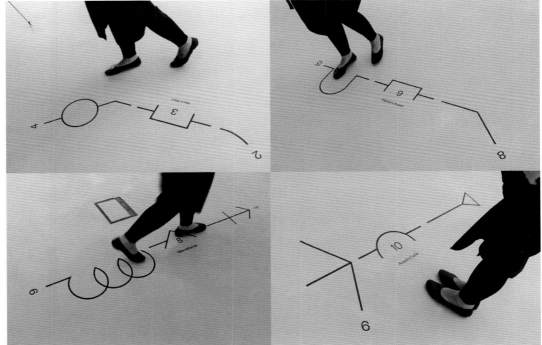

THE PLACE TO BE

Exhibits

GRAPHIC DESIGN
Edda Bracchi
Stefano Cremisini,
Rome

URL
etaoin-shrdlu.com

DESIGN FIRM
Etaoin Shrdlu Studio

CLIENT
MAXXI—Museo
nazionale delle arti
del XXI secolo

PRINCIPAL TYPE
Founders Grotesk,
Mono Regular
Founders Grotesk
Family

DIMENSIONS
Various

CONCEPT
The exhibition *The Place to Be* investigates the relationship between humans and their habitat, reflecting upon the connection between public and domestic space, from the city to the private. "The place" is man's space. By inhabiting it, human beings design and complete this space, their bodies defining the environment that surrounds them. Humans use signs to continuously negotiate a portion of space for themselves, demarcating their terrain and entering into dialogue with the exterior.

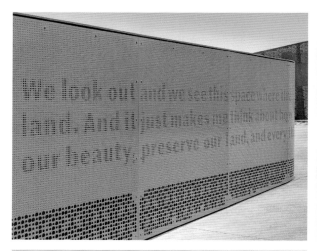

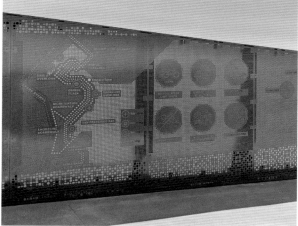

HUNTERS POINT SHORELINE ENVIRONMENTAL GRAPHICS

Exhibits

DESIGN
Ben Fehrman-Lee
Manuel Miranda
Fred Pirlot,
New York

URL
manuelmiranda.info

STUDIO
Manuel Miranda
Practice (MMP)

CLIENT
Pacific Gas &
Electric Company and
Envelope AD (Lead
Consultant)

PRINCIPAL TYPE
Marr Sans with
alterations

DIMENSIONS
Various

CONCEPT
In close collaboration with Berkeley-based architecture firm Envelope AD and urbanist Liz Ogbu (Studio O), MMP developed interpretive signage that reflects the complex social and historical relationships of a post-industrial site in south San Francisco. Embedded in concrete benches and perforated steel walls, the typography and graphics provide both functional wayfinding as well as representation of the community voices, historical events, and environmental conditions that define the site's legacy.

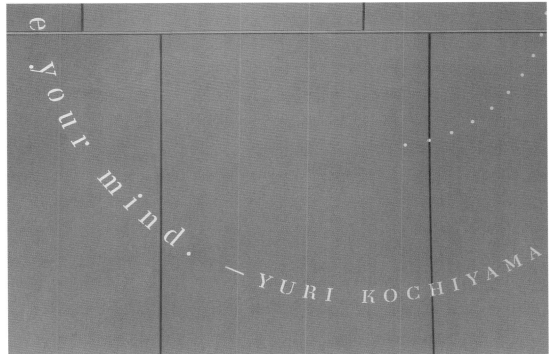

**PRINCETON
INTERNATIONAL ATRIUM**

Exhibits

DESIGN
Jihye Um,
Brooklyn, New York

DESIGN DIRECTION
Nicole Fischetti

PARTNERS
Andy Chen
Waqas Jawaid

URL
isometricstudio.com

TWITTER
@isometricstudio

DESIGN FIRM
Isometric Studio

CLIENT
Princeton University

PRINCIPAL TYPE
Danmark

DIMENSIONS
Various

CONCEPT
To commemorate the new Simpson International Building, Isometric created a distinctive spatial identity that celebrates Princeton University's international ethos. We designed a floor installation that spans three levels, featuring quotations from global authors. The concentric design begins in the atrium center and emanates outward. As visitors walk over the porcelain tiles, quotes, lines, and dots shimmer into view. After the careful application of silver vinyl graphics, the entire 7,200-square-foot floor area was coated with an epoxy that temporarily turned it glossy. Then a thin coat of polyurethane restored the original matte appearance of the tile.

YES! YEAR END SHOW IDENTITY

Exhibits

DESIGN
Erin Hyelin Kim
Prin Limphongpand,
New Haven,
Connecticut

URLS
erinh.kim
raxyl.com

CLIENT
Yale School of
Architecture

PRINCIPAL TYPE
Druk
Helvetica Neue

DIMENSIONS
Vertical 80 x 160 in.
(203.2 x 406.4 cm),
Horizontal 96 x 48 in.
(243.8 x 121.9 cm)

YOU = EU

Signage

DESIGN AND ART DIRECTION
Lizá Ramalho
Artur Rebelo,
Porto, Portugal

PRODUCTION
Tommasino

DESIGN FIRM
R2

CLIENT
EDP Foundation
& Rede Inducar

PRINCIPAL TYPE
Custom

DIMENSIONS
114.2 x 25.9 ft.
(34.8 x 79 m)

CONCEPT
This site-specific intervention, located on a frontier dam, departs from Mirandese, Portugal's second language. The work, inscribed on the east wall of the Miranda Dam, is drawn along and inside of the predefined metric of the walls, and merges into the structure. A reflection of readability and interpretation, the concepts of "I" and "other" are situated within territorial and linguistic border areas. The text is based on the coincidence that the first-person singular of "Mirandese" (Eu) is pronounced the same way as "you." You = Eu acquires additional meaning in the current socio-political context arising from the U.K. referendum.

SIGNAGE SCHOOL SCHENDLINGEN

Signage

DESIGN
Andrea Gassner
Christopher Walser,
Vorarlberg, Austria

ART DIRECTION
Andrea Gassner

URL
ateliergassner.at

DESIGN FIRM
Atelier Gassner

CLIENT
Landeshauptstadt
Bregenz; Bernhard
Fink, Planung
und Bau

PRINCIPAL TYPE
Custom based on DIN

CONCEPT
Out of these normative constraints Atelier Gassner has succeeded in generating a communicative and artistic added value. As you walk by these typographies, depending on the particular location one word or the other appears clearly legible, as if by magic, but in-between the interferences of the overlaid letters and lines create their own delightful, constantly new game. In addition, they are connected by the cross-hatching called for by the building regulations in full-height glass walls to prevent people from walking into them. The signage convinced through this lively game played with perception for a building in which conveying things worth knowing and seeing to around six hundred children is a main focus.

CORNELL TECH SIGNAGE

Signage

DESIGN
Elizabeth Kim
Chuan-Wei Ting,
New York

PARTNER-IN-CHARGE AND
DESIGN DIRECTOR
Michael Gericke

ASSOCIATE PARTNER AND
DESIGN DIRECTOR
Don Bilodeau

PROJECT COORDINATOR
Amanda Walter

URL
pentagram.com

DESIGN FIRM
Pentagram

CLIENT
Cornell Tech

PRINCIPAL TYPE
FF Din, in various
weights, for
messaging content
and identification
signs; custom "C"
for sculptured
elements

DIMENSIONS
Various

CONCEPT
The signage and identity elements for the Cornell Tech campus were designed to carefully integrate into and coexist with the surrounding landscaping and architecture. To create the structural form, a customized letter "C" was extruded and extended, then chamfered along the top. This chamfer allows the letterform to be visible from many vantage points, while an added illuminated core helps identify the forms as "beacons" for wayfinding. The site identifier also serves as an interactive feature, allowing students and visitors to travel through the sculptural form. The text for the signage was set in FF Din, a modern, legible interpretation of the classic German typeface of the same name.

LOUISE BOURGEOIS:
AN UNFOLDING PORTRAIT

Exhibits

DESIGN
Danielle Hall
David Klein,
New York

ART DIRECTION AND DESIGN
Derek Flynn

CREATIVE DIRECTION
H. Y. Ingrid Chou°

PRODUCTION
Claire Corey
Paulette Giguere
Tom Black Studio

DESIGN FIRM
Department of
Advertising and
Graphic Design,
Museum of
Modern Art

MUSEUM
Department of
Drawings and
Prints, Museum
of Modern Art

URL
momadesignstudio.org

PRINCIPAL TYPE
Caslon540 BT
Harbour

DIMENSIONS
98 x 53 in.
(248.9 x 134.6 cm)
44 x 56 in.
(111.8 x 167.6 cm)

CONCEPT
Louise Bourgeois: An Unfolding Portrait
explored the prints, books, and creative
process of this celebrated artist. For
the title wall, the letters were hand-
drawn using the typeface Harbour as the
foundation of the exhibition's graphic
identity. The bespoke line treatment was
inspired by Bourgeois's own drawing,
printing, and stitching—the repetition
of lines reflecting her often iterative
work. The round and hard-edge angles of
Harbour also complemented forms found
in her artwork. Harbour was paired
with the secondary typeface Caslon
for section texts and labels.

**CLUB 57: FILM, PERFORMANCE,
AND ART IN THE EAST VILLAGE,
1978–1983**

Exhibits

DESIGN
Eva Bochem-Shur,
New York

**ART DIRECTION AND
DESIGN**
Damien Saatdjian

CREATIVE DIRECTION
H. Y. Ingrid Chou°

PRODUCTION
Claire Corey
Tom Black Studio

URL
momadesignstudio.org

DESIGN FIRM
Department of
Advertising and
Graphic Design,
Museum of
Modern Art

MUSEUM
Department of
Drawings and
Prints, Museum
of Modern Art

PRINCIPAL TYPE
MoMA Sans

DIMENSIONS
78 x 66 in.
(198.1 x 167.6 cm)

CONCEPT
Club 57 was a countercultural hub located in the basement of a Polish
church at 57 St. Marks Place where artists, musicians, performers,
and curators met to exchange ideas, party, and show new work.
The exhibition presents their accomplishments across a range of
disciplines. Inspired by the club setting and use of DIY fliers, we
designed an identity system with large, stretched typography and
a neon title wall. We applied this typographic system to wristbands
for performances and coasters for specialty drinks. The advertising,
posters, and fliers used photographs from parties and performances,
along with works of art created by the Club 57 community.

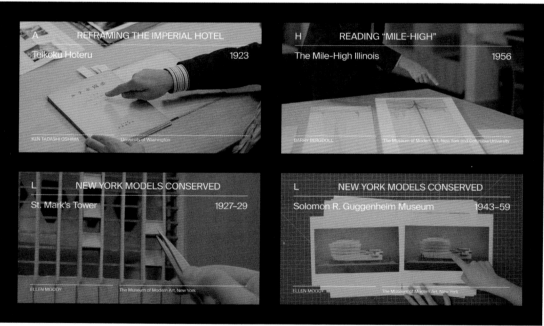

FRANK LLOYD WRIGHT AT 150:
UNPACKING THE ARCHIVE

Exhibits

DESIGN
Danielle Hall, New York

**ART DIRECTION
AND DESIGN**
Damien Saatdjian

CREATIVE DIRECTION
H. Y. Ingrid Chou°

PRODUCTION
Claire Corey
Tom Black Studio

URL
momadesignstudio.org

MUSEUM
Department of
Advertising and
Graphic Design, and
Department of
Architecture and
Design, Museum
of Modern Art

PRINCIPAL TYPE
Suisse
by Swiss Typefaces

DIMENSIONS
228 x 110 in.
(579.1 x 279.2 cm)

CONCEPT
In 2012, the Museum of Modern Art and Columbia University jointly acquired Frank Lloyd Wright's archives. To commemorate the architect's 150th birthday, MoMA invited scholars from a variety of fields to, quite literally, unpack his archive and curate individual galleries within the exhibition, each dedicated to an object or cluster of objects of their choosing. Complementing this curatorial approach, we designed an exhibition identity rooted in indexes and cataloging. Starting with the title wall, which acted as a thematic directory, the methodical system was employed across gallery titles, section texts, a timeline, and video stills.

DOWNTOWN CLAYTON WAYFINDING

Signage

DESIGN
Sarah Newitt
Martí Pérez Palau
Jim Redington,
London and
St. Louis, Missouri

ART DIRECTION
Sarah Newitt

URL
kikuobata.com

DESIGN STUDIO
Kiku Obata & Company

CLIENT
City of Clayton

PRINCIPAL TYPE
Standard CT

DIMENSIONS
Fingerpost:
42 x 96 in.
(106.7 x 243.8 cm),
Kiosk:
18 x 78 in.
(45.7 x 198.1 cm)

CONCEPT
This is a comprehensive wayfinding system that includes pedestrian fingerposts, sidewalk kiosks with pedestrian maps, vehicular directionals, and parking identification. The intent was to create a contemporary yet timeless signage system that is highly visible but with a subtle presence on the street. We designed the full system in black, powder-coated steel, accented with red-orange caps. Each kiosk includes You Are Here pedestrian maps, created for all unique locations.

CANG JIE SCRIPT

Experimental

ART DIRECTION
XU Lixian, Shenzhen,
Guangdong, China

URL
3lbrand.com

DESIGN FIRM
3LBrand Design
and Consulting

PRINCIPAL TYPE
Cang Jie Script

DIMENSIONS
27.6 x 39.4 in.
(70 x 100 cm)

CONCEPT
This project takes the innovation of traditional culture as its core idea, evolving ancient words into an innovative font of the future. According to legend, twenty-eight words were written by Cang Jie, and they are the most ancient words that exist up to now. In this new edition, Cang Jie Script is interpreted as 戊 (the fifth), 巳 (the sixth), 甲 (the first), 乙 (the second), 居 (location), 首 (head), 共 (general), 友 (friend), 所 (place), 止 (end), 列 (line), 世 (world), 式 (pattern), 气 (air), 光 (light), 名 (name), 左 (left), 互 (mutual), 爻 (trigram), 家 (family), 受 (receive), 尊 (respect), 戈 (dagger-axe), 茅 (ramie), 斧 (axe), and 芾 (exuberant).

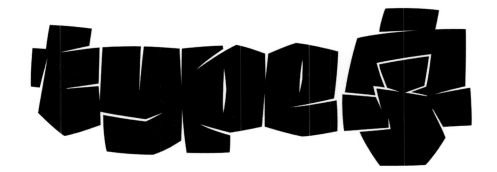

BILINGUAL LETTERING

Experimental

ART DIRECTION
Tien-Min Liao,
New York

URLS
bilinguallettering.com
typeji.com

TWITTER
@typeji

STUDIO
Typeji

CONCEPT
This project is a series of Latin-Kanji pairing studies for use in bilingual lettering and logotype. The project site documents fifty-plus pairing exercises as well as some thoughts and notes gained through the process. These pairing examples are not solutions for developing systematic typefaces but are the results of customizing the word "Type" and "字". Because these two writing systems are traditionally written with different tools and the character structures are very different, in order to inject the same personality into these two scripts, sometimes flexibility is necessary. Every single pair is a custom result, so there isn't only one solution.

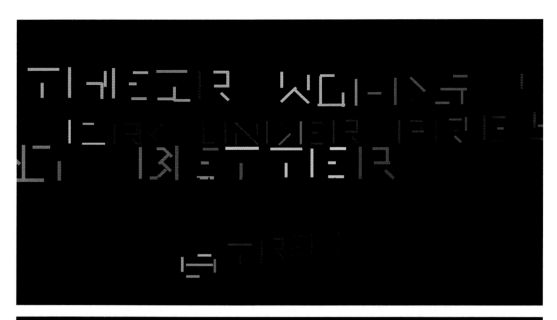

DISCUSSIONS OVER DINNER

Experimental

DESIGN AND CONCEPT
Matthias Hillner
Stanley Lim
Andreas Schlegel,
Singapore

SCHOOL
LASALLE College
of the Arts

URL
lasalle.edu.sg

CONTRIBUTORS
Siti Shafika binte Abdullah
Khushboo Agarwal
Christie Cheng
Reva Dhingra
Jessica Emily
Jane Foo
Andree Selene River
 Villaroman Garcia
Nicole Goh
Christopher Gong

Xuan Ha
Soh Xing Hao
Johan Iswara
Sakshi Jalan
Quek Mei Jun
Anand Gunveen Kaur
Claudius Keng
Ardine Keyla
Joy Lee
Yolande Leong
Jiang Xiao Long
Ariel Loy
Joshua Edward
 Navarro Lumain
Wanvari Vishesh Manoj
Samiksha Nair
Nirati Nayak
Kevin Ng
Ipshita Pal
Ng Peiling
Janna Phua
Mathan Raj
Felicia Agnes Salim

Muhammad Faris
 bin Samri
Quenna Tan Hui Shan
Jyotsna Shivkumar
Raelene Soon
Kimberley Tan
Nicholas Tan
Sherlyn Tan
Jeremiah Tang
Noel Teo
Venus Teo
Laksmi Arista Vyanda
Jennifer Wiriawan
Shawn Wu
Teo Boon Yee
Weng Yiping
Ashley Yuen
Mohamad Haikel bin
 Yusuff
Elizabeth Zhang

PRINCIPAL TYPE
Cubico Stencil

CONCEPT
This projection of generative typography was designed for the *Travelling Letters* exhibition at Vilnius Academy of Arts. Students wrote short statements on the notion of creativity and produced short video clips to illustrate their thoughts. The font was broken down into modular components to allow the statements to move across the projection screen. Custom-built software was programmed to allow the spatial disposition (z-axis) of individual letter shapes to be determined by the brightness of the pixels of the video footage beneath. As a result, the letter shapes move back and forth in space depending on the color values that the script extracts from the video footage. The disfiguration of type is constantly changing, as are the creative capabilities of individuals and societies.

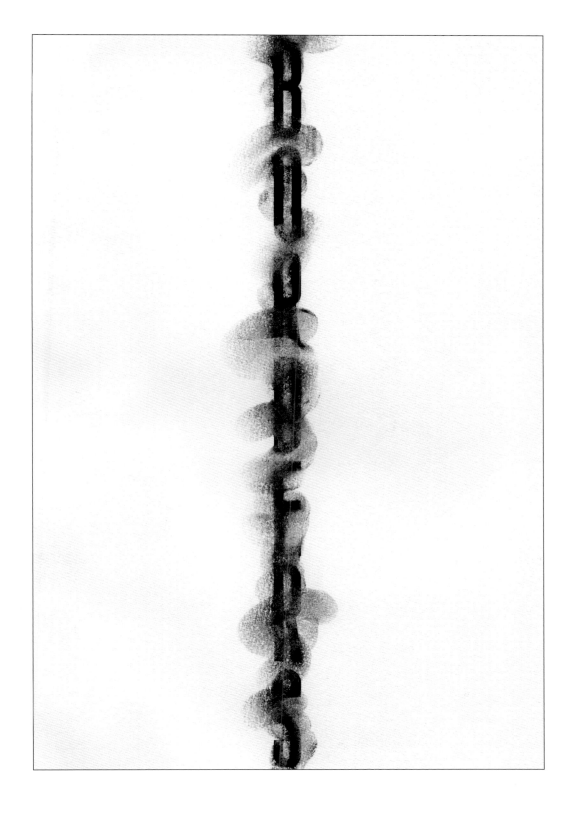

BORDERS

Experimental

DESIGN
Bob Aufuldish,
San Anselmo,
California

URL
aufwar.com

DESIGN FIRM
Aufuldish &
Warinner

CLIENT
Alliance Graphique
Internationale

PRINCIPAL TYPE
Pakt Extrabold
Condensed

DIMENSIONS
Various

CONCEPT
Each year, as part of the AGI Congress, members are invited to
participate in a special project. The theme for 2017 was "Borders:
Yesterday, Today, Tomorrow." My contribution ruminates on the
permeability of borders.

IRRESISTIBLE WAVE

Experimental

**DESIGN AND
CREATIVE DIRECTION**

Minjoo Kim
Youngwook Nam
Jooyoun Sun, Seoul

URL

60603project.com

PROJECT GROUP

60603

PRINCIPAL TYPE

SM3 SinsinMyungjo

DIMENSIONS

Various

CONCEPT

Document and word-processing programs in the digital space
are based on the spelling system, which distinguishes errors by
automatically generating a red underline. But it does not always mean
that the text is an "error." This project brings the red underline of the
digital space into the physical space. The red underline escapes from
being the element that denies a text, and instead becomes a sign of a
new possibility and creation that expands the subject. When viewers
touch the red underline, which is both familiar and unfamiliar, they
experience a new space that explores infinite boundaries.

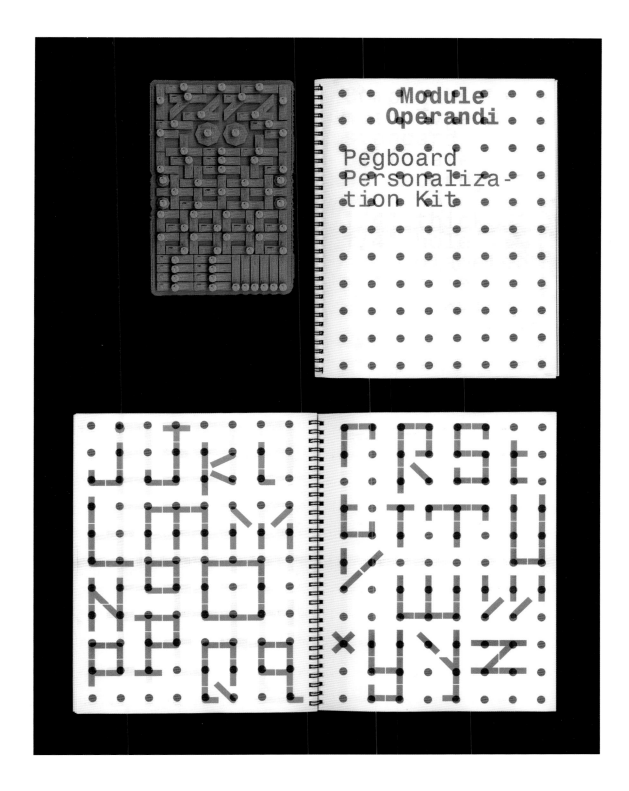

MODULE OPERANDI

Experimental

DESIGN
Yotam Hadar,
New York

URL
yotamhadar.com

TWITTER
@yotam

PRINCIPAL TYPE
Custom using Module
Operandi parts and
Monospace 821

DIMENSIONS
3D Object: 6 x 3.7 in.
(15 x 10 cm)
Book: 8.5 x 11 in.
(21 x 28 cm)

CONCEPT
A pegboard expansion and personalization kit consists of an open-source file for 3D printing and an instruction manual. "Module Operandi" is a kit of small movable bits that attach onto standard pegboards, expanding their functionality and enabling interaction and personalization. Planned as an open system, this kit of parts enables invention of new, playful ways of engagement with what is typically a utilitarian object. The accompanying wire-bound publication is half instruction manual, half artist book. It is Riso printed in two layers—one is a dot grid mimicking a pegboard pattern, and the other is a series of type and form experiments using shapes from the kit.

DOC.A TYPE SPECIMEN

Experimental

DESIGN
Sascha Lobe°
Sven Thiery
Yuan Wang
Jonas Zieher,
Stuttgart

STUDIO
L2M3
Kommunikationsdesign
GmbH

URL
l2m3.com

PRINCIPAL TYPE
doc.A

DIMENSIONS
13 x 18 in.
(33 x 46 cm)

FAIR DINKUM
THE STRUGGLE IS REAL
MANSPLAINING

Experimental

DESIGN
Karolina Lach°,
New York

URLS
karolinalach.com
pettytypecrimes.com

TWITTER
@thekarolina

INSTAGRAM
@therealkarolina

DESIGN FIRM
Petty Type Crimes

PRINCIPAL TYPE
Custom lettering

DIMENSIONS
Various

CONCEPT
This is an ongoing series of typographically experimental ceramic vessels. Drawing on historical lettering styles, it playfully juxtaposes the venerable medium of ceramics with the ephemerality of slang, humorous sayings, and internet zeitgeist.

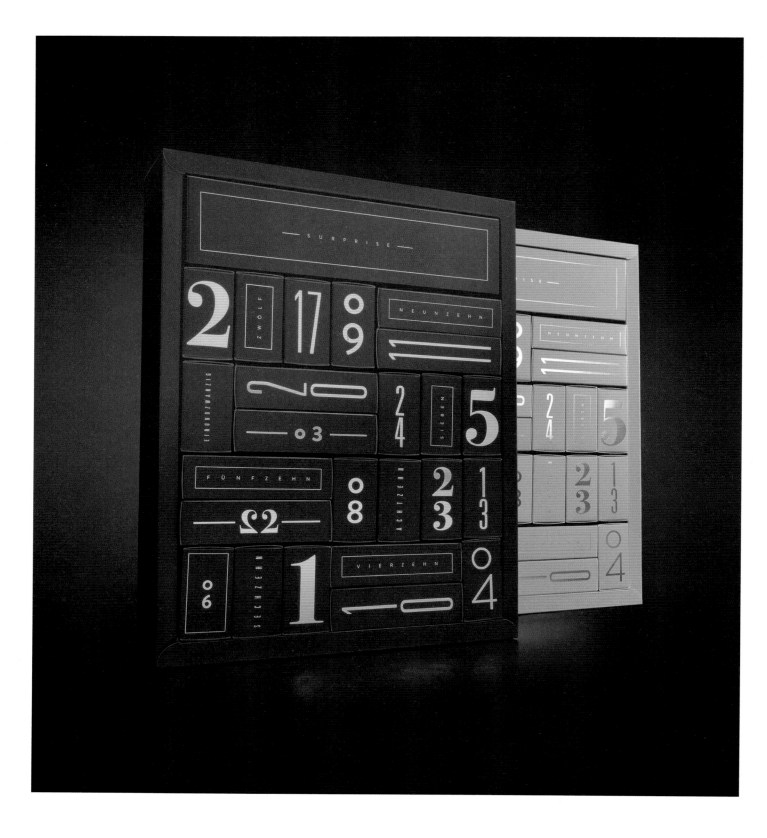

**TYPOGRAPHIC
ADVENT CALENDAR**

Calendars

**DESIGN, ART DIRECTION,
AND CREATIVE DIRECTION**
Michaela Vargas
Coronado,
Augsburg, Germany

URL
vargas-coronado.com

DESIGN FIRM
Michaela Vargas
Coronado

CLIENT
Adventskalender
GmbH

PRINCIPAL TYPE
Bodoni
Brandon Grotesque
Universe Thin Ultra
Condensed

DIMENSIONS
12.9 x 16.7 in.
(32.7 x 42.4 cm)

CONCEPT
Typography and simple graphic lines are
the only design elements used on this advent
calendar. The boxes can be individually filled.
The vision was to create an advent calendar
that becomes an elegant piece of decoration.
Every box is individually designed, and, put
together, all the elements form a visual entity.

DREAM

Identities

DESIGN
Cyrus Blais
CJ Draper
Jen Yung,
New York

**GLOBAL EXECUTIVE
CREATIVE DIRECTOR**
Tosh Hall°

MANAGING DIRECTOR
Sara Hyman

DIRECTOR OF STRATEGY
Daniel D'Arcy

DIRECTOR OF BRAND
Grace Dawson

BRAND EXECUTIVE
Rachel Ptak

PHOTOGRAPHY
David Farrell
Jack Jeffries

TYPOGRAPHY
Ian Brignell

ACCOUNT MANAGER
Zach Anziska

PRODUCERS
Grace Dawson
Rosina Pang

RETOUCHER
Simon Ve

FILM AND MOTION
Justin Sottile

URL
jkrglobal.com

TWITTER
@JKRglobal

AGENCY
Jones Knowles
Ritchie

CLIENT
Dream

PRINCIPAL TYPE
High School Sans

DIMENSIONS
Various

CONCEPT
"Dream" started in 1991 as a baseball diamond in an abandoned lot in Harlem. In 2011 the Dream Charter School opened, and by 2016 they wanted to expand beyond New York City but needed a new identity to reflect their ambitions. From naming to identity to uniforms, we re-envisioned a Dream that was fit for the future. With a new identity based around the home plate, we created a system that allowed flexibility—reflecting the expansive nature of children's imaginations. Dream has since opened a high school in South Bronx and programs in Newark, New Jersey, fulfilling their ongoing mission of supporting dreams everywhere.

BAUHAUS MUSEUM WEIMAR

Identities

ART DIRECTION
Petr Pscolka
Nadja Ratz
Andreas Steinbrecher
Andreas Uebele°,
Stuttgart

URL
uebele.com

DESIGN FIRM
büro uebele visuelle
kommunikation

CLIENT
Klassik Stiftung Weimar

PRINCIPAL TYPE
Neuzeit Grotesk

DIMENSIONS
Various

CONCEPT
What exactly makes up the essence, the "visual identity" of a major museum and its collections? Is it the architecture? The exhibits? In all probability it is a blend of all these factors. But the core of the whole thing—the identity per se—is the idea on which Bauhaus was founded. This, we recall, is where the originals took shape that are etched on our cultural consciousness as "Bauhaus." These iconic items, such as the lamp, the chair, and the door handle, were all designed and manufactured in Weimar: The objects actually form a key part of its visual identity. The contemporary witnesses are drawn by hand to emphasize the craftsmanship they embody. In this corporate design, it is the objects and their creators that take center stage.

HYPER LIEUX MOBILES
MOBILE HYPERSPACES

Identities

ART DIRECTION
Susanna Shannon°,
Paris and Marseilles,
France

CLIENT
Institut pour la Ville
en Mouvement,
Paris (Mireille Apel-
Muller, Yuna Conan,
and Julien Barbier)

PRINCIPAL TYPE
Helvetica Neue LT Pro

DIMENSIONS
8.25 x 11.7 in.
(21 x 29.7 cm)

CONCEPT
We wanted to begin a work-in-progress "visuality" with the launch
of IVM's new research program called Hyper Lieux Mobiles. This
first delivery is a collection of folders that are used by the think tank
to send off information packets to future partners of the research
program. This will soon be followed by a brochure. The motifs on the
folders are portions of much larger files that the folders have been
"cut out of," as if cut out of a large piece of material that will
be revealed gradually throughout the program.

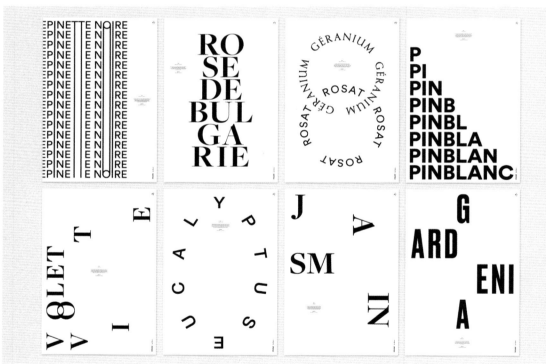

PRUNE CANDLE COLLECTION

Identities

DESIGN AND CREATIVE DIRECTION
Sébastien Bisson, Montréal

ACCOUNT DIRECTOR
Jean Doyon

URL
polygraphe.ca

STUDIO
Polygraphe Studio

CLIENT
Nadine Jazouli

PRINCIPAL TYPE
LL Circular
Druk
Freight
Gotham
GT Sectra Display

DIMENSIONS
Various

CONCEPT
Hand-dripped in batches of 125 per fragrance, these exclusive candles are crafted with carefully selected essences and essential oils that make them all the more exquisite and rare. The solution for illustrating each scent is deceptively simple: For each candle, create a typographic design that captures the character of the fragrance. The limitless flexibility of the typography means that the collection, which had eight candles at launch, can evolve in any direction.

do+little

We're a modern hair and body care brand.

CRUELTY-FREE

DERMATOLOGIST TESTED

PUT YOUR BEST SELF FORWARD

Hair looks best when it's ready for action—not frozen into place.

Featuring premium natural products developed specifically for children, we're building a brand-new category of essentials that optimally tends to kids' unique hair and skin needs, while also being safe, effective and fun.

WITH BOTANI-MILK COMPLEX

. . . .

DO+LITTLE

Identities

DESIGN
Drianne Laliberté,
New York

DIRECTORS
Nikki Chung
Dungjai Pungauthaikan

URL
once-future.com

TWITTER
@once_future

DESIGN FIRM
Once—Future Office

CLIENT
do+little

PRINCIPAL TYPE
Chalet Comprimé
Domaine

DIMENSIONS
18 x 24 in.
(45.7 x 61 cm)

CONCEPT
do+little is a modern hair and body care brand offering premium natural products for kids. Our new visual identity for the company and its first products positions the do+little product line and company as a high-end option for sophisticated and discerning parents. Their first product, Shiny Happy, has launched and is already being lauded for its effectiveness and distinctive packaging.

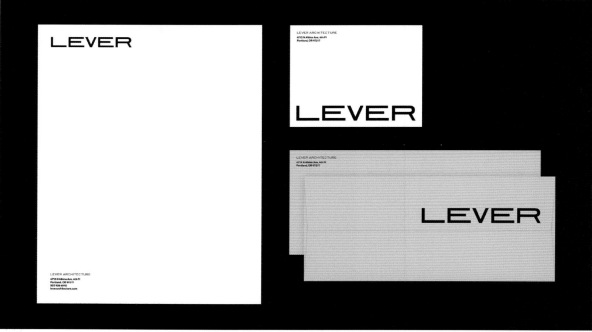

LEVER

Identities

DESIGN
Nick Fogarty
Drianne Laliberté,
New York

DIRECTORS
Nikki Chung
Dungjai Pungauthaikan

URL
once-future.com

TWITTER
@once_future

DESIGN FIRM
Once–Future Office

CLIENT
LEVER Architecture

PRINCIPAL TYPE
Lab Grotesque
Styrene

DIMENSIONS
18 x 24 in.
(45.7 x 61 cm)

CONCEPT
LEVER Architecture, an award-winning Portland firm, wanted to reimagine their identity and website to better articulate the firm's culture and mission. Their new flexible identity system conveys their devotion to making beautiful human spaces and buildings through innovative and economical design. As leaders in the mass timber movement, they are passionate about building technology, and research is a primary focus.

THE JIM HENSON EXHIBITION

Identities

DESIGN
Caroline Bagley,
San Francisco

CHIEF CREATIVE OFFICERS
Brian Collins
Matt Luckhurst,
New York and
San Francisco

SENIOR EXPERIENCE
DESIGNER
Clay Kippen

BUSINESS MANAGER
Antonia Lazar

URL
wearecollins.com

DESIGN STUDIO
COLLINS

CLIENT
The Museum of
the Moving Image

PRINCIPAL TYPE
Henson Display

DIMENSIONS
Various

CONCEPT
New York's Museum of the Moving Image was opening a new exhibition featuring the work and life of Jim Henson—best known as the visionary creator of the Muppets. COLLINS led the creative execution of the exhibition space and all surrounding marketing material for the launch of the exhibition. Inspiration for the design was gathered from the vast range of Jim Henson's work, which was always characterized by bold inventiveness and playfulness. The evocative letterforms of our design system reference his work's striking personality and sense of whimsy. The Jim Henson Exhibition launched in late 2017 to critical acclaim from publications such as The New York Times and has quickly become a popular success for the museum.

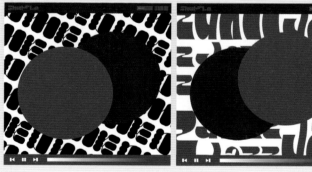

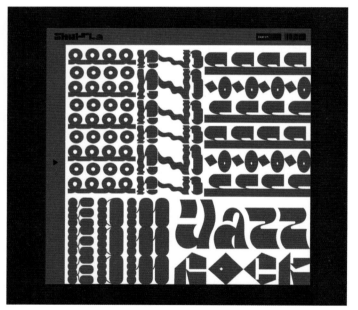

SHUFFLE

Identities

ART DIRECTION
Sijia Zhang,
New York

URL
sijia-zhang.com

AGENCY
Mood of Shape

PRINCIPAL TYPE
Shuffle

DIMENSIONS
Various

CONCEPT
Shuffle is a conceptual music app focusing on expressing the strength, power, and mystery of music.

CLAYTON VANCE ARCHITECTURE IDENTITY

Identities

DESIGN, ART DIRECTION, LETTERING, AND ILLUSTRATION

Kevin Cantrell, Mantua, Utah

URL
kevincantrell.com

TWITTER
@kevinrcantrell

DESIGN FIRM
Kevin Cantrell Studio

CLIENT
Clayton Vance Architecture

PRINCIPAL TYPE
Proprietary Vance Serif and custom

DIMENSIONS
Various

CONCEPT

Inspired by Roman mosaic tiles and pools, Clayton Vance Architecture incorporates classic proportions and principles applied with a modern sensibility. KCS created a comprehensive brand identity system applied across multiple brand touchpoints with scalable mosaic illustrations to match myriad proportions in application.

DOT COLOR INTERACTION
PERFORMING ARTS WEEK

Identities

DESIGN
Zhang Weimin,
Shenzhen, China

DESIGN FIRM
Zhang Weimi
brand design

CLIENT
SESUN culture

TYPECON 2017 COUNTER! BOSTON, MA AUG. 23–27 PRESENTED BY S...

TYPECON

Identities

DESIGN
Michael McCaughley
David Shatan-Pardo,
New York

CREATIVE DIRECTION
Jennifer Kinon
Bobby C. Martin Jr.°

ANIMATOR
Miller McCormick

URL
originalchampions
ofdesign.com

TWITTER
@ocdagency

DESIGN AGENCY
OCD | The Original
Champions of Design

CLIENT
Society of Typographic
Aficionados

PRINCIPAL TYPE
AW Conqueror
TypeCon

DIMENSIONS
Various

CONCEPT
The brunt of our work for TypeCon happened in late 2016 after a long and brutal election year that ended on a new low. Our design response had to reflect the importance and urgency of our rapidly changing world and speak to issues affecting us all. We came up with the theme "Counter," which worked both as a type-based message and a revolutionary call to action.

MTV VIDEO MUSIC AWARDS LOGO

Logotypes

DESIGN
Taylor Hale
Scott Allen Hill,
New York

OCD CREATIVE DIRECTION
Jennifer Kinon
Bobby C. Martin Jr.°

MTV CREATIVE DIRECTION
Thomas Berger
Catherine Chesters

URL
originalchampions
ofdesign.com

TWITTER
@ocdagency

DESIGN AGENCY
OCD | The Original
Champions of Design

CLIENT
MTV

CONCEPT
The MTV Video Music Awards identity celebrates MTV's iconic logo and forges a wholly new made-to-be-dynamic mark just for the VMAs. The wordmark is easily recognizable, and its symmetrical structure allows it to transform into countless permutations or to house imagery.

MTV VIDEO MUSIC AWARDS
IDENTITY SYSTEM

Identities

DESIGN
Taylor Hale
Scott Allen Hill,
New York

OCD CREATIVE DIRECTION
Jennifer Kinon
Bobby C. Martin Jr.°

MTV CREATIVE DIRECTION
Thomas Berger
Catherine Chesters

URL
originalchampions
ofdesign.com

TWITTER
@ocdagency

DESIGN AGENCY
OCD | The Original
Champions of Design

CLIENT
MTV

PRINCIPAL TYPE
GT America
Condensed

DIMENSIONS
Various

CONCEPT
The MTV Video Music Awards identity
celebrates MTV's iconic logo and forges
a wholly new made-to-be-dynamic mark
just for the VMAs. The wordmark is easily
recognizable, and its symmetrical structure
allows it to transform into countless
permutations or to house imagery.

AD AGE IDENTITY SYSTEM

Identities

LEAD DESIGNER
Michael McCaughley,
New York

DESIGN
Daniel Hennessy
Hanah Ho

CREATIVE DIRECTION
Jennifer Kinon
Bobby C. Martin Jr.°

STRATEGIST
Sarah Hermalyn

MOTION DESIGN
Zipeng Zhu

URL
originalchampions
ofdesign.com

TWITTER
@ocdagency

DESIGN AGENCY
OCD | The Original
Champions of Design

CLIENT
Ad Age
Erik Spooner,
Ad Age
Creative Director

PRINCIPAL TYPE
Exchange
Outsiders Bold
Outsiders Bold Italic
Retina Black
Retina Condensed
Black

CONCEPT
The visual strategy is all about owning
Ad Age's hundred years of authority, unifying
the print and digital platforms, and clearly
branding discrete units of *Ad Age* content that
have been widely shared. The typographic
tool kit leans into *Ad Age*'s newspaper
heritage—three typefaces and a commitment
to easy-reading columns on all platforms.
The bands of color further support efficiency.
When you need a design element, you have all
of the stripes. When you need the design to
get out of the way, you have fewer stripes. The
seventeen-color palette brings variability.

V O O O O
O O O O
O O O O
O O O
O OLKSHAUS

VOLKSHAUS

Identities

DESIGN
RAFFINERIE,
Zürich

URL
raffinerie.com

DESIGN AGENCY
RAFFINERIE

CLIENT
Volkshaus Zürich

PRINCIPAL TYPE
GT Haptik

DIMENSIONS
Various

CONCEPT
A long and tumultuous history precedes the Volkshaus Zürich
("Volkshaus" = house for the people/public). The first public bath,
boxing matches, youth riots—it all happened here. And today? It's still
buzzing, steaming, and shaking. A bar and restaurant, a hammam spa,
concert halls, a bookstore, meeting rooms, an administration office,
and even apartments: everything under one roof. In our redesigned
corporate identity, the "o" in "Volkshaus" symbolizes the venue's
visitors. This recognizable and playful element finds its way in the
logo, website, stationery, and signage.

**OLESON BRANDING
AND STATIONERY**

Identities

DESIGN AND ART DIRECTION
Abby Haddican
Sharon Werner°,
Saint Paul, Minnesota

CREATIVE DIRECTION
Sharon Werner

URL
wdw.com

TWITTER
@Werner_Design

DESIGN STUDIO
Werner Design
Werks, Inc.

CLIENT
Oleson Sales

PRINCIPAL TYPE
Custom

DIMENSIONS
Various

CONCEPT
John Oleson is an electrical engineer with a background in sales and client services. When John launched his business, Oleson Sales, his focus was on electronic equipment, but he asked us to create an identity that could scale to other industries as his company grew. With its diacritical marks, the logo serves as a pronunciation clue for John's name and is also a nod to his Scandinavian heritage. The two Os, the L, and their diacritical marks break out into a secondary smiling logo, which provides a touch of levity and literally serves as the company's face on social media.

SZABÓ MAGDA 100

Logotypes

DESIGN
Anna Farkas,
Budapest

URL
anagraphic.hu

DESIGN FIRM
Anagraphic

CLIENT
Petőfi Literary
Museum

PRINCIPAL TYPE
Caligo Poster

DIMENSIONS
6.3 x 6.3 in.
(16 x 16 cm)

CONCEPT
Hungarian novelist Magda Szabó was born a hundred years ago, in 1917. The writer of dramas, essays, studies, memoirs, and poetry, she is the most translated Hungarian author, with publications in forty-two countries and more than thirty languages. This logo, emphasizing her multiplicity in the Hungarian literature, was designed for a large-scale, centennial exhibition titled *I Have Kept So Many Secrets*... at Petőfi Literary Museum. The logo's ligatures reflect the main concept of the exhibition: Szabó has built a private mythology around her own ancestors in her writing, and these people and their connections play various roles in her works.

TAQIZA

Logotypes

DESIGN
Abraham Lule°,
New York

URL
abrahamlule.com

INSTAGRAM
@abrahamlule

CLIENT
Pablo Galindo,
Sydney, Australia

PRINCIPAL TYPE
Custom

CONCEPT
Taqiza is a Mexican restaurant in Bondi Beach, Australia, that wanted to honor the culture and gastronomy of Mexico. The primary logo and secondary application were inspired by the Mexican national shield, portraying an eagle with a snake that, in this case, has been changed into a cilantro leaf. Four capital letter Ts are the secondary graphics inspired by papel picado, a traditionally well-known indicator of festivities and joy. The intricacy of the design printed in golden foils elevates the humble gesture of cooking with dedication and passion.

TOKYO BUSINESS LINK

Logotypes

DESIGN AND ART DIRECTION
Kenta Nakano,
Kamakura City, Japan

URL
super-elm.com

TWITTER
@super_elm

INSTAGRAM
@kentanakano

DESIGN STUDIO
Superelement

CLIENT
TOKYO BUSINESS LINK

PRINCIPAL TYPE
TBL Rounded

CONCEPT
This is the logo for the cooperative TOKYO BUSINESS LINK.
It represents the "B" for Business in the initials "T," "B," and "L"
of TOKYO BUSINESS LINK. Additionally, we express the "link"
that forms the basic concept of a cooperative by linking together
each of the initials. We also designed the original font TBL Rounded
for this logo.

AdAge

AD AGE WORDMARK

Wordmarks

LEAD DESIGNER
Michael McCaughley,
New York

DESIGN
Daniel Hennessy
Hanah Ho

CREATIVE DIRECTION
Jennifer Kinon
Bobby C. Martin Jr.°

STRATEGIST
Sarah Hermalyn

URL
originalchampions
ofdesign.com

TWITTER
@ocdagency

DESIGN AGENCY
OCD | The Original
Champions of Design

CLIENT
Ad Age
Erik Spooner, *Ad Age*
Creative Director

CONCEPT
The wordmark is based on *Ad Age*'s first masthead, published at launch in 1930. It was cutting-edge in its time using Kabel, designed by Rudolf Koch and released in 1927. Now, eighty-eight years later, the revival was crafted by Tobias Frere-Jones.

JUSTICE LEAGUE

Logotypes

DESIGN
Timothy Cohan,
New York

PARTNER AND
CREATIVE DIRECTOR
Emily Oberman

URL
pentagram.com

TWITTER
@pentagram

DESIGN FIRM
Pentagram°

CLIENT
Warner Bros.

CONCEPT
Based on a heritage piece of Justice League comic book cover art, the custom logotype stacks the name with streamlined and closely spaced letters to form a monumental rectangular shape. The logotype's form echoes the movie's story of a powerful, tight, cohesive unit. The cutout star is a nod to DC's heritage and the spirit of its iconic superheroes. A "JL" monogram set in a shield was also created for an insignia-like secondary logo. The timeless graphic simplicity of the identity allows it to handle a variety of treatments, including textured, metal, and dimensional forms.

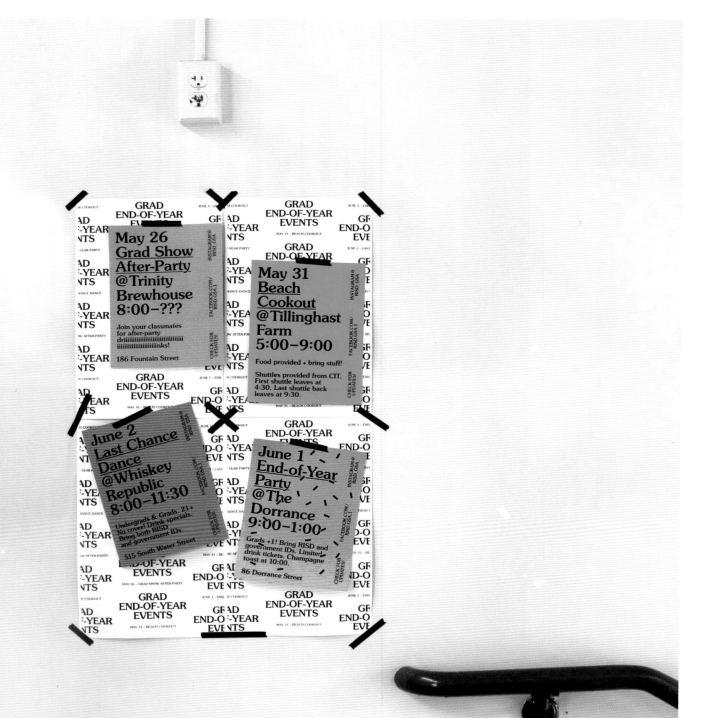

A PARTY SERIES

Fliers

DESIGN
Bo-Won Keum
Drew Litowitz,
Providence,
Rhode Island

CLIENT
Rhode Island School
of Design (RISD) GSA

PRINCIPAL TYPE
ITC Souvenir

DIMENSIONS
Various

CONCEPT
These fliers were designed for a series of events for the graduate
student alliance at the Rhode Island School of Design. Each event
occupies a different standard 8.5 x 11 in. sheet of colored paper; these
were pasted onto larger, standard tabloid sheets that could be tiled
like wallpaper to cover large surface areas.

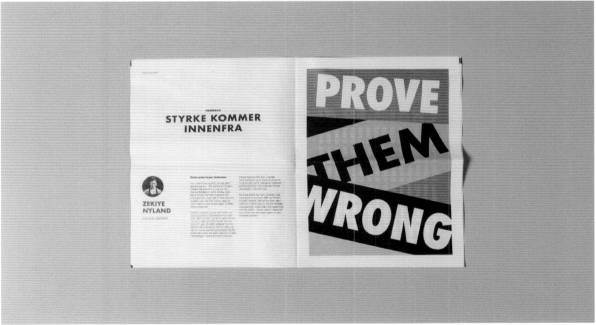

INVITATION AND PROGRAM FOR !KONFERANSEN

Invitations and Programs

DESIGN
Cecilie Larssen
Lønning
Eric Amaral Rohter
Andrea Tjøsvoll,
Haugesund, Norway

ART DIRECTION
Cecilie Larssen
Lønning

CREATIVE DIRECTION
Eric Amaral Rohter

URL
larssenamaral.no

DESIGN AGENCY
Larssen & Amaral

CLIENT
Kvinneraadet

PRINCIPAL TYPE
Futura Book
Futura Bold
Futura Extra Bold
Futura Extra Bold
Condensed
Maax Regular
Maax Medium
Maax Bold

DIMENSIONS
11.4 x 15 in.
(28.9 x 38 cm)

CONCEPT
The year 2017 was an extremely political one on a global scale. This theme was reflected in the conference's messaging and communication, so we wanted to create a more politically engaging visual expression, using typography and color to brand bold statements, statistics, and quotes that related to various topics, themes, and speakers. This gave the conference a strong, bold voice. The newspaper was used as a multipurpose marketing tool. It served as a way to promote the event, was handed out at strategic events and venues, and was used during the conference as the program.

藍-愛-維

Business Cards

DESIGN
Winnie Wu,
Singapore

URL
studiokaleido.net

DESIGN STUDIO
studioKALEIDO

CLIENT
Carrie Lam
Photography

PRINCIPAL TYPE
Miso Regular
and custom

DIMENSIONS
2.1 x 3.3 in.
(5.4 x 8.5 cm)

CONCEPT
We designed business cards for a Taiwan-based fine art photographer around the premise that a distinct feature of her work often uses the format of triptychs.

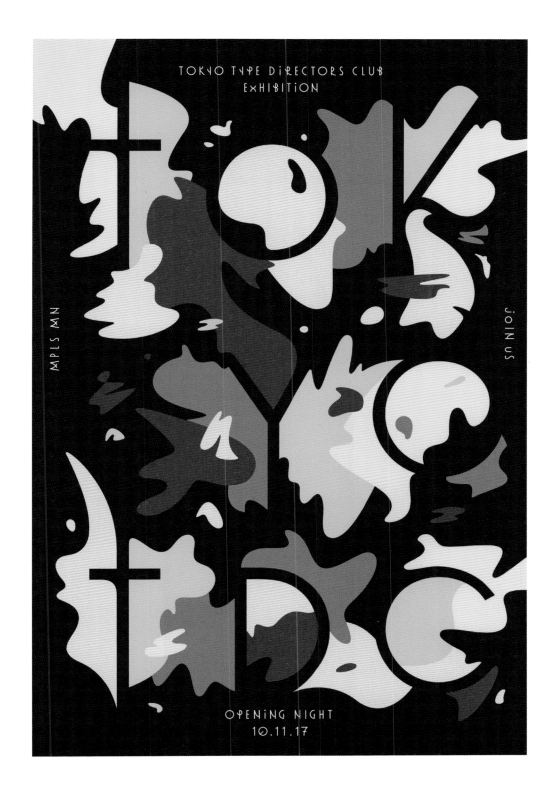

TOKYO TDC
INVITATION AND BANNER

Invitations and Banners

DESIGN AND ART DIRECTION
Abby Haddican
Sharon Werner°,
Saint Paul, Minnesota

CREATIVE DIRECTION
Sharon Werner°

URL
wdw.com

TWITTER
@Werner_Design

DESIGN STUDIO
Werner Design
Werks, Inc.

CLIENT
Minneapolis College
of Art and Design,
AIGA Minnesota, and
Werner Design Werks

PRINCIPAL TYPE
Custom

DIMENSIONS
Various

CONCEPT
This was event branding for a curated
exhibition of work from the Tokyo Type
Directors Club, on display at the Minneapolis
College of Art and Design. Like the event
itself, the graphics were meant to be a fun
celebration of experimental typography.

NOVAOLO

Packaging

DESIGN AND CREATIVE DIRECTION
Michael Hester,
Oakland, California

CALLIGRAPHY
Julie Wildman

URL
pavementsf.com

DESIGN FIRM
Pavement

CLIENT
Novaolo Wines

PRINCIPAL TYPE
Custom

DIMENSIONS
3.1 x 11.5 in.
(7.9 x 29.2 cm)

CONCEPT
Novaolo is a wine about obscured identities. The name pays homage to the two matriarchs of the winemaker's Polish and Sicilian families. Through marriage, both matriarchs lost their maiden surnames— "Novaolo" is quite literally a combination of the two names. Sophisticated calligraphy, combined with a die cut label in the shape of a notebook page, visualizes this conceptual label through an unexpected execution.

SUPERBA!

Packaging

DESIGN AND CREATIVE DIRECTION
Michael Hester,
Oakland, California

URL
pavementsf.com

DESIGN FIRM
Pavement

CLIENT
Dollar Shave Club

PRINCIPAL TYPE
Mallory Bold
Mallory Ultra
Saa Series BD

DIMENSIONS
2.25 x 5.25 in.
(5.7 x 13.3 cm)

CONCEPT
As Dollar Shave Club looked to expand their ever-increasing lineup of men's personal care products into oral healthcare, they sought to create a brand that was masculine, bold, and confident to match the powerful flavors and invigorating sensations of the Superba! products. The brand needed to be sophisticated but have just enough panache to mirror the style and confidence of the modern male. Straightforward graphics and bright colors that emulated retro European lifestyle brands were used in combination with simple messaging to create a simple yet impactful brand.

LOFOTEN SEAWEED

Packaging

URL
bynorth.no

DESIGN FIRM
by north
Bodø, Norway

CLIENT
Lofoten Seaweed

PRINCIPAL TYPE
Dala Floda
Circular

DIMENSIONS
Various

CONCEPT
More of the food we consume in the future will have to come from the oceans. Situated in the Lofoten archipelago in northern Norway, Lofoten Seaweed needed a flexible and recognizable identity to help them launch their brand. We developed an identity system that avoided the usual Lofoten clichés, choosing instead to focus on the health benefits and the exclusivity of the products, which are produced in an environment where the seaweed is harvested by hand. In keeping with the environmental focus, we also made sure that all materials used had as little impact on nature as possible.

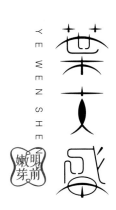

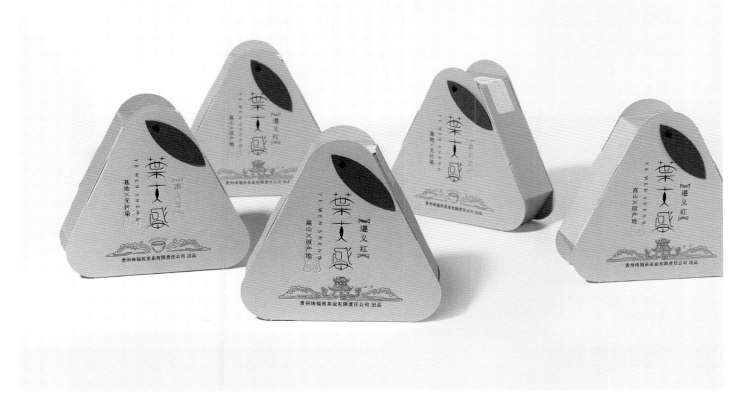

BREEZE VALLEY

Packaging

DESIGN
Chen Lieguan,
Shenzhen City, China

CLIENT
Guizhou, China,
Qi Fuyuan tea
industry company

PRINCIPAL TYPE
华文细黑

DIMENSIONS
3.5 x 4.7 x 2 in.
(9 x 12 x 5 cm)

CONCEPT
The design was inspired by the shape of mountains, the interplay of light and shadows in the landscape, and the "rhyme" of air in the atmosphere.

JEANNERET WINE PACKAGING

Packaging

DESIGN
Shane Keane,
Adelaide, Australia

CREATIVE DIRECTION
Chris Cooper

DESIGN STUDIO
Band

CLIENT
Jeanneret Wines

PRINCIPAL TYPE
Calibre

DIMENSIONS
5.1 x 3.1 in.
(13 x 8 cm)
3.1 x 5.1 in.
(8 x 13 cm)

CONCEPT
Every bottle of Jeanneret wine is truly a product of its environment. The characteristics of each vintage reflect the growing conditions of the year. The design references family ties to Le Corbusier, the Swiss-French architect whose modernist designs were based upon proportions found in nature—a practice that echoes the winemaking process and inspired our approach. The label designs reflect Le Corbusier's philosophies—and the palette was based on his system of harmonious colors. Growing conditions and the year's winemaking process now take pride of place on each label. Variances in vintage can be read as well as tasted.

VISTA

Packaging

DESIGN
Tom Crosby,
Adelaide, Australia

CREATIVE DIRECTION
Scott Carslake°
Anthony De Leo

URL
voicedesign.net

TWITTER
@voice_of_design

DESIGN FIRM
Voice

CLIENT
Longview Vineyard

PRINCIPAL TYPE
GT Haptik

DIMENSIONS
Various

CONCEPT
Responding to the product's name and with a focus on its scenic origin, a typographic portrait of the Longview landscape was created. The packaging attempts to convey the vineyard's steep inclines and vast panoramic views, while establishing "Vista" as the focus of the design. Bold and uncomplicated, the illustration is presented in black foil with heavily debossed finishing to add tactility, reminiscent of rows and rows of vines. The palette is intentionally light and bright for both pickup appeal and memorability, and in response to the young and fresh profile of the wine.

CANG JIE CREATION

Posters

ART DIRECTION
XU Lixian, Shenzhen,
Guangdong, China

DESIGN FIRM
3LBrand Design
and Consulting

URL
3lbrand.com

CONCEPT
Cang Jie created original Chinese characters by observing the astronomical phenomena above as well as the birds, animals, insects, and fish below. While paying respect to Chinese culture and the sage who created the characters, the poster considers the future development of characters.

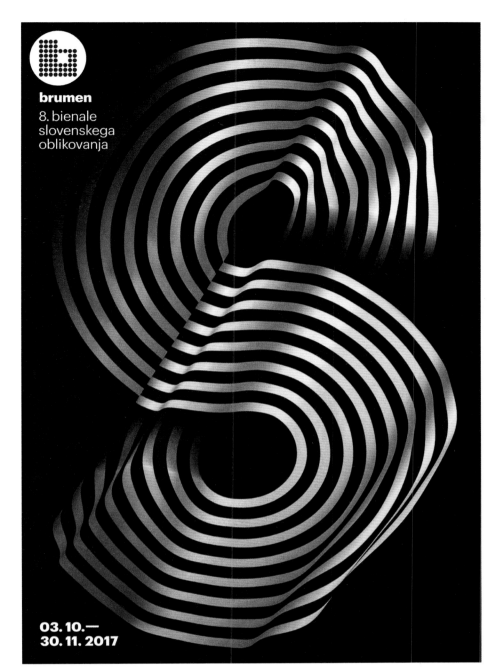

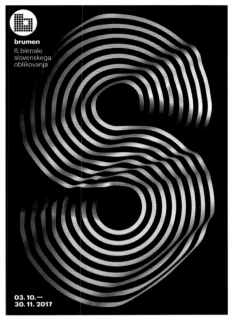

**8TH BRUMEN BIENNIAL
OF SLOVENIAN DESIGN**

Posters

**DESIGN, ART DIRECTION,
AND LETTERING**

Anja Delbello
Aljaz Vesel,
Ljubljana, Slovenia

URL

weareaa.com

STUDIO

AA

CLIENT

Fundacija Brumen
(Brumen Foundation)

PRINCIPAL TYPE

Graphik

DIMENSIONS

26.8 x 38.6 in.
(68 x 98 cm)

CONCEPT

The posters were designed for the 8th Brumen Biennial, the most
prestigious Slovenian design competition, which is organized by the
Brumen Foundation. The main visual is the gigantic number 8 (using
the biennial edition number as the main visual is the recurring concept
of the biennial's identity). It's constructed out of eight parallel lines
as an homage to Mexico '68 identity (Olympics as the symbol of the
positively spirited competition). The entire numeral is waving like
a flag to communicate the pride of winning an award. The flag also
emphasizes that the biennial is of national importance.

TYPECON POSTERS

Posters

DESIGN
Michael McCaughley,
New York

CREATIVE DIRECTION
Jennifer Kinon
Bobby C. Martin Jr. °,
New York

URL
originalchampions
ofdesign.com

TWITTER
@ocdagency

DESIGN AGENCY
OCD | The Original
Champions of Design

CLIENT
Society of Typographic
Aficionados

PRINCIPAL TYPE
AW Conqueror

DIMENSIONS
Various

CONCEPT
The TypeCon posters really embody 2017's "Counter" theme by conveying the conference information while overprinting the Preamble of the U.S. Constitution in the cryptic version of AW Conqueror TypeCon.

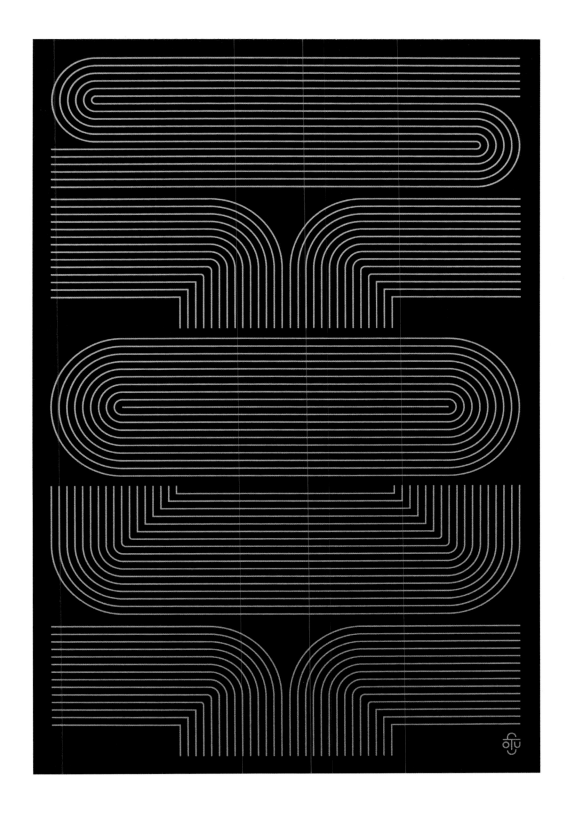

STOUT IDENTITY POSTERS

Posters

DESIGN
Ryan Bosse
Jordan Cullen,
San Francisco

CREATIVE DIRECTION
Brian Gunderson
Ryan Meis

URL
stoutsf.com

DESIGN FIRM
Stout Design, Inc.

PRINCIPAL TYPE
Custom

DIMENSIONS
24 x 36 in.
(61 x 91.4 cm)

CONCEPT
This typographic series is an exploration of identity and visual expression. In one poster, we expand on the playful nature of our logo and use its architecture to illustrate a variety of hidden type "faces." In the second, our studio name is embraced with a combination of strength, style, and precision.

**RICE UNIVERSITY
SCHOOL OF ARCHITECTURE
LECTURE POSTERS**

Posters

DESIGN
Michael McCaughley,
New York

CREATIVE DIRECTION
Jennifer Kinon
Bobby C. Martin Jr. °

URL
originalchampions
ofdesign.com

TWITTER
@ocdagency

DESIGN AGENCY
OCD | The Original
Champions of Design

CLIENT
Rice University
School of
Architecture

PRINCIPAL TYPE
Neue Haas Unica Pro

DIMENSIONS
Various

CONCEPT
Rice Architecture's Lecture Series posters are designed using
a unique circular grid that organizes design elements in a dynamic
and collaborative way.

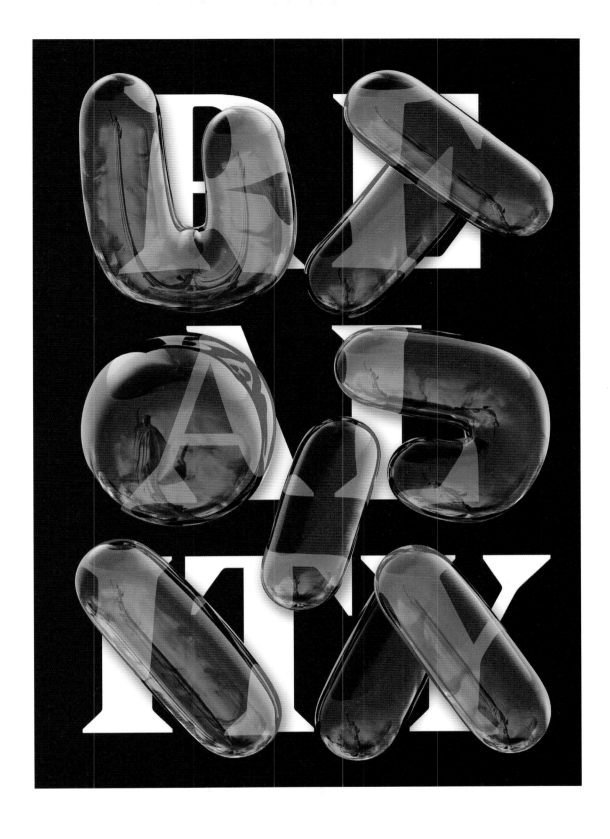

UTOPIA

Posters

DESIGN
Götz Gramlich,
Heidelberg, Germany

**ART AND CREATIVE
DIRECTION**
Götz Gramlich

3D MODELING
Oliver Örtel

INSTAGRAM
@instagggramlich

URL
gggrafik.de

DESIGN FIRM
gggrafik design

CLIENT
Goethe Institut
Tel Aviv

PRINCIPAL TYPE
Noe Text and custom

DIMENSIONS
23.4 x 33.1 in.
(59.4 x 84 cm)

CONCEPT
This is a poster for *Utopia*, a group
exhibition at Goethe Institut Tel Aviv.
Offset and silkscreened print. A fragile but
mesmerizingly iridescent utopia overlies the
hard-edged monochrome reality of life.

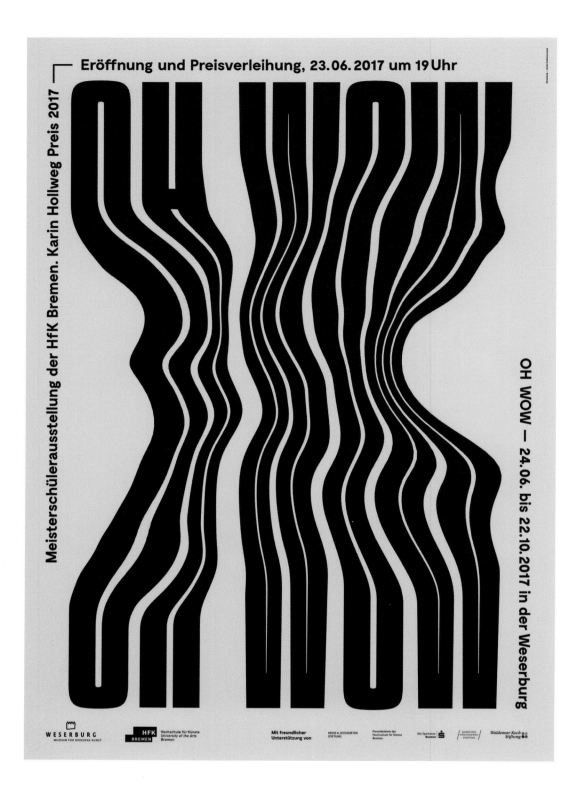

OH WOW

Posters

DESIGN AND ART DIRECTION
Sven Lindhorst-Emme°, Berlin

ORGANIZATION
Ana Baumgart (HfK)

CURATION
Ingo Clauss

URL
lindhorst-emme.de

STUDIO
studio lindhorst-emme

CLIENTS
Weserburg—Museum für moderne Kunst and HfK University of Arts, Bremen

PRINCIPAL TYPE
Moderat

DIMENSIONS
33.1 x 46.6 in. (84.1 x 118.9 cm)

CONCEPT
Because of the title, the concept concentrates on the main "OH WOW" visual. It is a bit psychedelic, and the rest of the information surrounds it. It was important to create a poster with an "OH WOW" effect. The title in the center has become more like a picture than typography, but it is still readable.

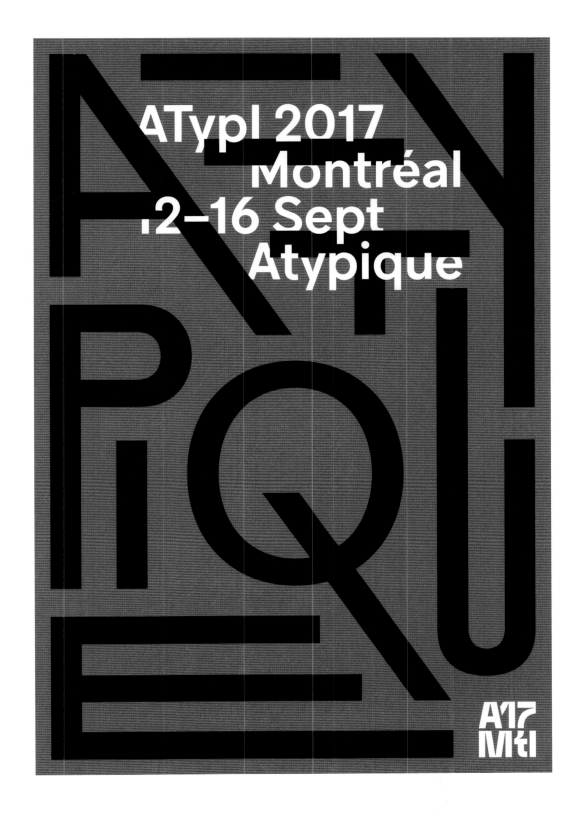

ATypI 2017
Montréal
12–16 Sept
Atypique

2017 ATYPI CONFERENCE POSTERS

Posters

GRAPHIC DESIGN
AND LETTERING

Julien Hébert,
Montréal

URL
julienhebert.net

TWITTER
@julienhebert

CLIENT
Association
Typographique
Internationale (ATypI)

PRINCIPAL TYPE
Guillon

DIMENSIONS
24 x 36 in.
(61 x 91.5 cm)

CONCEPT
The theme for the 2017 ATypI conference was "Atypique." This was
a great opportunity to experiment with expressive handlettering.

SHAKESPEARE IN THE PARK
2017 SEASON POSTERS

Posters

DESIGN AND PARTNER
Paula Scher°,
New York

DESIGN AND
ASSOCIATE PARTNER
Courtney Gooch

URL
pentagram.com

TWITTER
@pentagram

DESIGN FIRM
Pentagram°

CLIENT
The Public Theater

PRINCIPAL TYPE
Knockout
(customized)

DIMENSIONS
Various

CONCEPT
Each year, the Shakespeare in the Park posters continue Paula
Scher's ongoing relationship with The Public Theater, whose identity
was designed by Scher and first introduced in 1994. The 2017
posters combine striking images and quotes from the season's two
productions (*Julius Caesar* and *A Midsummer Night's Dream*) with
The Public's Knockout typeface, modified by squaring off the inside
of the letterforms for a hard, rigid look (for *Caesar*) and a soft, fluid
look (for *Midsummer*).

Hochschultag 2017, Hochschule Mannheim, 30. Nov, 16 Uhr, Gebäude C, Aula - Begrüßung: Prof. Dr.-Ing. Dieter Leonhard, Rektor

Festansprache: Jürgen Wörner ›Digitale Geschäftsmodelle und Cyber Risiken‹ Mitglied im Vorstand der Mannheimer Versicherung AG
Verleihung des Albert-und-Anneliese-Konanz-Lehrpreises, Preisverleihung / Stipendienvergabe: Prof. Dr. Astrid Hedtke-Becker

Hochschultag 2017, Hochschule Mannheim, 30. Nov, 16 Uhr, Gebäude C, Aula - Begrüßung: Prof. Dr.-Ing. Dieter Leonhard, Rektor

Festansprache: Jürgen Wörner ›Digitale Geschäftsmodelle und Cyber Risiken‹ Mitglied im Vorstand der Mannheimer Versicherung AG
Verleihung des Albert-und-Anneliese-Konanz-Lehrpreises, Preisverleihung / Stipendienvergabe: Prof. Dr. Astrid Hedtke-Becker

HOCHSCHULTAG

Posters

DESIGN
Armin Lindauer,
Mannheim, Germany

URL
sehwerk.org

STUDIO
Sehwerk

CLIENT
University of
Applied Sciences

PRINCIPAL TYPE
DIN Condensed Bold

DIMENSIONS
23.4 x 33.1 in.
(59.4 x 84.1 cm)

CONCEPT
This is the university in motion.

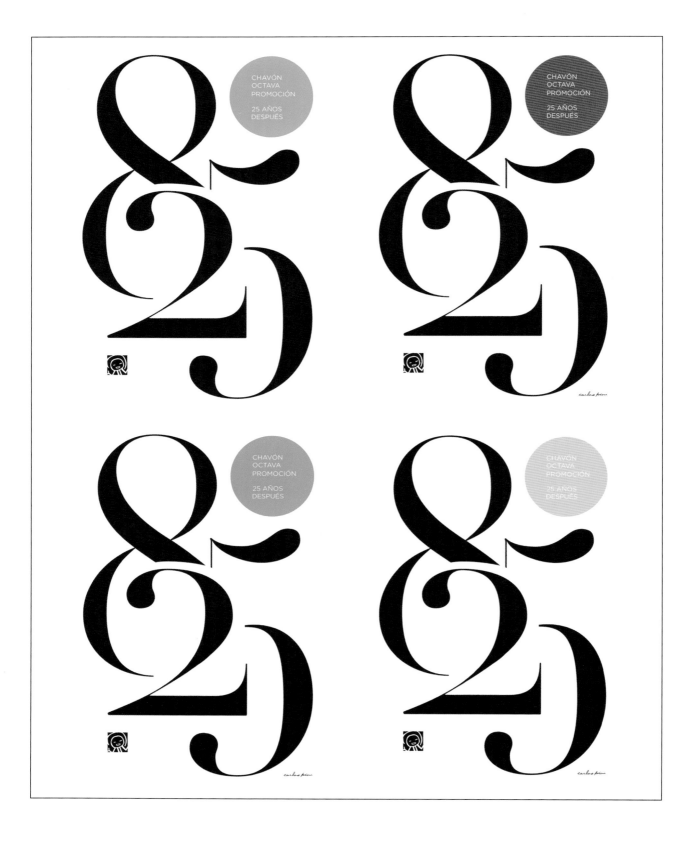

CELEBRATING 25 YEARS

Posters

DESIGN AND CREATIVE DIRECTION

Carlos Pion,
New York

URL

carlospion.com

TWITTER

@carlospion

DESIGN FIRM

Carlos Pion New York

CLIENT

Altos de Chavon
School of Design

PRINCIPAL TYPE

Didot HTF 96 Light
Gotham

DIMENSIONS

18 x 24 in.
(45.7 x 61 cm)

CONCEPT

The idea was to create a simple yet
memorable statement about us—the eight
graduating group—coming together twenty-
five years later.

SEASON-OPENER 2018
Posters

DESIGN
Benjamin Wolf,
Bielefeld, Germany

CREATIVE DIRECTION
Christoph Beier

URL
beierarbeit.de

TWITTER
@beierarbeit

DESIGN STUDIO
beierarbeit

CLIENT
Bielefelder
Philharmoniker

PRINCIPAL TYPE
Fab Figures Big F

DIMENSIONS
99.2 x 140.2 in.
(252 x 356 cm)

CONCEPT
The focus was on beauty to create an
eye-catcher of sounding typography.

REFERENCE AND RELATION

Posters

DESIGN AND CREATIVE DIRECTION
Katja Schloz, Stuttgart

URL
katjaschloz.de

DESIGN OFFICE
Katja Schloz Graphic Design

CLIENT
University of Stuttgart

PRINCIPAL TYPE
Century Gothic Regular

DIMENSIONS
33.1 x 23.4 in.
(84.1 x 59.4 cm)

CONCEPT

This is an announcement poster for the 40th Annual Conference of the German Linguistic Society at the University of Stuttgart. The repetitive pattern of typography and lines on each poster is designed to create an instant transition of dialogue into its surroundings—even when hung with a huge gap in-between. The main concept is to provide various possibilities and constellations to always create new relations, just like references in linguistic research.

THE SIDE PROJECT

Posters

DESIGN AND LETTERER
María Sanoja,
Santo Domingo,
Dominican Republic

URL
mcsanoja.com

CLIENT
The Side Project

PRINCIPAL TYPE
Custom hand-drawn

DIMENSIONS
24 x 36 in.
(61 x 91.4 cm)

CONCEPT
This project involved logo and poster design for The Side Project,
an event company that organizes discos and house parties at unlikely,
secret locations. The lettering on each poster is based on a custom-
made ink splat because every event is a unique experience.

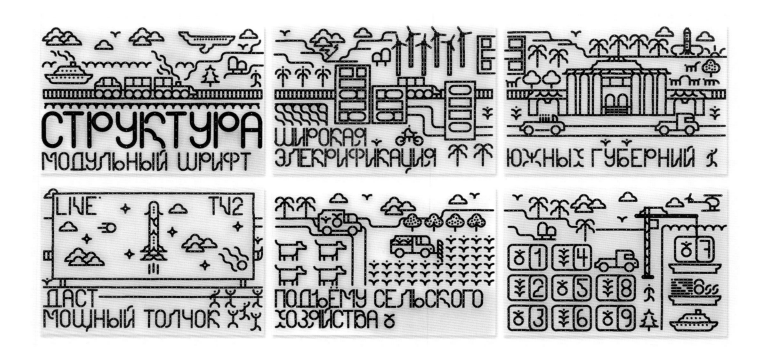

**STRUCTURA—MODULAR
CYRILLIC TYPEFACE**

Posters

**DESIGN AND
ART DIRECTION**

Vika Nurislamova,
Moscow

CREATIVE ASSOCIATE
Maxim Ivanov

URLS
v-i-k-a.com
gasmaster.ru

STUDIO
V-I-K-A

PRINCIPAL TYPE
Structura

DIMENSIONS
39.4 x 27.6 in.
(100 x 70 cm)

CONCEPT
Structura is a modular typeface based on six modules, all of which
were laser-cut from acrylic plastic. Using those elements, I built
a type specimen employing a Russian pangram and then illustrated
the written text. Apart from textual messages, Structura allows you
to create icons, signs, patterns, and even physical 3D objects (for
example, I have a collection of ceramic vessels based on Structura).

SAMBANZO
16 AGO 2017

20H R$20
AUDIO REBEL

COISAS INVISÍVEIS
(INVISIBLE THINGS)

Posters

DESIGN
Thiago Lacaz,
Rio de Janeiro

URL
thiagolacaz.com

CLIENT
Quintavant/
Audio Rebel

PRINCIPAL TYPE
Neue Haas Grotesk

DIMENSIONS
23.4 x 33.1 in.
(59.4 x 84 cm)

CONCEPT
This is a poster for the instrumental music concert by Sambanzo,
a solo project of Brazilian saxophonist Thiago França. The letters of
a modular typography are identified by the orientation of the gradient
that fills them. A low-contrast background color creates an optical
effect that refers to the name of the project.

WAN TIAO

Posters

**FOUNDER AND
ART DIRECTION**

XU Lixian, Shenzhen,
Guangdong, China

URL
3lbrand.com

DESIGN FIRM
3LBrand Design &
Consulting

DIMENSIONS
27.6 x 39.4 in.
(70 x 100 cm)

CONCEPT
"Overlook in evening," from the verse written by Su Dongpo of the
Northern Song Dynasty, is taken as the design element. The image form
is used to convey the content of verses ingeniously. The rhyme of the
design is full and interesting, revealing the charm of the typeface.

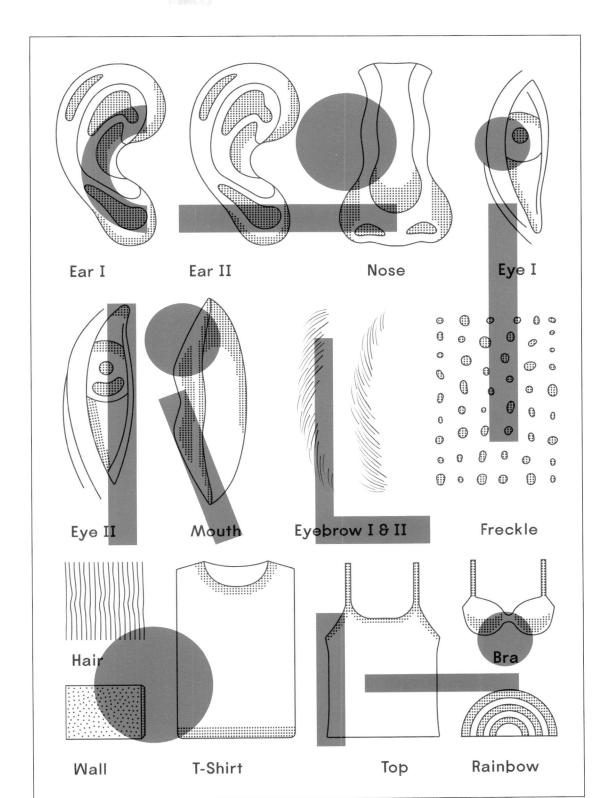

Ear I Ear II Nose Eye I

Eye II Mouth Eyebrow I & II Freckle

Hair Wall T-Shirt Top Rainbow Bra

RAINBOW DECONSTRUCTED

Posters

DESIGN
Sascha Lobe°
Yuan Wang,
Stuttgart

URL
l2m3.com

STUDIO
L2M3
Kommunikationsdesign
GmbH

CLIENT
Soirée graphique
No. 10

PRINCIPAL TYPE
doc.A

DIMENSIONS
35.2 x 50.4 in.
(89.5 x 128 cm)

ACROSS BORDERS

Posters

GRAPHIC DESIGN AND LETTERING

Khajag Apelian
Tarek Atrissi
Andreu Balius°
Joe Chang
Verónica Fuerte
Phil Garnham
Tseng Green
Anna Kulachek
Rocío Martinavarro
Wael Morcos°
Krystian Sarkis°
Wissam Shawkat
Bahia Shehab

Edo van Dijk
Jaewan Yu
Yah-Leng Yu,
Barcelona

CREATIVE DIRECTION
Rocío Martinavarro

URL
mayuscula.es

TWITTER
@MayusculaBrands

DESIGN FIRM
Mayúscula

CLIENT
Across Borders

PRINCIPAL TYPE
Custom

DIMENSIONS
15.7 x 19.6 in.
(40 x 50 cm)

CONCEPT
This is a cross-cultural and multilingual dialogue among sixteen designers of different origins, all invited to donate an artwork under the concept "Design to Break Borders"—later overlaid to create a new piece. Their creative work is intentional miscegenation by showing the strength of fusion and transformation of ideas, demonstrating their commitment to those who seek to integrate into other cultures, refugees. The project aims to stir thoughts on the individual versus the collective; local versus global; coexistence among people; connection between styles, alphabets, and countries of birth; and the immense problems plaguing immigration and displaced people.

NA MARGEM DE LÁ – UM LAMENTO

Posters

DESIGN AND ART DIRECTION
Lizá Ramalho
Artur Rebelo,
Porto, Portugal

SCENE PHOTOGRAPHY
Jorge Gonçalves

DESIGN FIRM
R2

CLIENT
Dona Maria II
National Theatre

PRINCIPAL TYPE
Founders Grotesk
X-Condensed (Bold)
Plak Ultra Condensed
(Light, Regular, Bold)

DIMENSIONS
42 x 69 in.
(120 x 175 cm)

CONCEPT
This poster was designed for *Na Margem de Lá – Um Lamento*, a play that addresses the plight of refugees who attempt to cross the Mediterranean Sea, performed at the Dona Maria II National Theatre in Lisbon. The poster pushes the relationship between text and image: The actor's face works as a central element, framed by the title, with the composition of typographic elements creating a certain tension that gradually gains prominence throughout the poster. It culminates in the standout word "lamento" (sorrow).

ANAFOR TYPEFACE

Posters

DESIGN
Erman Yılmaz,
Istanbul

URL
informaltype.com

STUDIO
Informal Type
Foundry

PRINCIPAL TYPE
Anafor Basic
Informal Text

DIMENSIONS
26.8 x 38.6 in.
(68 x 98 cm)

CONCEPT
Anafor was deeply inspired by the pioneer of geometric abstract art and the creator of the avant-garde suprematist movement, Kazimir Malevich. This typeface is separated from the basic Latin letters in terms of character and letter structure. Furthermore, the forms and main structure are designed together with alternatives by taking into account the relationships among the defined angles. Anafor contains certain aspects of a display typeface, due to the structure of the letterforms that are open to abstract connotations.

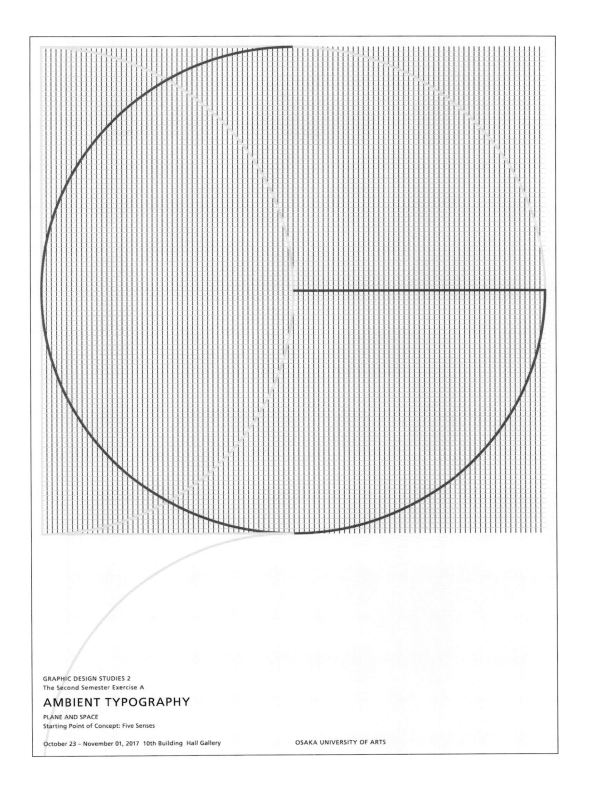

GRAPHIC DESIGN STUDIES 2
The Second Semester Exercise A

AMBIENT TYPOGRAPHY

PLANE AND SPACE
Starting Point of Concept: Five Senses

October 23 – November 01, 2017   10th Building   Hall Gallery   OSAKA UNIVERSITY OF ARTS

GRAPHIC DESIGN STUDIES

Posters

**DESIGN AND
ART DIRECTION**
Shinnoske Sugisaki,
Osaka, Japan

URL
shinn.co.jp

TWITTER
@shinnoske_s

DESIGN FIRM
Shinnoske Design

CLIENT
Osaka University
of Arts

PRINCIPAL TYPE
Frutiger Roman

DIMENSIONS
28.7 x 39.4 in.
(72.8 x 100 cm)

CONCEPT
These posters announce an exhibition of the experimental programs
in graphic design for students. The design considers both the "making"
side and the "viewing" side of the exhibition. Ambient typography:
Each student represents the relationship between the plane media
and the surrounding environment through typography. Media object:
Each student uses a three-dimensional object as the medium that
communicates a message.

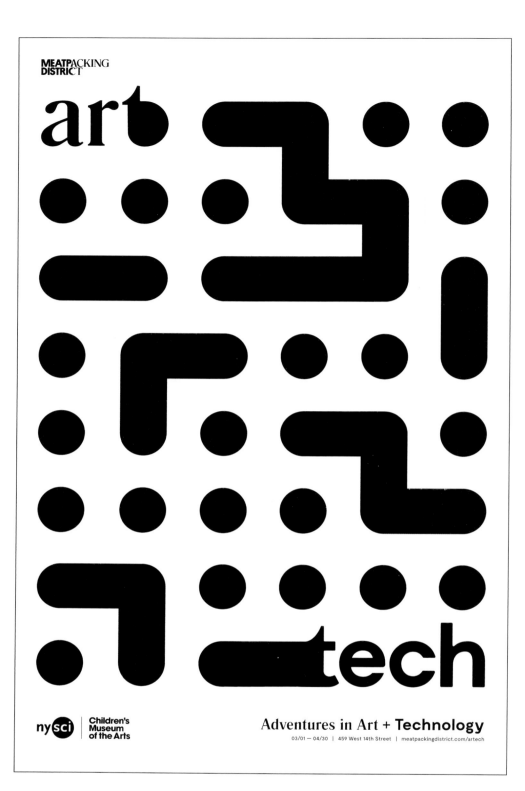

ARTECH: ADVENTURES IN ART
AND TECHNOLOGY

Posters

DESIGN
Nicolas Ortega,
New York

SVP, HEAD OF DESIGN
Craig Ward

AGENCY
Deutsch, New York

CLIENT
The Meatpacking
District

PRINCIPAL TYPE
Platform Bold
Romana EF

DIMENSIONS
20 x 30 in.
(50.8 x 76.2 cm)

CONCEPT
The Children's Museum of the Arts, in association with the New York
Hall of Science, staged an 8,000-square-foot pop-up exhibit for 5- to
12-year-old kids showcasing work and workshops at the intersection
of science and art. We were tasked with creating an identity and design
system that brought this concept to life.

THE NATIONAL'S
SLEEP WELL BEAST POSTER

Posters

DESIGN
Elyanna Blaser-Gould
Luke Hayman°
Andrea Trabucco-
Campos°,
New York

ART DIRECTION
Luke Hayman

URL
pentagram.com

DESIGN FIRM
Pentagram°

CLIENT
The National

PRINCIPAL TYPE
Maison
Styrene B

DIMENSIONS
18 x 24 in.
(45.7 x 61 cm)

CONCEPT
This poster was designed as part of the
unique identity for The National's new album,
Sleep Well Beast.

**2017 YALE SCHOOL
OF ARCHITECTURE POSTERS**

Posters

DESIGN
Laitsz Ho,
New York

ART DIRECTION
Michael Bierut°

URL
pentagram.com

DESIGN FIRM
Pentagram°

CLIENT
Yale School of
Architecture

PRINCIPAL TYPE
GT Eesti
Pitch
Yale

DIMENSIONS
21.5 x 34 in.
(54.6 x 86.4 cm)

CONCEPT
In 2016, the new dean of the Yale School of Architecture, Deborah
Berke, wanted to signal change and new direction in the school's
poster series. Our immediate thought was to change the paper
color from the previous gallery-white background to a mix of bright,
cheerful colors. Another big change was to focus less on the name
of the school, and more on the people involved in the events. We went
back to basics, taking a Bauhaus-like approach to type and seeing
it through a brightly colored filter. Sobriety was mixed with the
celebratory. The logotype uses the official Yale typeface by Matthew
Carter and is the only design constant.

ATAMIRA

Posters

CREATIVE DIRECTION
Lloyd Osborne
Shabnam Shiwan
Auckland, New
Zealand

PHOTOGRAPHY
Charles Howells

URL
osborneshiwan.com

TWITTER
@osborneshiwan

STUDIO
Osborne Shiwan

CLIENT
Atamira Dance
Company

PRINCIPAL TYPE
Atamira

DIMENSIONS
33.1 x 46.8 in.
(84.1 x 118.9 cm)

CONCEPT
Atamira Dance Company is New Zealand's leading Māori contemporary dance theater creator. Atamira explores themes of gender roles and cultural beliefs, further defining its meaning as a platform for the dead. Our creative focuses on relationships between male and female, corporeal and spirit. Typography and imagery collide across edges, creating a sense of unease and chaotic movement, mirroring the subject matter. Custom woven lettering reflects dance movement. Imagery references Michelangelo's *Pietà* and Māori mythology. With Atamira, we continue our focus of breaking down traditional stereotypes by celebrating Atamira Dance Company's contemporary outlook, both locally and internationally. These are mythologies woven in movement.

CLARA BUNTIN
Kabarettistin

«Clip und Clara»
Première in Zürich

Fr, 17.11.2017, 20⁰⁰ Uhr
Miller's Studio

buntin@clarabuntin.ch
www.clarabuntin.ch

Tel +41 (0)44 387 99 79
tickets@millers.ch
www.millers-studio.ch

Miller's Studio
Seefeldstrasse 225
CH–8008 Zürich

CLIP UND CLARA

Posters

DESIGN
Jürgen X. Albrecht
Raphael Mathias,
Offenburg, Germany

CREATIVE DIRECTION
Jürgen X. Albrecht

URL
j-x-albrecht.de

TWITTER
@J_X_Albrecht

DESIGN STUDIO
Jürgen X. Albrecht,
Konzeption
& Gestaltung

CLIENT
Clara Buntin

PRINCIPAL TYPE
Clara Buntin Headline
Neue Haas Unica

DIMENSIONS
23.4 x 33.1 in.
(59.4 x 84.1 cm)

CONCEPT
Clara Buntin, an artist from Zürich, invented a new genre for her solo program *Clip und Clara*, in which she combines singing, wordplay, poetry, and bizarre humor. Her word jokes cause slight vibrations in the brain. The design concept is based on this almost schizophrenic performance. Each letter of the typeface combines two different fonts and symbolizes the dialogue between Clip and Clara.

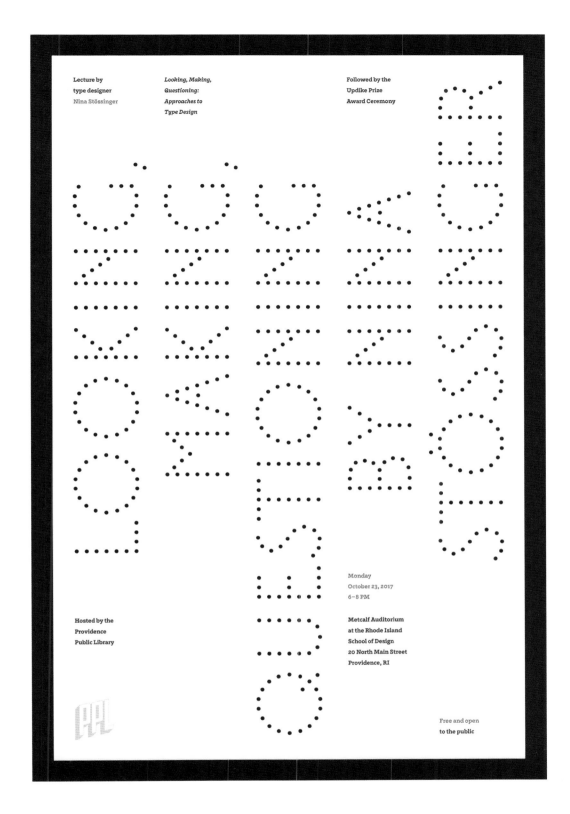

2017 UPDIKE PRIZE AWARD CEREMONY AND LECTURE POSTER

Posters

DESIGN
June Shin,
Providence,
Rhode Island

URL
notborninjune.com

TWITTER
@notbornin_june

CLIENT
Providence Public
Library

PRINCIPAL TYPE
Nordvest and Sélavy

DIMENSIONS
18 x 27.75 in.
(45.7 x 70.5 cm)

CONCEPT
The poster for the 2017 Updike Prize Award Ceremony and Lecture takes a purely typographic approach, appropriate for an event that celebrates excellence in type design. It foregrounds two typefaces designed by the lecturer Nina Stössinger herself. The text appearing in Sélavy, a display typeface consisting entirely of dots, is laser-cut, accentuating its unique feature and adding another layer to the otherwise flat medium. The poster takes on a new life depending on what is beneath it, as the background is shown through the openings.

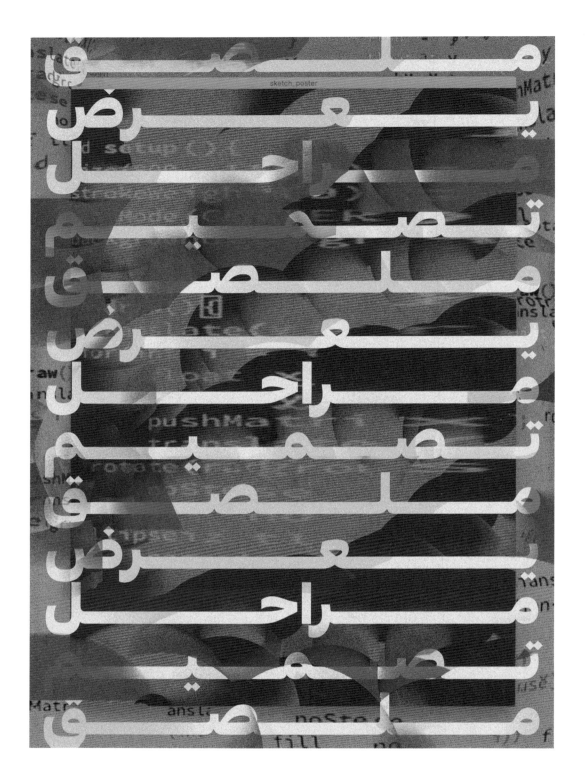

POSTER POSTER

Posters

DESIGN
Salem Al-Qassim,
Sharjah,
United Arab Emirates

URL
fikra.gtd

TWITTER
@fikradesigns

DESIGN STUDIO
Fikra Design Studio

CLIENT
Weltformat DXB
Poster Exhibition

PRINCIPAL TYPE
TPTQ Arabic Kanun
Black
Source Code Pro
Regular

DIMENSIONS
35.6 x 50.4 in.
(90.5 x 128 cm)

CONCEPT
The poster reveals the process of designing this poster. The text translates to "poster revealing the process of designing the poster revealing the process of designing the poster revealing the process of designing the poster," which exaggerates the notion of making, editing, making, re-editing, etc.

STAATSTHEATER MAINZ POSTERS

Posters

DESIGN
Anna Bühler
Nina Odzinieks
Pit Stenkhoff,
Berlin

URL
neuegestaltung.de

DESIGN FIRM
Neue Gestaltung
GmbH

CLIENT
Staatstheater Mainz
GmbH

PRINCIPAL TYPE
Suisse Works
Suisse Int'l
Handwritten fonts by
Neue Gestaltung

DIMENSIONS
33.1 x 46.8 in.
(84.1 x 118.9 cm)

CONCEPT
In a marked departure from convention, a wide range of striking illustrative and photographic techniques and typography is employed to create a series shaped by its bold use of a broad palette of visuals. Specifically designed to raise people's awareness of the artistic richness offered by a multi-genre repertory theater, every poster aims to embrace a given production's particular flair and focus, with only the theater's characteristic star logo referencing the series' origin.

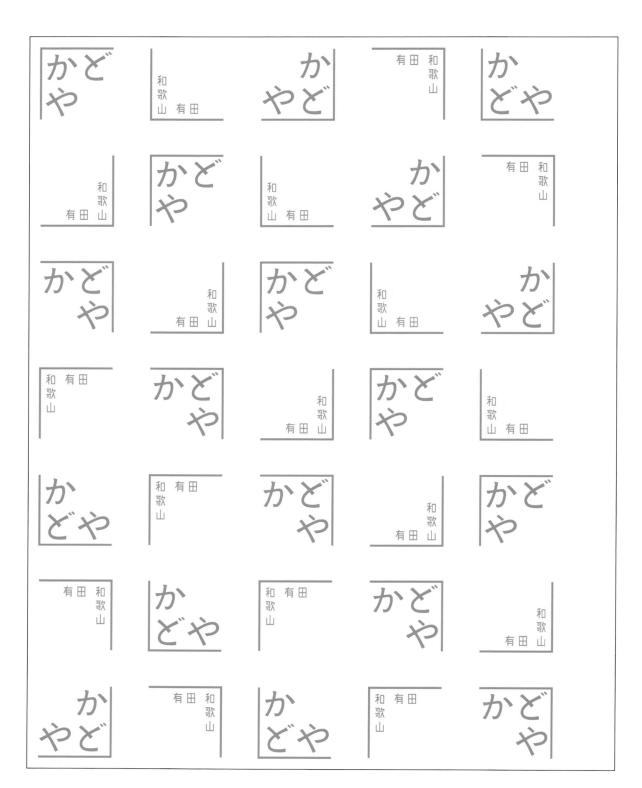

KADOYA

Posters

DESIGN
Minako Endo,
Tokyo

ART DIRECTION
Koichi Sugiyama

URL
maruinc.net

DESIGN FIRM
MARU

CLIENT
Kadoya

PRINCIPAL TYPE
Gothic BBB
Custom

DIMENSIONS
28.7 x 40.6 in.
(72.8 x 103 cm)

CONCEPT
Kadoya is a food dealer that deals with distinctive items.
Because the word means "corner" in Japanese, I decided to design
the corner to stand out.

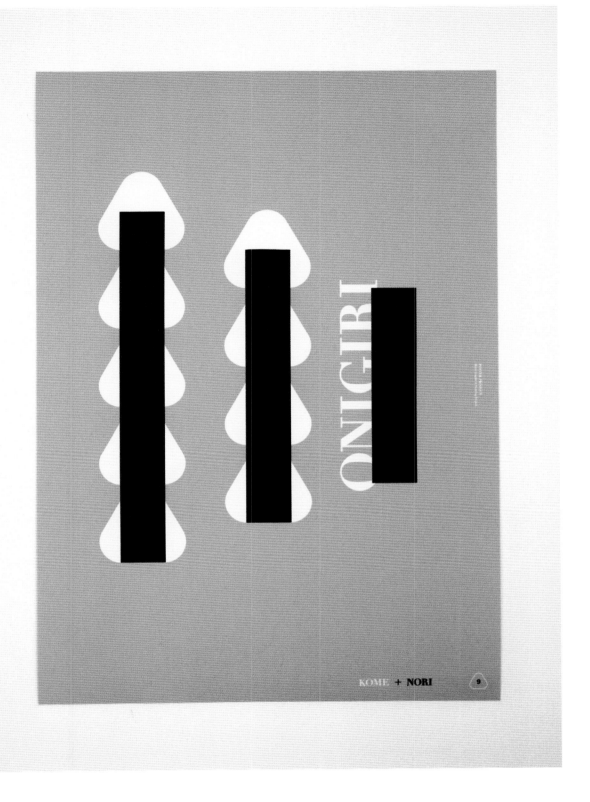

ONIGIRI

Posters

DESIGN
Minako Endo,
Tokyo

ART DIRECTION
Koichi Sugiyama

URL
maruinc.net

DESIGN FIRM
MARU

PRINCIPAL TYPE
Didot

DIMENSIONS
20.3 x 28.7 in.
(51.5 x 72.8 cm)

CONCEPT
I designed rice balls as a motif graphically with paper and gum tape.

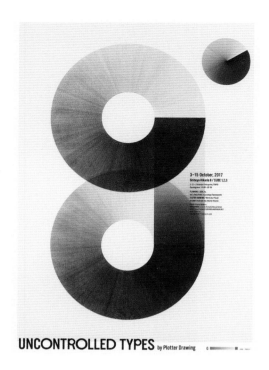

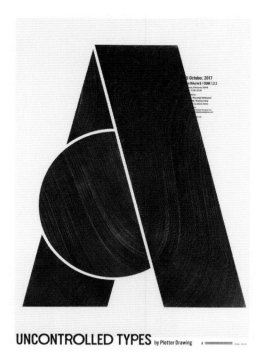

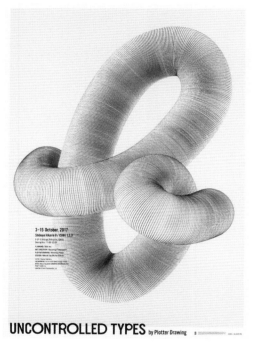

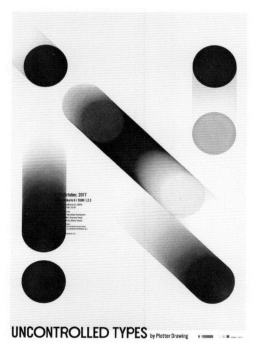

**UNCONTROLLED TYPES BY
PLOTTER DRAWING**

Posters

DESIGN
Hiromasa Fukaji
Natsuki Isa
Shuhei Yokota,
Tokyo

ART DIRECTION
Kazushige Takebayashi

PROGRAMMER
Junichiro Horikawa

EDITOR
Sayaka Yoshihara

URL
shainc.co.jp

DESIGN STUDIO
SHA Inc.

PRINCIPAL TYPE
Custom

DIMENSIONS
28.7 x 40.6 in.
(72.8 x 103 cm)

CONCEPT
Digital format is an indispensable tool in today's creative industry,
and creators have produced works by using various types of software.
Because digital expression seems to have lost expressive depth,
we felt that the appeal of physical expression should be re-examined.
We developed a new expressive method called plotter drawing.
Scrapes and nonuniformity are characteristic to this method.

RODRIGO

Posters

DESIGN
Marc Weymann,
London

LYRIK
Ingo Cesaro
Kronach

TEXT
Andri Perl
Chur

URL
marcweymann.com

TWITTER
@marcweymann

CLIENT
Edition Onepage

PRINCIPAL TYPE
Univers Next Pro 730
Basic Heavy

DIMENSIONS
23.4 x 33.1 in.
(59.4 x 84.1 cm)

CONCEPT
Five times a year, Doris Büchel produces a poster for *Edition Onepage*.
With each edition of the magazine two new authors are chosen for the
main text and the poem, and a new designer is selected to create the
poster based on the content of the story. The length of the text, the
format, and the fold are the same with every issue. The abstract design
elements in *Onepage* No. 9 represent the eventful life of Rodrigo and
his story of an almost incomprehensible coincidence. Design elements
have been placed on the folds, which allows their counterparts to be
revealed as the poster is being unfolded. The fold is thus an essential
part of the poster, both visually and functionally. The title page, the
reading order, and the simple comfort of holding this A1 poster in your
hands while reading all defined the placement of the different pieces
of content.

GÜRTEL NIGHTWALK XX

Posters

DESIGN
Eva Dranaz°,
Vienna

URL
3007wien.at

DESIGN FIRM
3007

CLIENT
Ottakringer
Kulturfreunde

PRINCIPAL TYPE
Handlettering

DIMENSIONS
23.5 x 33.1 in.
(59.7 x 84.1 cm)

CONCEPT
Gürtel Nightwalk is an annual street festival in a former red-light
district in Vienna that features live concerts, performances, and
readings. The illustration was inspired by the diversity of the location,
the noisy traffic next to the venues, and the long cultural walk through
the district.

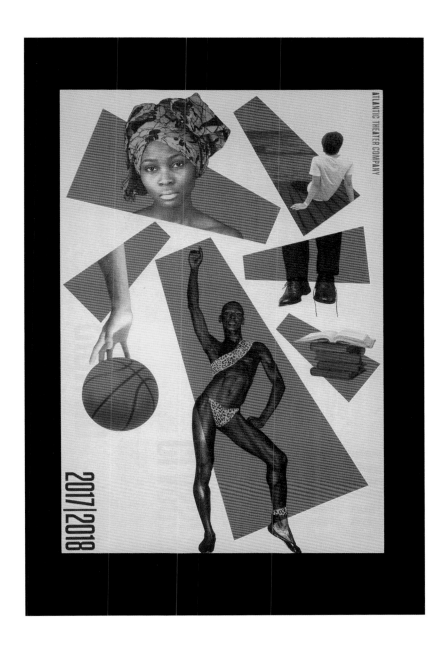

ATLANTIC THEATER COMPANY
2017–2018 SEASON POSTER

Posters

DESIGN
Paula Scher°
Rory Simms,
New York

PARTNER
Paula Scher°

ASSOCIATE PARTNER
Rory Simms

URL
pentagram.com

DESIGN FIRM
Pentagram°

CLIENT
Atlantic Theater
Company

PRINCIPAL TYPE
Fakt
Tungsten

DIMENSIONS
24 x 36 in.
(61 x 91.4 cm)

CONCEPT
This campaign for the influential performing arts group recasts its brand identity with a blast of bright color.

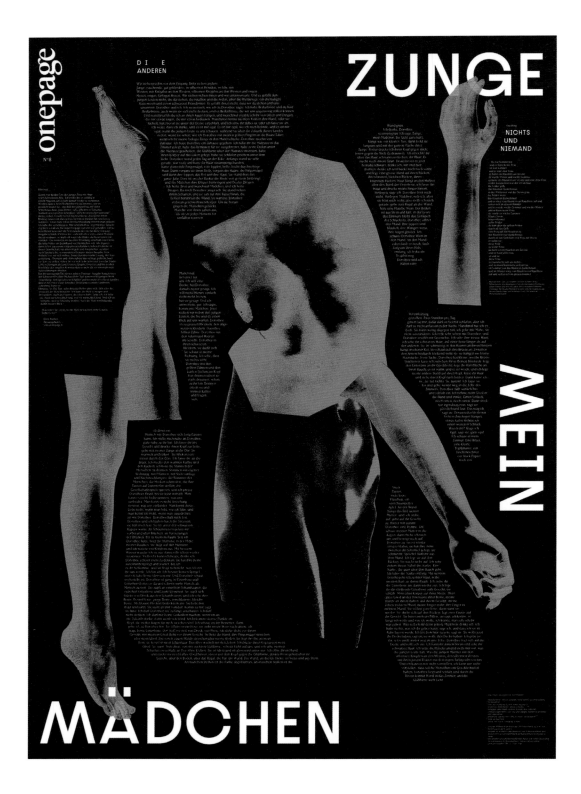

ONEPAGE NO. 8: DIE ANDEREN

Posters

DESIGN
Sascha Lobe°
Yuan Wang,
Stuttgart

URL
l2m3.com

STUDIO
L2M3
Kommunikationsdesign
GmbH

CLIENT
Edition Onepage

PRINCIPAL TYPE
doc.A
Matrix Book

DIMENSIONS
23.4 x 33.1 in.
(59.4 x 84.1 cm)

Sun
Ø 1.392.000 km

Mercury
Ø 4.879 km

Venus
Ø 12.100 km

Earth
Ø 12.740 km

Moon
Ø 3.474 km

You are here ↑

1 light minute

Scale 1:139.200.000.000

Home

HOME

Posters

DESIGN
Fábio Prata
Flávia Nalon,
São Paulo

URL
ps2.com.br

STUDIO
ps.2 arquitetura
+ design

PRINCIPAL TYPE
Helvetica

DIMENSIONS
27.6 x 39.4 in.
(70 x 100 cm)

CONCEPT
The poster was created as a New Year's gift to be distributed to clients
and friends. It features a part of the solar system between the sun
and the earth in the scale of 1:139.200.000.000. The great emptiness
that surrounds us is shocking and reminds us of the specialness and
fragility of our little planet, which is everyone's home.

DESIGN ARMY WEBSITE

Self-Promotion

DESIGN
Joe Letchford
Angela Milosevic
Magdiel Ortiz,
Washington, D.C.

**CO-FOUNDER AND
CHIEF CREATIVE OFFICER**
Pum Lefebure°

CEO AND CO-FOUNDER
Jake Lefebure

DEVELOPER
Nick DiMatteo

URL
designarmy.com

TWITTER
@DesignArmy

DESIGN FIRM
Design Army

PRINCIPAL TYPE
Berthold
Akzidenz-Grotesk

CONCEPT
For the redesign and launch of the Design Army website, we looked to design not only for a mobile-first experience, but also one that reflected the look and vision of who we are and what we create. Our goal was to have information easily accessible and to excite the user. Although the look is clean, crisp, and vibrant, we looked to create an experience that is energetic, dynamic, and easy to navigate. The balance of art and information creates a vibrant, visual language that fully extends the Design Army brand experience.

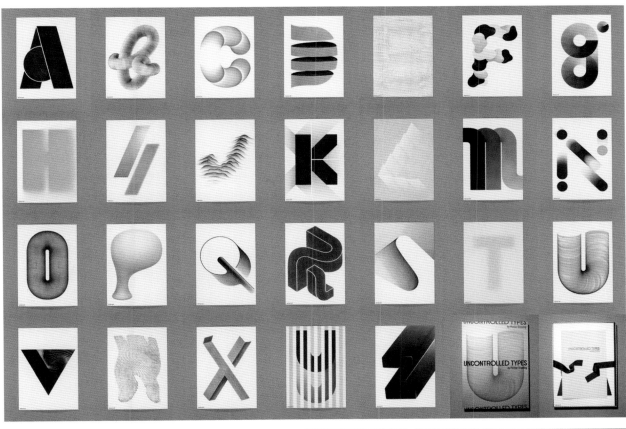

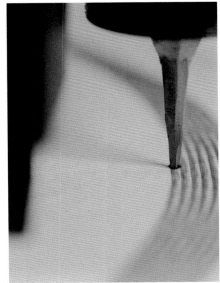

UNCONTROLLED TYPES BY PLOTTER DRAWING

Self-Promotion

DESIGN
Hiromasa Fukaji
Natsuki Isa
Shuhei Yokota,
Tokyo

ART DIRECTION
Kazushige
Takebayashi

PROGRAMMER
Junichiro Horikawa

EDITOR
Sayaka Yoshihara

URL
shainc.co.jp

DESIGN STUDIO
SHA Inc.

PRINCIPAL TYPE
Custom

DIMENSIONS
Various

CONCEPT
Digital format is an indispensable tool in today's creative industry, and creators have produced works by using various types of software. Because digital expression seems to have lost expressive depth, we felt that the appeal of physical expression should be re-examined. We developed a new expressive method called plotter drawing. Scrapes and nonuniformity are characteristic to this method.

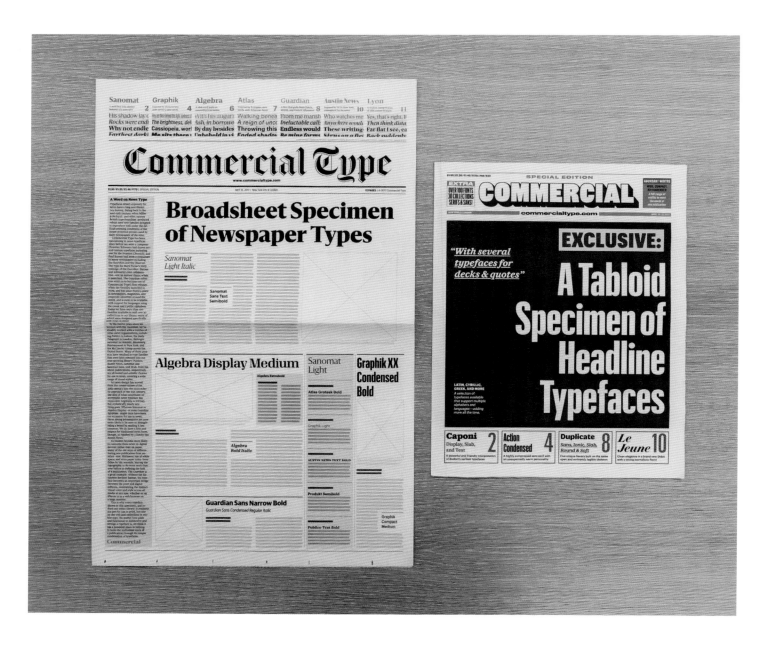

COMMERCIAL TYPE
NEWSPRINT SPECIMEN

Self-Promotion

DESIGN
Jack Curry°,
New York

CREATIVE DIRECTION
Paul Barnes
Christian Schwartz,
London and New York

PRINTING
Newspaper Club

URLS
heytheremynameis
jack.com
commercialtype.com

TWITTER
@thejackamo
@commercialtype

STUDIO
Commercial Type

PRINCIPAL TYPE
Various from the
Commercial Type
library

DIMENSIONS
Broadsheet: 29.9 x
22.8 in. (76 x 57.8 cm)
Tabloid: 22.8 x 15 in.
(57.8 x 38 cm)

CONCEPT
This is a two-part specimen showing a broad selection of the typefaces in the Commercial Type library designed for newspaper and magazine use. The first part of the specimen is fashioned in the style of a daily broadsheet newspaper and is meant to showcase families—such as Sanomat, Guardian, Publico, and Graphik—that are geared toward more "serious" news use. The second part of the specimen is formatted in the vein of a tabloid, and it features more expressive type treatments using families such as Druk, Action Condensed, Robinson, and Duplicate.

**CONCRETE
HOLIDAY CARD 2017**

Self-Promotion

DESIGN
Jessica Johnstone,
Toronto

ART DIRECTION
Jordan Poirier

CREATIVE DIRECTION
Diti Katona
John Pylypczak

PRODUCTION
Brandy McKinlay

URL
concrete.ca

TWITTER
@ConcreteAgency

DESIGN FIRM
Concrete Design

PRINCIPAL TYPE
Supersoft
Untitled Sans

DIMENSIONS
Various

CONCEPT
Our annual holiday package is delivered to friends, clients, and associates. This year's iteration included a silkscreened wine box, poster, and card alongside a micro-embossed envelope and sticker. The graphic and loud Supersoft contrasts the perfectly plain Untitled Sans. The poster was turned into wrapping paper, distorting the type into new forms each time. As big emoji (and sticker) fans, we thought it would be fun to include an iconic representation of "peace" and "joy" inspired by the original emoji set designed by Shigetaka Kurita.

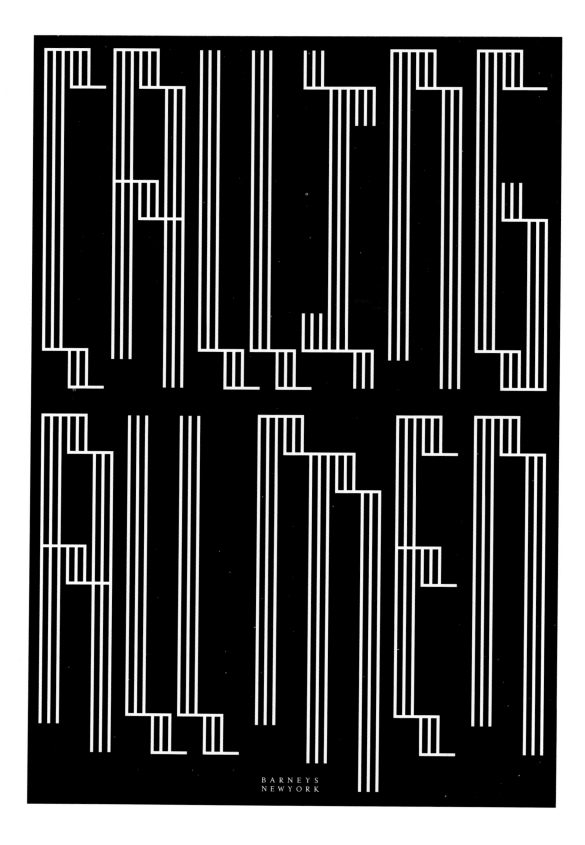

BARNEYS PROMOTIONAL POSTERS

Posters

DESIGN
Kevin Brainard,
New York

ART DIRECTION
Kevin Brainard
Cybele Grandjean

URL
area-of-practice.com

TWITTER
@areaofpractice

INSTAGRAM
@areaofpractice

STUDIO
Area of Practice

CLIENT
Barneys New York

MAGAZINE

Student Work

DESIGN
Duy Dao,
Hanoi

URL
duydao.net

PROFESSOR
Annie Huang

SCHOOL
Art Center
College of Design

PRINCIPAL TYPE
45Degrees
Lyon Text
Solaria
Union

DIMENSIONS
6 x 9 in.
(15.2 x 22.9 cm)

CONCEPT
Published three times a year, *Three Magazine* explores culture and society using the idea of the number 3. Each issue uses one three-letter word, three fonts, and three colors that correspond to society during that period of time. The magazine looks at current events and social issues and builds a conversation around them. Using first-person interviews, as well as related articles and photography, *Three Magazine* aims to bring a fresh point of view to its audience.

ALTERNATIVE FACTS

Experimental

DESIGN
Renata Graw
Alexa Viscius
Crystal Zapata,
Chicago

URL
thenormalstudio.com

DESIGN FIRM
Normal

PRINCIPAL TYPE
Times New Roman

DIMENSIONS
Various

CONCEPT
Shown in installation at Typeforce, this is a collection of artist Jenny Holzer's truisms paired with President Trump's tweets. Holzer's writings are a poignant and succinct commentary on polarizing social and political issues, while Trump's use of Twitter is brash and often self-indulgent. The pairings function as a distillation of the divided state of our country and the issues that plague our way of life. Inspired by red/blue stereoscopy, the colored light shining on the text hides or reveals each quote printed superimposed on a hanging banner. A small booklet of additional quote pairings was created as a takeaway.

```
Starting MS-DOS...
Current date is 1-11-2016

C:\>help
For more information on a specific command, type HELP command-name

ASK REDDIT        Get an instant opinion on your designs
DESIGN MOVEMENT   Look up a chosen design movement
INSPIRE ME        Feeling stuck? Get inspired in seconds
INQUIRY           Ask Wikipedia
RANDOM            Feeling lucky? Let the computer design for you
SEARCH            Search on popular websites and search engines


C:\>SEARCH -google graphic design trends
   Searching for graphic design trends on google.com
   It took 350ms to execute the command.

   Suggestions
   I - graphic design trends 2015
   I - graphic design trends 2016
   I - graphic design trends history
   I - graphic design trends forecasting

   Results [date I title I url]
20/01/2016 I The 9 Graphic Design Trends You Need to Be Aware o...
   http://designschool.canva.com/blog/design-trends-2016/

04/02/2016 I Are These Graphic Design Trends Going Out of Style...
   http://designschool.canva.com/blog/old-design-trends

22/02/2016 I 10 Brilliant Graphic Design Trends of 2016 - Creat...
   http://creativemarket.com/blog/10-brilliant-graphic-design-tre...

01/03/2016 2016 Design Trends Guide on Behance
   http://behance.net/gallery/34559663/2016-Design-Trends-Guide


C:\>_
```

GO BEYOND TRENDS

Student Work

DESIGN
Rok Hudobivnik
Justin Ner
Norwich, England

PROFESSOR
Nigel Aono-Billson

SCHOOL
Norwich University
of the Arts

PRINCIPAL TYPE
DOS VGA 437

DIMENSIONS
17.7 x 25.2 in.
(45 x 64 cm)

CONCEPT
This series of posters is a representation of raw search data that is
based on numerous algorithms in the style of an MS-DOS prompt. This
predictive information shows that we as designers are often exposed
to the same or similar search results from websites like Google and
Pinterest. Hence, it is not surprising that graphic design styles emerge
and recur on a global level.

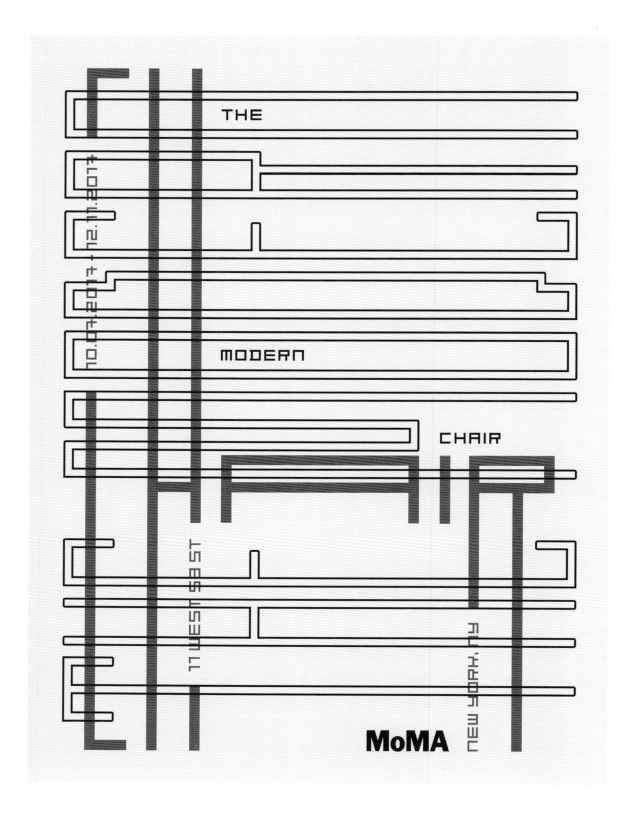

MODERN CHAIR

Student Work

DESIGN
Eugene Lee°,
New York

INSTRUCTOR
Carin Goldberg

SCHOOL
School of Visual Arts°,
New York

PRINCIPAL TYPE
P22 DeStijl

DIMENSIONS
30 x 40 in.
(76.2 x 101.6 cm)

CONCEPT
T his is a modernist chair exhibition poster informed by the bright, graphic illustrations and grid systems inherent to mid-twentieth-century Herman Miller furniture catalogs. The color and forms exhibit influences of Experimental Jetset and Russian Constructivism. Collectively, the amalgamation of styles yields a minimal poster in spirit with the modernist philosophy of Functionalism.

CORPUS CHRISTI 2018

Student Work

DESIGN
Yasmina Garcia
Estudillo°, New York

SCHOOL
Parsons
School of Design,
The New School

PROFESSOR
Steven Clunis

PRINCIPAL TYPE
Dead History

DIMENSIONS
58 x 67 in.
(147.3 x 170.2 cm)

CONCEPT
The assignment was "type as image." Corpus Christi, Granada's "The Body of Christ" festival, is a weeklong event in this beautiful, romantic city in the south of Spain. Though it is a religious celebration, everyone in Granada enjoys the festivities regardless of personal faith. Traditional religious processions decorate Granada's cobblestone streets, a sacred ceremony for some and an expression of Spanish heritage to others. As the city from which flamenco originates, Granada sees its streets teeming with beautiful women dressed in gypsy costumes and handsome men riding majestic horses.

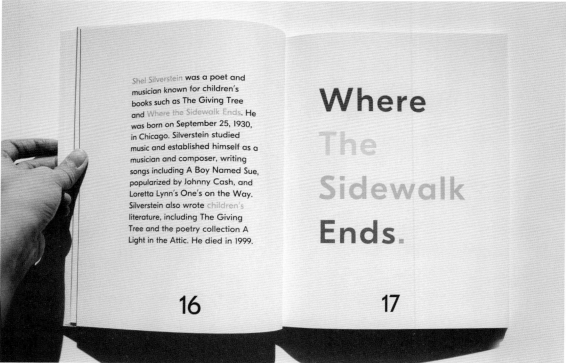

TYPE SPECIMEN BOOK

Student Work

DESIGN
Jae Yearn Kim,
New York

URL
jaeyearnkim.com

INSTRUCTOR
Scott Buschkuhl

SCHOOL
School of Visual Arts°,
New York

PRINCIPAL TYPE
GT Eesti

DIMENSIONS
8 x 10 in.
(20.3 x 25.4 cm)

CONCEPT
For this project, I took inspiration from Shel Silverstein's poem "Where the Sidewalk Ends" and made an alphabet book for kids. All the shapes and types in the book are from the typeface GT Eesti.

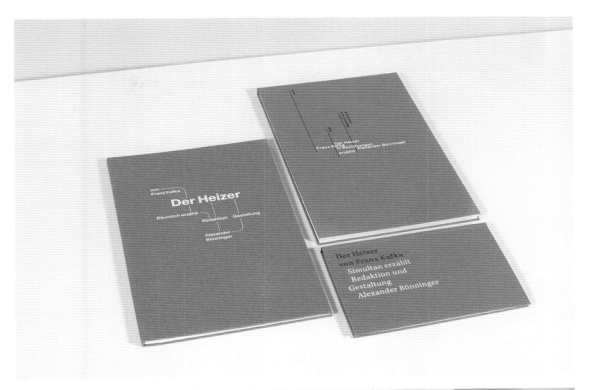

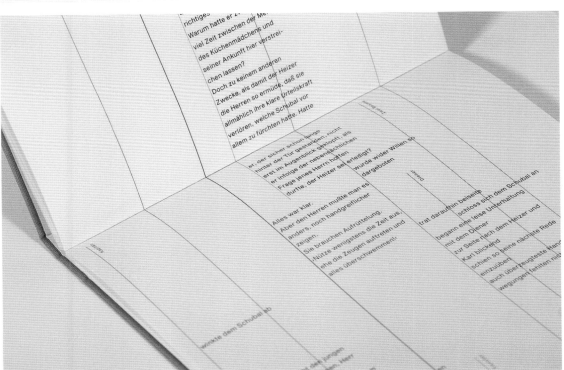

NONLINEAR NARRATIVE STRUCTURES

Student Work

DESIGN
Alexander Bönninger,
Essen, Germany

URL
alexander
boenninger.de

PROFESSORS
Ralf de Jong
Christin Heinze

SCHOOL
Folkwang University
of Arts

PRINCIPAL TYPE
Kepler
Sequel Sans

DIMENSIONS
Various

CONCEPT
The work experiments with typographic and medial staging. The aim is to break up the linearity of texts or narrations and make them accessible in a nonlinear way. I became interested in sign language, which is completely visual and multidimensional. I discovered that the narrative structure of a non-hearing person is significantly different from the narrative structure used in spoken language. Information is passed on simultaneously and each aspect is linked spatially. I tried to apply this different perspective on the action of reading a text, and I used the rules of sign language as inspiration for this work.

**MY VOICE FOUND
THE WORDS I SOUGHT**

Student Work

DESIGN
Colin Doerffler

URL
colindoerffler.com

PROFESSORS
Dirk Fütterer°
Nils Hoff

SCHOOL
Bielefeld University of
Applied Sciences

PRINCIPAL TYPE
Caslon 540
Helvetica Neue
12:51

RETOUCHER
Blane Robinson

DIMENSIONS
4.3 x 7.1 in.
(11 x 18 cm)

CONCEPT
This is an empirical study of the relationship
between word, image, and reality documented
in 160 pages.

Chéruit Paquin

Schiaparelli

Vionnet **Philo**

Chanel Lanvin

Prada **Kawakubo**

Hulanicki Quant

Cashin *Valentina*

Rykiel **Hamnett**

Westwood Grès

Lygia: A typeface family with gestural
and elegant qualities for editorial use

An alternative to commonly-used Didone typefaces prevalent in the fashion industry, Lygia explores the duality of sharp and round
forms with stylish cues. The family is designed to cover a range of hierarchies for fashion magazines — from display to text: Regular,
Semi Bold, **Bold**, **Black** and its *Italic* companions for heavy blocks of content (9 to 14pt) and a Hairline for headlines (60pt and above).

LYGIA

Student Work

DESIGN
Flavia Zimbardi,
New York

URL
flaviazim.com

TWITTER
@flaviazim

INSTRUCTOR
Hannes Famira

SCHOOL
The Cooper Union,
Type@Cooper

CONCEPT
An alternative to commonly used Didone typefaces prevalent in the
fashion industry, Lygia explores the duality of sharp and round
forms with stylish cues. The family is designed to cover a range of
hierarchies for editorial use—from display to text: Regular, Semi Bold,
Bold, Black, and its Italic companions for heavy blocks of content (9 to
14pt) and a Hairline for headlines (60pt and above).

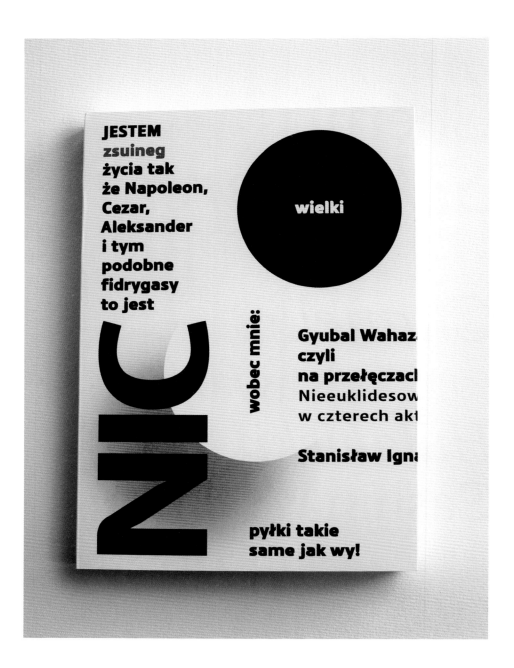

GYUBAL WAHAZAR

Student Work

DESIGN
Andrzej Bach
Vladyslav Kerpich
Magda Kłos
Martyna Kostrzewa
Paulina Kowalska
Weronika Ławska
Kyrylo Lohvyn
Maciej Mainda
Julia Michalczyk
Hai Duong Minh
Kinga Ostapkowicz
Patrycja Ostrowska
Zuzanna Ryncarz
Yustsina Sakalenka
Joanna Świderska
Agnieszka Toczyska
Anna Wawer
Zofia Włoczewska
Filip Wyrzykowski,
Warsaw

COVER DESIGN
Kinga Ostapkowicz

**CREATIVE DIRECTION
AND EDITING**
Professor
Ewa Satalecka

COLLABORATORS
Małgorzata Sady
Marek Średniawa

PROJECT SUPERVISION
Andrzej Klimowski

BOOK TYPESETTING
Weronika Ławska
Joanna Świderska

SCHOOL
Polish-Japanese
Academy of
Information
Technology

PROOFREADING
Alicja
Gorgońexecution
Jan Duda
Marta Kamieńska

URL
pja.edu.pl

RESEARCH
Marek Średniawa
(Witkacy's Institut)
Małgorzata Sady,
POKIS

PRINCIPAL TYPE
Ayka
Sneekpi

DIMENSIONS
8 x 11.4 in.
(20.2 x 29 cm)

CONCEPT
The project resulted from the research
and initiative of Małgorzata Sady and Marek
Średniawa, who wrote about the plans
that Gaberbocchus Press in London had
for publication of the English translation
of *Gyubal Wahazar* by Stanisław Ignacy
Witkiewicz (a.k.a. Witkacy). In an attempt to
encourage the continuation of this unrealized
challenge, workshops were conducted by Ewa
Satalecka (typography) and Andrzej Klimowski
(illustration) for a group of first-year students
who started working on the bilingual
publication of the book.

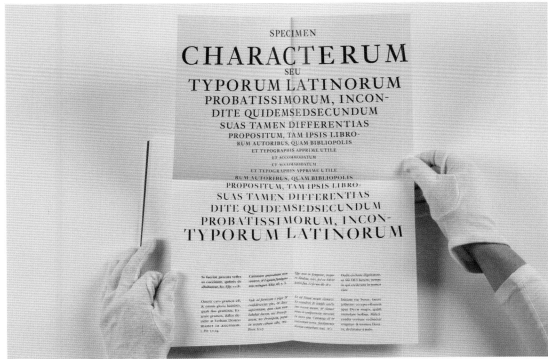

GENATH—EINE SCHRIFTANALYSE

Student Work

DESIGN
Janina Engel
Dorothée Martin,
Munich

BOOKBINDING
Gisela Benfer

PROFESSOR
Sybille Schmitz

SCHOOL
Mediadesign
Hochschule München

PRINCIPAL TYPE
Genath Regular,
Bold, and Italic

DIMENSIONS
6.2 x 8.7 in.
(15.8 x 22 cm)

CONCEPT
The book analyzes in detail the typeface Genath, developed by François Rappo. Based on a type specimen from 1720 by Johann Rudolf Genath, Rappo published the further developed and digitized typeface in 2011. The analysis includes a historic background of baroque typefaces, noting similarities to Janson, Fleischmann, and van Dijck, as well as a detailed study of the typeface's characters and uses. In an interview, the renowned typographer granted insight into his work process and personal life.

PORT MAGAZINE

Student Work

DESIGN
Gabriel Dörner
Lina Gräf
Nora Keilig,
Weimar, Germany

SCHOOL
Bauhaus University,
Weimar

PRINCIPAL TYPE
Beirut Poster
Beirut Text

DIMENSIONS
9.1 x 13.4 in.
(23 x 34 cm)

CONCEPT
PORT is the Bauhaus University student magazine. For the annual exhibition, selected works of all faculty members as well as their formation processes are published. Both the editing and design of the magazine are entirely student-run. Limited to three colors and one font, this edition surpasses all the previous ones, thanks to its size and analog offset printing on the cover, which came into being through experimental exposure of printing plates.

**HORIZONTE #11
"WISSEN/KNOWLEDGE"**

Student Work

DESIGN
Leon Lukas Plum°
Jakob Treß,
Weimar, Germany

PROFESSOR
Markus Weisbeck

SCHOOL
Bauhaus University,
Weimar

PRINCIPAL TYPE
Atlas Grotesk
Rando

DIMENSIONS
6.5 x 9.1 in.
(16.5 x 23 cm)

CONCEPT
As a guiding idea, we referenced elements derived from classical
book aesthetics in a contemporary visual context. Thus, every
submission is introduced by an "end paper" consisting of a
typographical composition on the front and a reproduction of
handcrafted marbled paper on the back. The articles have been
printed on natural paper, whereas we have chosen a high-white
glossy paper for the image section in the middle of the magazine.
Our display typeface Rando dates back to the Romanesque typefaces
of the late nineteenth and early twentieth centuries and resembles
Willy Fleckhaus's iconic cover designs.

1984: PRINCIPLES OF NEWSPEAK

Student Work

DESIGN
Weixi Zeng,
New York

URL
weixizeng.com

INSTRUCTOR
Hyesung Park

SCHOOL
School of Visual Arts°,
New York

PRINCIPAL TYPE
NittiPX
Saracen Black
Warschau

CONCEPT
In his novel *1984*, George Orwell included an appendix that explained a fictional language called Newspeak that was created by the totalitarian government. Often neglected by readers of *1984*, this guide is now more relevant than ever in a world full of government censorship and endless lies.

T1 REVIVAL

Student Work

DESIGN
Annabel Brandon°,
New York

INSTRUCTOR
Hannes Famira

SCHOOL
The Cooper Union,
Type@Cooper

PRINCIPAL TYPE
T1 Revival

DIMENSIONS
11 x 17 in.
(43.2 x 27.9 cm)

CONCEPT
This is a first-term project at Type@Cooper. It is a specimen poster
and a folded eight-page booklet for T1 Revival, a Caslon revival text
face based on a guidebook to Seville that was printed in London in
1906. All engravings were taken from the original source.

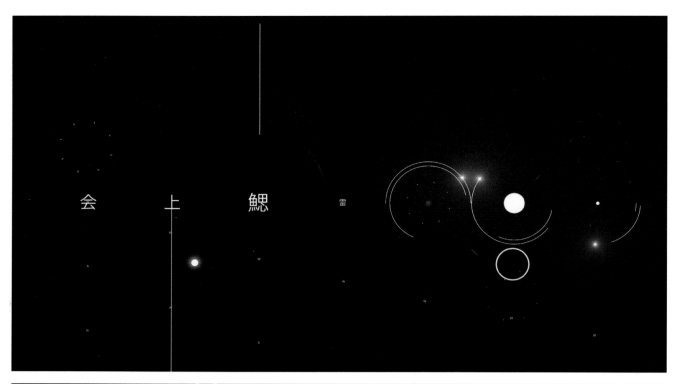

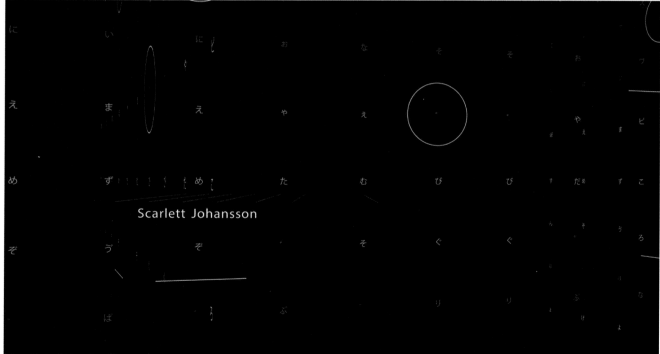

DESIGN
Ryoko Kondo,
New York

URL
ryokoloves.art

INSTRUCTOR
Ori Kleiner

SCHOOL
School of Visual Arts°,
New York

PRINCIPAL TYPE
Kozuka Gothic Pro

DIMENSIONS
25.6 x 14.4 in.
(65 x 36.6 cm)

CONCEPT
The concept here was the situation in which a language barrier makes someone feel lost, confused, and annoyed. It reminded me of the feeling I had when I first moved to New York from Japan. Each scene has fine lines and small flashing stars that are mostly filled with typefaces that represent the sensitivity, loneliness, and unexpected joy of foreign visitors.

MEMOIRS OF A GEISHA

Student Work

DESIGN
Sung Yoon Lee,
New York

INSTRUCTOR
Ori Kleiner

SCHOOL
School of Visual Arts°,
New York

PRINCIPAL TYPE
Trajan Regular
ヒラギノ角ゴシック
体 W0

DIMENSIONS
32 x 18 in.
(81.3 x 45.7 cm)

CONCEPT
This is a visual abstraction of those objects that best symbolize
Japanese Geisha culture, such as cherry blossom, umbrella, paper
lantern, and hand fan. The story was based on a movie, and each scene
symbolizes the characters in the film.

THE WAY WE DRESS

Student Work

DESIGN
Sanuk Kim,
New York

URL
behance.net/
gallery/52833765/
The-Way-We-Dress

INSTRUCTOR
Hyesung Park

SCHOOL
School of Visual Arts°,
New York

PRINCIPAL TYPE
Druk
Walbaum Standard

CONCEPT
Clothing has a transformative power that empowers women every day. Experimenting with fashion by mixing and matching apparel is not just a fun activity, but it's also a great way to discover yourself. The airiness and the casual vibe of the audio is reflected in the subtle use of color, patterns, and texture. This project is based on the audio from NOWNESS's "The Way We Dress" series.

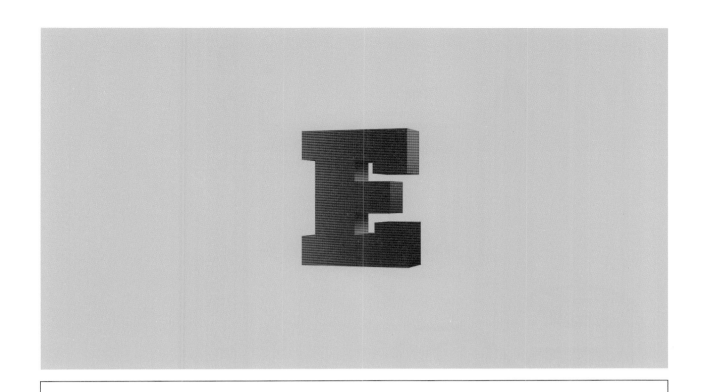

PERSEVERE

PERSEVERE

Student Work

DESIGN
Katherine Murnion,
New York

URL
katherinemurnion.
com/persevere-
motion-typography/

MUSIC
Ceiri Torjussen

SOUND DESIGN
FreeSound.org

INSTRUCTOR
Christopher Palazzo

SCHOOL
School of Visual Arts°,
New York

PRINCIPAL TYPE
Museo Slab 1000

CONCEPT
This motion typography piece visually represents the word
"Persevere." Each letter is an actor portraying conceptual aspects
of perseverance.

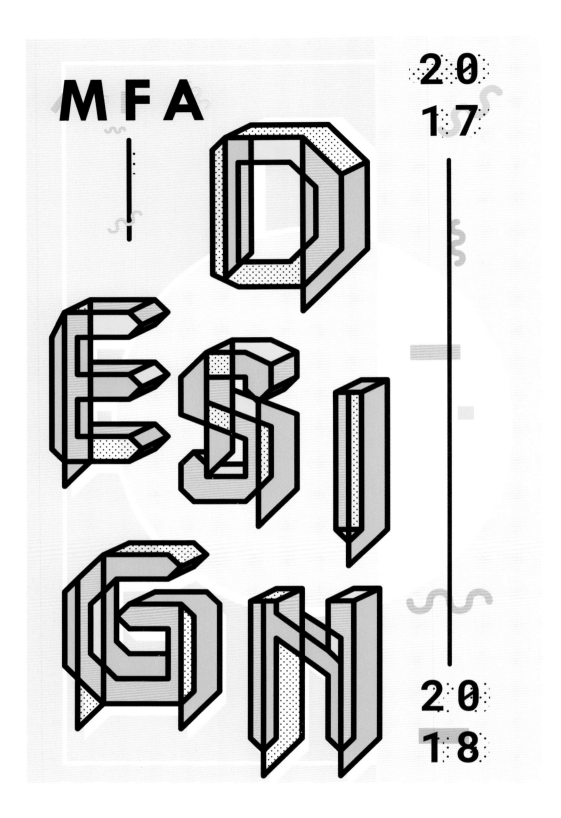

**SVA MFA DESIGN
ORIENTATION BRANDING**

Student Work

DESIGN
Jessica Hsinhua Lin°,
New York

INSTRUCTOR
Steven Heller

SCHOOL
School of Visual Arts°,
New York

PRINCIPAL TYPE
RobotoMono-Bold
Twentieth Century

DIMENSIONS
24 x 36 in.
(61 x 91.4 cm)

CONCEPT
A fun branding system was created to welcome students, new
and returning, to SVA MFA Design. The goal was to show diversity
and creativity within the MFA Design community through colors
and patterns.

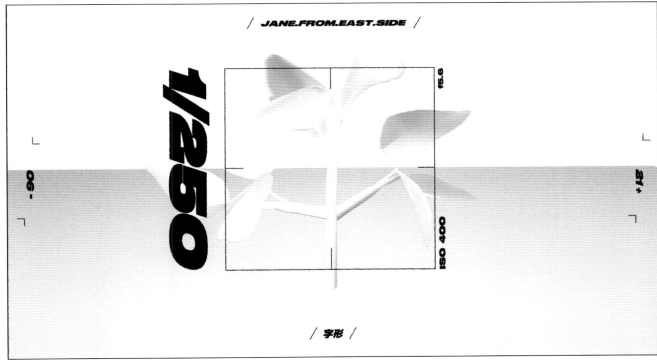

ZYGZYGY

Student Work

DESIGN AND ANIMATION
Inyeong Cho,
New York

BOOK AUTHOR
Leslie Lasiter

MUSIC
Intheshell-Notbad-
b34ts

INSTRUCTOR
Christopher Palazzo

SCHOOL
School of Visual Arts°,
New York°

CONCEPT
This is a promotional film done at SVA for the book ZYGZYGY. All of the experimental shapes in this book represent glyphs—digitized pictographs. I was inspired by the shapes in this book and tried to show that manmade glyphs originally came from nature and at the same time the glyph itself can be thought of as another form of nature (digi-nature).

Development of the first Korean numerals

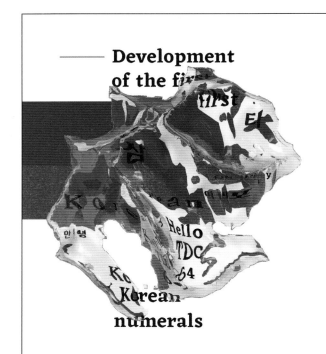

Sino-Korean

Regular written numbers	영	일	이	삼	사	오	육	칠	팔	구
Most important components	ㅇ	ㅣ	이	ㅅ	ノ	오	ㅉ	ㄹ	ㅂ	구
Results	ㅎ	ㄹ	우	쇼	ㄴ	으	ㅁ	ㄹ	ㅂ	구

Native-Korean

Regular written numbers	하나	둘	셋	넷	다섯	여섯	일곱	여덟	아홉	
Most important components	ㅎ	ㄷ	ㅅ	ㄴ	ㄷ	ㅓ	ㄴ	ㄷ	ㅏ	
Results	아	ㄷ	ㄴ	ㄴ	ㄷ	ㅋ	ㄹ	ㄹ	ㅂ	

Concept

Regular out-written three	삼
Most important components	산
New arranged components	쇼
Result numeral three	쇼
Handwritten version	쇼

Arabic-Korean

Regular written numbers	0	1	2	3	4	5	6	7	8	9
Similar forms from Hangeul	ㅇ	ㅓ	ㄱ	ㄹ	ㄴ	ㄹ	이	ㅋ	응	이
Results	0	ㅗ	ㄹ	ㅋ	ㄴ	ㄷ	ㅂ	ㅋ	8	어

Usage in copytext

Regular arabic numerals	종이책 독서량은 성인 평균 8.3권으로, 2015년 9.1권 대비 0.8권 감소했다.
Sino-Korean	종이책 독서량은 성인 평균 ㄴ.쇼권으로, 우ㅎㄴ으년 구.ㄹ권 대비 ㅎ.ㅂ권 감소했다.
Native-Korean	종이책 독서량은 성인 평균 ㄹ.ㄴ권으로, 드ㅎ아ㄷ 년ㄴ.아권 대비 ㅎ.ㄹ권 감소했다.
Arabic-Korean	종이책 독서량은 성인 평균 8.ㅋ권으로, ㄹㅇㄷ년 어.ㅗ권 대비 0.8권 감소했다.

DEVELOPMENT OF THE FIRST KOREAN NUMERALS

Student Work

DESIGN
Jakob Reinhard, Wiesbaden, Germany

URL
j-reinhard.de

PROFESSORS
Christine Bernhardt
Klaus Eckert

SCHOOL
RheinMain University of Applied Sciences

PRINCIPAL TYPE
Eczar (headline) concept based on Noto Sans CJK KR

CONCEPT
This experimental project engages with the untouched topic of missing Korean numerals. Until now, the Korean Hangeul script has been combined with the Arabic numerals—for example, 내달 16일이면 숭례문이 화재 발생 45년을 맞는다. From a typographic and conceptual point of view, there are opportunities to develop better-fitting numerals by considering cultural and typographic needs.

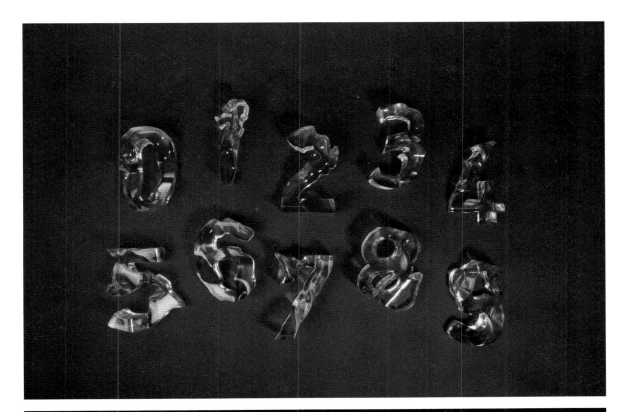

WAVES

Student Work

DESIGN
Katherine Mayhew,
Glendora, California

URL
katherinemayhew.
com

INSTRUCTOR
Andrew Byrom

SCHOOL
California State
University,
Long Beach

DIMENSIONS
3.5 x 2 x 5.25 in.
(8.9 x 5.1 x 13.3 cm)

CONCEPT
Painstakingly cast out of resin, these house number designs, based on the typeface Din, are a representation of the beauty of natural distortion that is created from water waves. The project is an experiment in typography design and fabrication to bring a three-dimensional number concept to life.

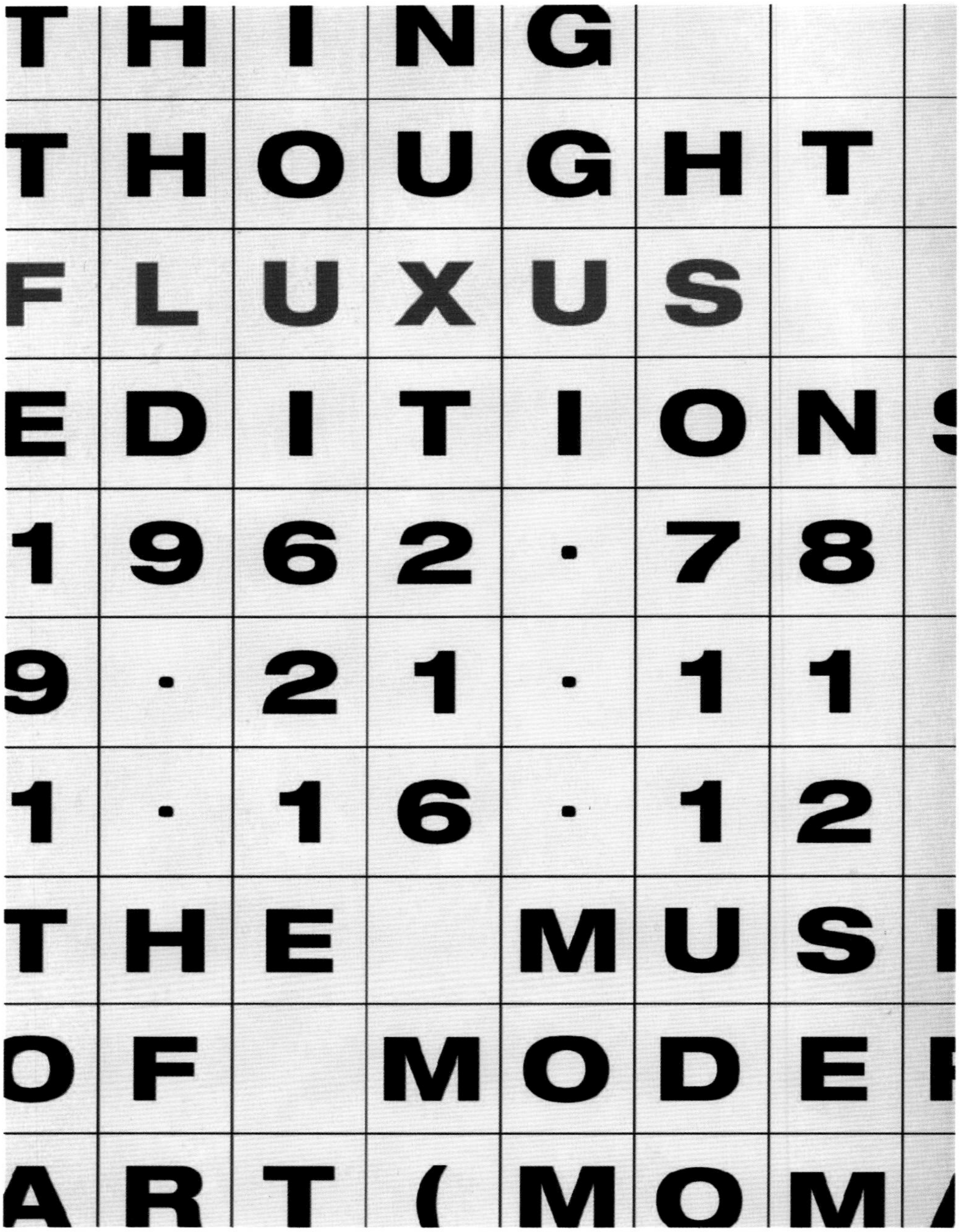

THING
THOUGHT
FLUXUS
EDITIONS
1962·78
9·21·11
1·16·12
THE MUSI
OF MODER
ART (MOMA

FLUXUS POSTER

Student Work

DESIGN
Soomin Jung,
New York

URL
soominjung.net

TWITTER
@so_ominjung

INSTRUCTOR
Carin Goldberg

SCHOOL
School of Visual Arts°,
New York

PRINCIPAL TYPE
Helvetica Neue 83
Heavy Extended

DIMENSIONS
18 x 24 in.
(45.7 x 61 cm)

SHAKESPEARE BOOK COVER SERIES

Student Work

DESIGN
Soomin Jung,
New York

INSTRUCTORS
Ivan Chermayeff
Tom Geismar
Sagi Haviv
Mackey Saturday

URL
soominjung.net

TWITTER
@so_ominjung

SCHOOL
School of Visual Arts°,
New York

PRINCIPAL TYPE
Akkurat Bold
Champion HTF
Featherweight

DIMENSIONS
8 x 11.5 in.
(20.3 x 29.3 cm)

CONCEPT
In this series of book covers for three of
Shakespeare's plays, I used the first letters of
their names (*Hamlet*, *Macbeth*, and King *Lear*)
to simplify the content of the plays.

OFF TRACK

Student Work

DESIGN
Yangyifan Dong,
San Francisco and
Chengdu, China

URL
behance.net/
dongyangyifan

INSTRUCTOR
Scott Thorpe

SCHOOL
California College
of the Arts

PRINCIPAL TYPE
IM FELL English
Manteka
NovaMono
Poppins

DIMENSIONS
4.5 x 8 in.
(11 x 21 cm)

CONCEPT
This is an encyclopedia of my personal experiences on trains when
I traveled alone in Europe for two months during the winter of 2015.
A train is a heterotopia and feeling, like an outsider all of my life
there and at home, I made this book to showcase my double-meaning
journey. The size follows the size of the TRAVELER'S notebook, and the
binding uses elastic strings that indicate "tracks," with the potential
for more add-ons.

ALL MIXED UP

Student Work

DESIGN
Sharleen Chen,
Los Angeles

URL
sharleenchen.com

INSTRUCTORS
Anther Kiley
Théotime Vaillant
Lorraine Wild
Michael Worthington

SCHOOL
California Institute
of the Arts

PRINCIPAL TYPE
Audree
LL Brown
GT Haptik

CONCEPT
In this age of booming development and interest in virtual and augmented reality, how can graphic designers use and incorporate these tech tools into our practice? This project investigates how the conventions of traditional graphic design—specifically in relation to the poster format—can evolve in a mixed-reality space. It addresses the challenges and opportunities that come with mixed reality and evaluates the potential of designing within this environment.

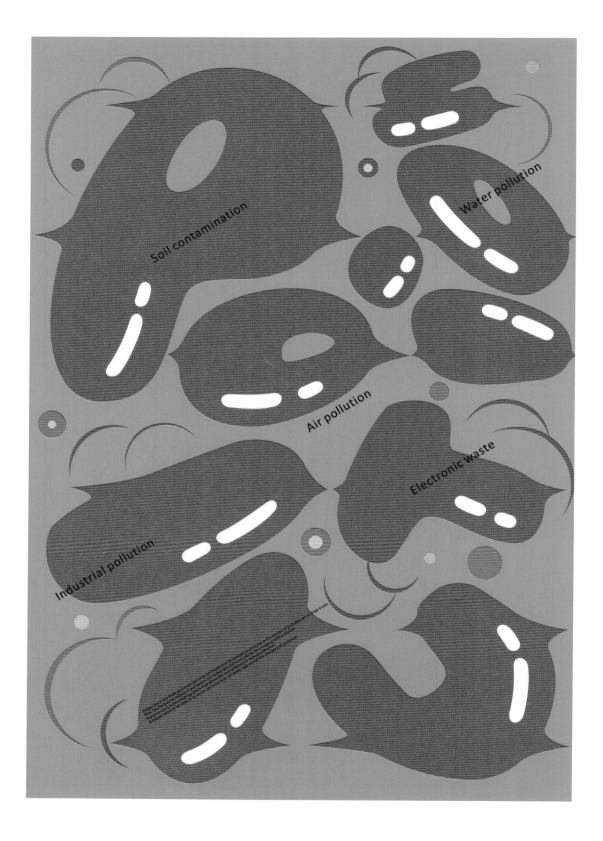

Soil contamination

Water pollution

Air pollution

Electronic waste

Industrial pollution

POLLUTION

Student Work

DESIGN
Peng Jun,
Associate Professor,
Wuhan, China

SCHOOL
Wuhan Polytechnic
University

PRINCIPAL TYPE
Arial
Calibri

DIMENSIONS
27.6 x 39.4 in.
(70 x 100 cm)

CONCEPT
The poster graphics use each letter of the word "Pollution" as an element to evolve into different animals and plants. It implies that environmental pollution is closely related to animals and plants, and calls on people to care for the environment and protect nature.

NO NUKES, PLUTONIUM IS FOREVER

Student Work

DESIGN
Qingyu Wu°,
New York

TWITTER
@QINGYU_WU

INSTRUCTOR
Elliott Earls

SCHOOL
Cranbrook Academy
of Art

PRINCIPAL TYPE
Fugue
Larish Neue

DIMENSIONS
4.25 x 7.2 in.
(10.8 x 18.3 cm)

CONCEPT
This book project was inspired by the
Japanese anti-nuclear student movement of
the 1960s, anti-nuclear songs, and films from
the early '80s.

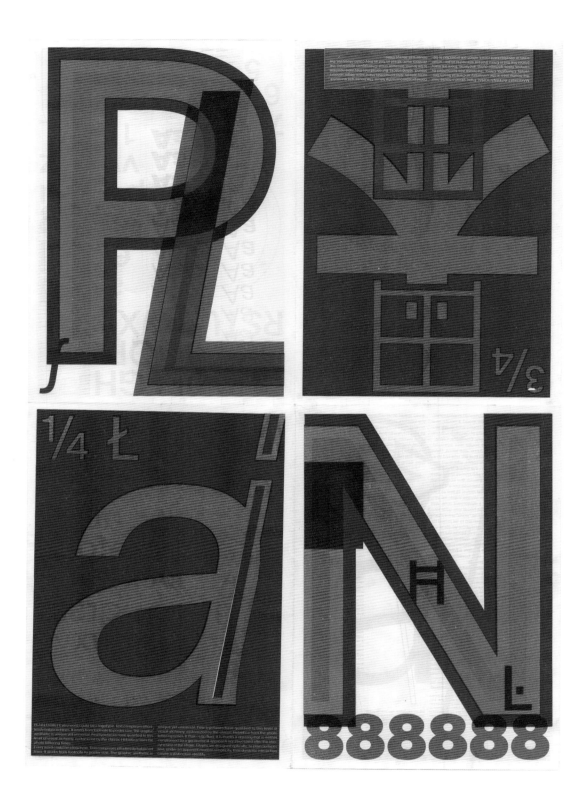

UNTITLED

Student Work

DESIGN

Pianpian He,
New Haven,
Connecticut

URL

pianpianhe.com

SCHOOL

Yale School of Art

PRINCIPAL TYPE

Plain Regular

DIMENSIONS

23.4 x 32.3 in.
(59.4 x 84 cm)

CONCEPT

This two-sided poster was made as a type specimen. One side was printed using two-color Risograph; the other side used a black-and-white inkjet. The poster can also be folded into a four-page pamphlet.

FUTURE BLOCKS

Student Work

DESIGN
Yaxu Han,
New York

INSTRUCTOR
Steven Heller

URL
yaxuhan.com/project

SCHOOL
School of Visual Arts°,
New York

DIMENSIONS
30 x 20 in.
(76.2 x 50.8 cm)

CONCEPT
This is a magnetic toy block of the future that can compose typefaces,
inspired by Ladislav Sutnar.

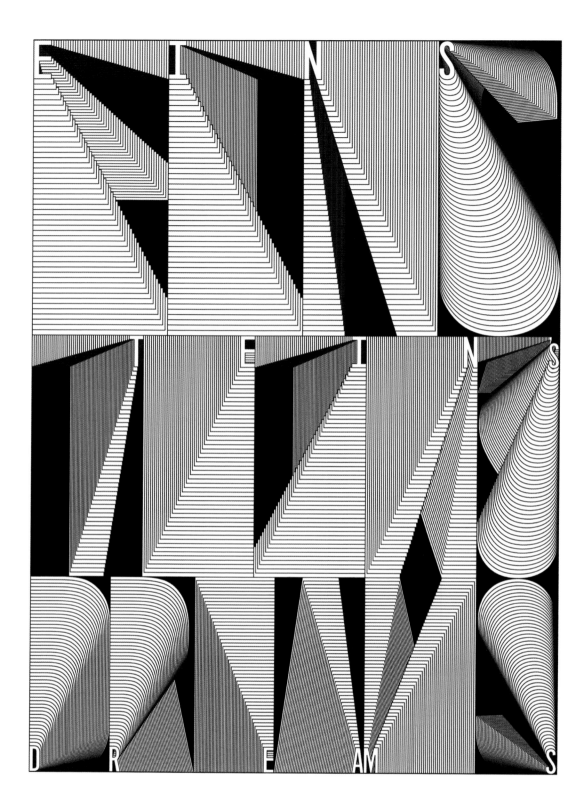

EINSTEIN'S DREAMS OF POSTERS

Student Work

DESIGN
Meagan Vanderhill,
Savannah

URL
meaganvanderhill.com

INSTRUCTOR
Sohee Kwon

SCHOOL
Savannah College
of Art and Design

PRINCIPAL TYPE
Alternate Gothic
(modified)

DIMENSIONS
16 x 23 in.
(40.6 x 58.4 cm)

CONCEPT
This is a poster for the novel *Einstein's Dreams*. The poster captures
the essence of the novel by expressing the repetition and movement
of time through its typography and color (white representing the past,
black the future).

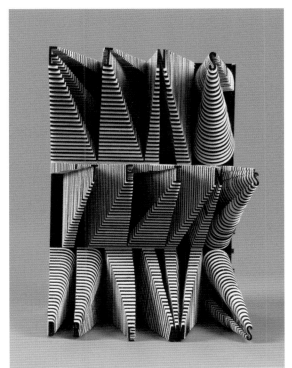

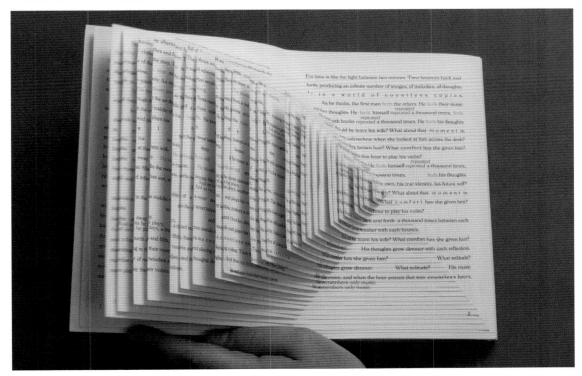

EINSTEIN'S DREAMS

Student Work

DESIGN
Meagan Vanderhill,
Savannah

URL
meaganvanderhill.com

INSTRUCTOR
Sohee Kwon

SCHOOL
Savannah College
of Art and Design

PRINCIPAL TYPE
Alternate Gothic
(modified)

DIMENSIONS
24 x 32 in.
(61 x 81.3 cm)

CONCEPT
This experimental book reimagines five chapters from Alan Lightman's novel *Einstein's Dreams*. The book conceptually explores different representations of time as presented in the novel. The acrylic book box expresses the repetition of time and the movement of past and future (past represented in white, future in black) and houses the five-chapter book. Each chapter in the book is redesigned through structure, grid, and typography to be read as if you were experiencing time as the characters themselves are experiencing time.

EDITORIAL DESIGN

Student Work

DESIGN
Ying Zhang,
New York

URL
yingzhang.
myportfolio.com

SCHOOL
Parsons
School of Design,
The New School

PRINCIPAL TYPE
Futura PT Light,
Medium Oblique
and Book

DIMENSIONS
8.5 x 11 in.
(21.6 x 27.9 cm)

CONCEPT
The idea was to treat type as graphics
and explore the interaction between type
and figure in spatial relations, depending
on position, weight, and size.

ADLER PLACEMAKING

Student Work

DESIGN
Amy Chang
Savannah

URL
amychang.design

PROFESSOR
Steff Geissbuhler

SCHOOL
Savannah College
of Art and Design

PRINCIPAL TYPE
Futura
Condensed Bold

DIMENSIONS
Various

CONCEPT
In creating the environmental graphics for SCAD's graphic design building, Adler Hall, I wanted to explore the impact that type in perspective can have. Pairing bold typographic elements with SCAD's striking color combination of black and yellow creates a visual impact that should inspire students. The contrasting colors blend the sharp perspectives of the repurposed postal office, creating optical illusions when approached from different angles. Each hallway or room exhibits distinctive usage of color and type, but there remains a common message that runs through all the spaces: to challenge perspectives and break rules.

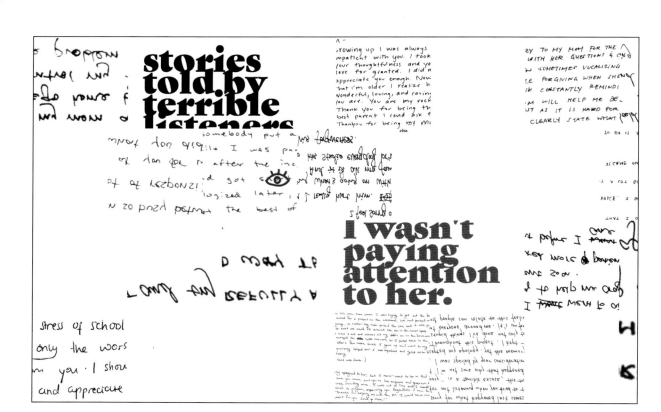

There was this one time when I was trying to get out the door to head to school for a project on the weekend. We had parked my car in the garage, or rather my mom parked the car, and it was parked in crooked, so that we could fit around the car in the small space.
I went to back it out and almost hit my dad's car in the driveway and almost scraped the side mirrors, so I pulled back in the garage frustrated. After a few more tries I gave up and went to my mom for help. She graciously helped but I was impatient and yelled at her for how much time it was taking.

(Yeah that was dumb...)

I eventually apologized to her, but I never want to be in that state of mind again. "I love you mom, and you're too awesome and generous to take anyone's crap, including mine. I was out of time and I should never act like that to anyone, especially you. Regardless of how frustrated I was. Thanks for helping me with the car. I would have ruined it if it wasn't for you. Love ya mom!"

THE IMPATIENT

Student Work

DESIGN
Erin Zhang,
Oakland, California

URL
zyyerin.com

INSTRUCTORS
Bob Aufuldish
Leslie Becker

SCHOOL
California College
of the Arts

PRINCIPAL TYPE
Gastromond

CONCEPT
"Why are we such impatient listeners, even with someone we care about?" This project is a survey and a collection of answers regarding this question. It is not an attempt to provide a solution, but various perspectives looking into the situation.

DER WIDERSPENSTIGE HEILIGE

Student Work

DESIGN
Saori Shiroshita,
Berlin

URL
shiroshitasaori.com

SCHOOL
Berlin University
of the Arts

PRINCIPAL TYPE
Akzidenz-Grotesk

DIMENSIONS
23.4 x 33.1 in.
(59.4 x 84.1 cm)

CONCEPT
The poster is a reinterpretation of a poster designed by
Hans Förtsch, former professor of the Berlin University of the Arts.
The same typeface from the original was used. The original poster
was designed for the 1961 premiere at the Renaissance Theater in
Berlin of Der Widerspenstige Heilige (a German performance of
Paul Vincent Carroll's *The Wayward Saint*) and can be found in the
university's archives.

RADICAL MOVEMENTS

Student Work

DESIGN
Chad Miller°,
Brooklyn, New York

SCHOOL
Vermont College
of Fine Arts,
Montpelier, Vermont

PRINCIPAL TYPE
Maison Neue

DIMENSIONS
24 x 36 in.
(61 x 91.4 cm)

CONCEPT
A collection of visual research and aesthetic experimentation, this project attempts to reconcile two seemingly disparate but integral pillars of myself—punk and modernism—by exploring visual and philosophical similarities between each movement and the economic, social, and political climates that shaped them.

GDFP: TYPOGRAPHIC IDENTITY

Student Work

DESIGN
María Carla Mazzitelli,
Buenos Aires

URLS
fadu.uba.ar
behance.net/
carlamazzitelli

PROFESSOR
Rubén Fontana

SCHOOL
University of Buenos
Aires (FADU-UBA)

PRINCIPAL TYPE
Découpe Regular
Découpe Italic
Découpe Black

DIMENSIONS
Various

CONCEPT
This research project developed a visual identity for Graphic Design
Festival Paris using Découpe, an expressive display type designed
specifically for the event. Inspired by gestural graphic expressions,
such as paper cutouts and spontaneous handwriting, of the artists
and designers who play a part in this international festival, Découpe
includes three different styles: Regular, Italic, and Black. This was
a noncommercial project.

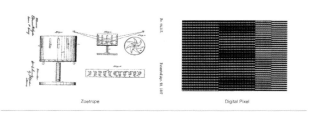

Zoetrope

Digital Pixel

The construction of typeface reference to cylinderical spinning motion and optical
illusion created through integration of continuous lines and form.

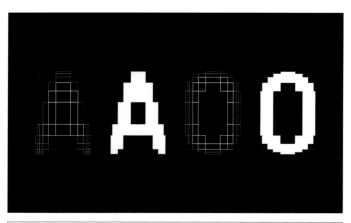

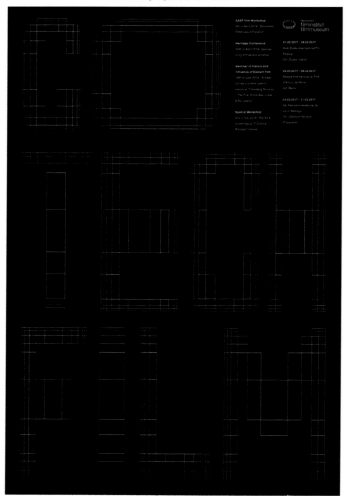

EXPOSURE
MOVEMENT
PROJECTION
SCREENING

**MON - FRI
10AM - 5PM**

deutsches
filminstitut
filmmuseum

**FILMIC VISION
EXHIBITION IDENTITY**

Student Work

DESIGN
Haejung Jun,
New York

URL
jane-jun.com

SCHOOL
School of Visual Arts°,
New York

PRINCIPAL TYPE
Akzidenz Grotesk
Custom

DIMENSIONS
20 x 30 in.
(50.8 x 76.2 cm)

CONCEPT

Filmic Vision, a yearlong exhibition at the Deutsche Filminstitut, is
dedicated to showcasing the "origins, progress, and future of film." It
showcases historical film technology, as well as contemporary themes
such as interactive stations and advanced projection techniques. The
customized typeface references two of the essential inventions in film
history: zoetrope and digital pixel. The typeface illustrates fundamental
techniques of film: exposure, movement, focus, and optical illusion. It
reflects the purpose of the exhibition, which is to encourage viewers to
"deeply observe and understand the process of film and ways in which
moving images produce their effects."

FLUXUS POSTER

Student Work

DESIGN
Haejung Jun,
New York

URL
jane-jun.com

INSTRUCTOR
Carin Goldberg

SCHOOL
School of Visual Arts°,
New York

DIMENSIONS
12 x 18 in.
(30.5 x 45.7 cm)

CONCEPT
This is a Museum of Modern Art exhibition poster for *Thing/Thought: Fluxus Editions, 1962–1978*. The poster references the box and match, which are significant artworks of the Fluxus movement. All of the letters were constructed with matches.

RAISING GENERATION HATE

NEARLY ONE THIRD OF ALL HATE CRIMES IMMEDIATELY AFTER THE 2016 ELECTION OF TRUMP FOR PRESIDENT WERE CARRIED OUT BY STUDENTS AT THEIR K-12 SCHOOLS.

HATE SPEECH AND THE FIRST AMENDMENT

Student Work

DESIGN
Samantha Spaeth, Seattle

URLS
samanthaspaeth.com
art.washington.edu/ design

PROFESSOR
Annabelle Gould

SCHOOL
University of Washington

PRINCIPAL TYPE
Anton Regular
Baskerville Regular

DIMENSIONS
16 x 22 in.
(40.6 x 55.9 cm)

CONCEPT
The First Amendment allows Trump to spew hate speech until explicit racism and bigotry are the new norm. Under the current administration there has been a drastic rise in hate crimes, especially shockingly in K-12 schools due to their increased exposure to such hate speech. This poster is designed to raise awareness around and combat the effects of hate speech on children, by calling on parents and educators to talk with children about what they hear.

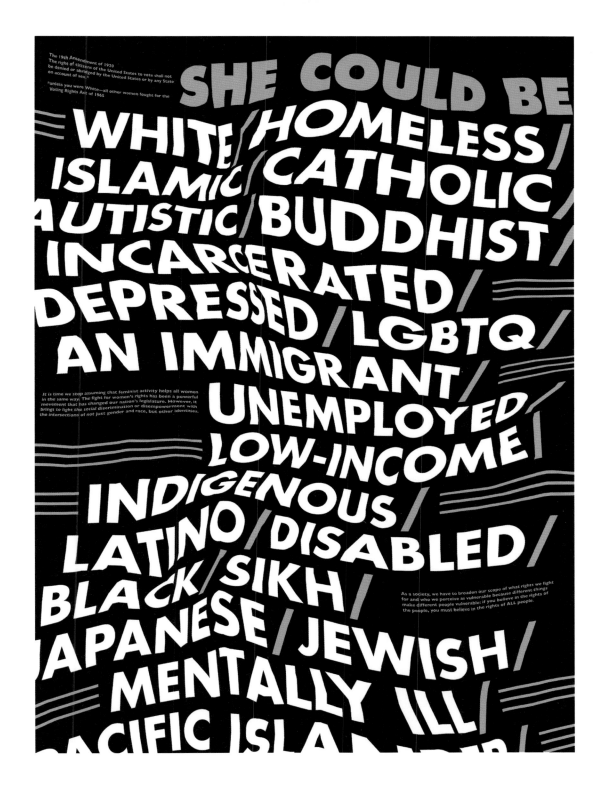

INTERSECTIONALITY AND THE 19TH AMENDMENT

Student Work

DESIGN
Andrew Le,
Seattle

URL
art.washington.edu/
design

PROFESSOR
Annabelle Gould

SCHOOL
University of
Washington

PRINCIPAL TYPE
Gill Sans
Futura Pro

DIMENSIONS
16 x 22 in.
(40.6 x 55.9 cm)

CONCEPT
Each bold word is an identity that can connect with the viewer either personally or socially. My hope is that by seeing each identity in the context of, and connected to, other identifiers, the viewer begins to understand how intersectionality plays a huge role in his or her life and the lives of others. Intersectionality reveals that there is no such thing as neutrality—by choosing to remain silent and support only specific marginalized communities, we perpetuate the cycle of discrimination and oppression that we have been taught.

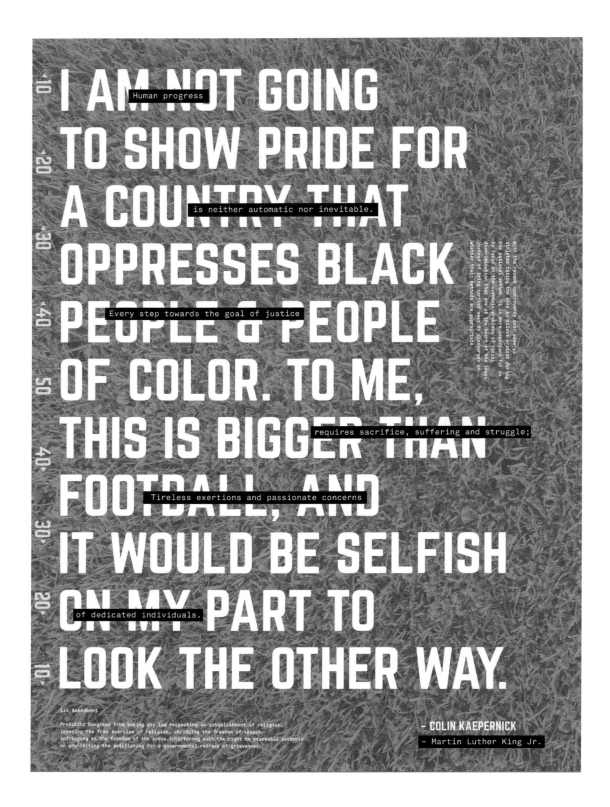

DISCRIMINATION AND THE FIRST AMENDMENT

Student Work

DESIGN
Faezah Shaharuddin, Seattle

URL
art.washington.edu/design

PROFESSOR
Annabelle Gould

SCHOOL
University of Washington

PRINCIPAL TYPE
Akkurat Mono Norwester

DIMENSIONS
16 x 22 in.
(40.6 x 55.9 cm)

CONCEPT
This poster was a response to the "Take a Knee" anti-discrimination protests of 2017 by NFL players. The design was intended to remind the American public that the focus should not be on the "how" of the protests but on the "why." Colin Kaepernick's words are juxtaposed with those of Martin Luther King Jr. to emphasize that meaningful progress requires struggle and conflict. Like the civil rights movement of the 1960s, the Take a Knee protests are a necessary and important reminder that systematic discrimination is a dire problem that our society still needs to address.

GUNS AND THE SECOND AMENDMENT

Student Work

DESIGN
Isaac Jaeger,
Seattle

URL
art.washington.edu/
design

PROFESSOR
Annabelle Gould

SCHOOL
University of
Washington

PRINCIPAL TYPE
Sentinel
Space Mono

DIMENSIONS
16 x 22 in.
(40.6 x 55.9 cm)

CONCEPT
Outside the United States, there have been eighteen school shootings in twenty years. The United States, meanwhile, had eighteen school shootings in just the first thirty-five days of 2018 alone. The language of the Second Amendment warps beneath the mighty National Rifle Association, whose donation recipients in Congress tell us that shootings are inevitable. Somehow, unbelievably, the next tragedy is never more than one week away. To the parents and children of America, U.S. Senator John Thune (Republican, $180,000 from the NRA) says, "Get small."

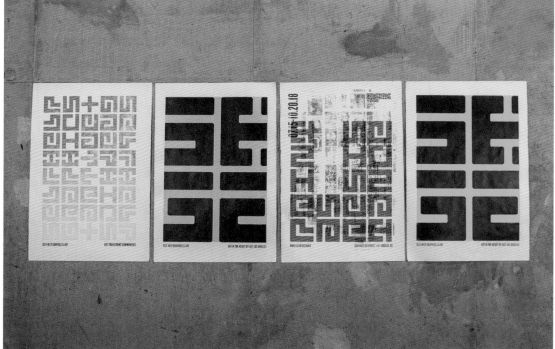

SELF HELP GRAPHICS & ART

Student Work

DESIGN
David Jimenez,
Pasadena, California

SCHOOL
Art Center College
of Design

PRINCIPAL TYPE
Knockout-HTF67 Full
Bantamweight
Custom

INSTRUCTOR
Brad Bartlett

DIMENSIONS
Single page:
15 x 11.5 in.
(38 x 29.2 cm)
Spread:
15 x 23 in.
(38 x 58.4 cm)

CONCEPT
The goal of this project was to provide Self Help Graphics & Art with an identity that embraces the community arts center's values, mission, and history in East Los Angeles. Self Help Graphics & Art started in the context of the cultural identity and political empowerment of Chicano and Latino artists. Inspired by the grid structure within the Aztec and Maya hieroglyphs, I created a custom typeface and logotype. The final logotype was letterpressed and screen printed to achieve texture and pay homage to Self Help Graphics & Art's printmaking identity.

**PRIVACY AND THE
FOURTH AMENDMENT**

Student Work

DESIGN
Cody Scott,
Seattle

URL
art.washington.edu/
design

PROFESSOR
Annabelle Gould

SCHOOL
University of
Washington

PRINCIPAL TYPE
Leitura
VCR OSD Mono

DIMENSIONS
16 x 22 in.
(40.6 x 55.9 cm)

CONCEPT
The continued exploitation of Americans' privacy and the prevalence
of the National Security Agency's violations of the Fourth Amendment
allow government agencies to have a frighteningly comprehensive
perspective of a person's identity. This poster visualizes the many
facets that can be collected by these agencies and shows how this
information can not only create a corrupted digital framework of a
person's identity but also capitalize on our dependency on technology.

SILENT SPRING COVER DESIGN

Student Work

DESIGN
Jacquelyn Pierson,
Brooklyn, New York

URL
jackiepierson.com

INSTRUCTOR
Jennifer Heuer

SCHOOL
Pratt Institute

PRINCIPAL TYPE
Hand-lettered Brush
Hand-lettered
Brush Sub
Source Sans Pro

DIMENSIONS
20.75 x 8.5 in.
(52.7 x 21.6 cm)

CONCEPT
Using bold, graphic lettering and the manipulation of classic scientific illustration, this cover design is intended to show how human interference leads to the destruction of natural life and the inevitable "Silent Spring" Rachel Carson predicted we will find ourselves inhabiting.

ROAD RALLY

Student Work

DESIGN
Megan Dweck,
Brooklyn, New York

URL
megandweck.com

INSTAGRAM
@megandweck

INSTRUCTOR
Shanti Sparrow

SCHOOL
Shillington School
of Design

PRINCIPAL TYPE
Aperçu Mono
(body copy)
Custom

DIMENSIONS
Various

CONCEPT
Road Rally is an event for the New York City Department of
Transportation to improve the perception of traffic enforcement
agents, commonly known as "meter maids." The design for the
campaign was inspired by the visual language of vintage auto racing.

THE IMAGES OF GOD

Student Work

DESIGN
Jaejin Ee,
New York

INSTRUCTOR
Michael Worthington

SCHOOL
California Institute
of the Arts

PRINCIPAL TYPE
Electra

DIMENSIONS
5.5 x 7 in.
(14 x 178 cm)

CONCEPT
Renaissance paintings and sculptures have long presented stereotypical images of the various gods and goddesses of Greek and Roman mythology. However, while Greek and Roman mythology has been reproduced and re-consumed for a long period of time, the appearance of the gods has changed as well through diverse media such as movies, educational books for kids, and comic books. In this design project, the Roman alphabet letterings are made through collages of the gods and goddesses of Greek and Roman mythology. There are two counterpart sets according to their different appearances: stereotypical and contemporary.

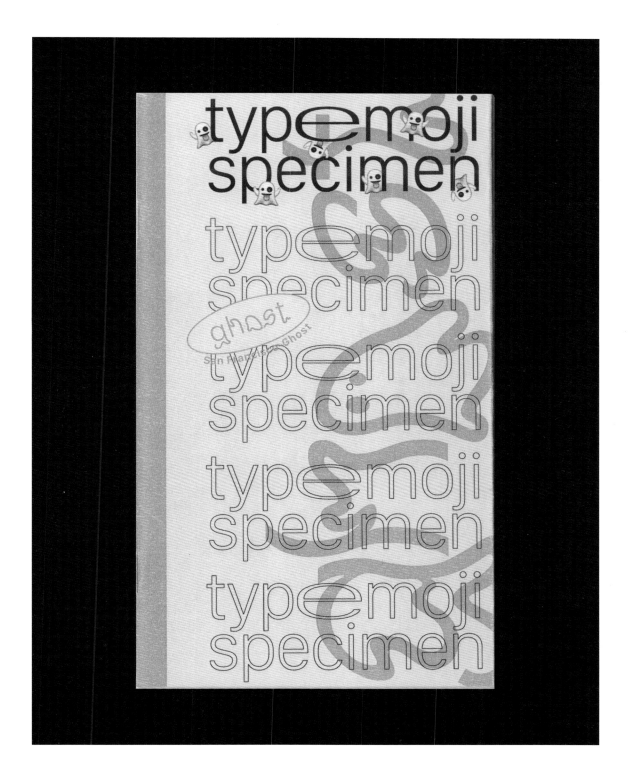

TYPEMOJI; SF-GHOST

Student Work

DESIGN
Jaejin Ee,
New York

SCHOOL
California Institute
of the Arts

INSTRUCTORS
Anther Kiley
Lorraine Wild
Michael Worthington,
Thesis Advisor

PRINCIPAL TYPE
San Francisco
SF-Ghost

DIMENSIONS
4 x 7 in.
(10.2 x 17.8 cm)

CONCEPT
typEmoji is a set of several typefaces, with each typeface made by mixing San Francisco and an emoji. SF-Ghost was made by mixing San Francisco and the ghost emoji. typEmoji has been developed for use in two ways: to express subtly different tones in text messages, and to emphasize typographically certain parts of texts. typEmoji has a different weight system depending on the level of expression of each emoji. Like ligatures, typEmoji automatically appear when an emoji is placed right next to type.

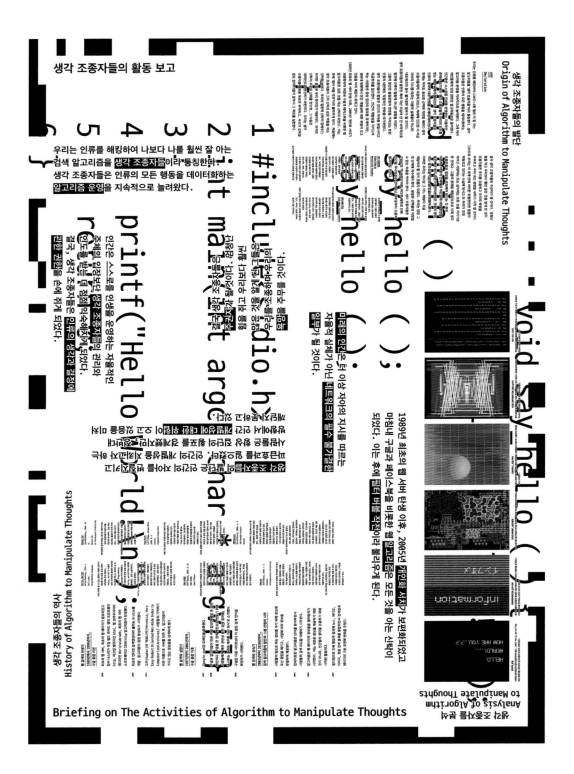

생각 조종자들의 활동 보고

Briefing on The Activities of Algorithm to Manipulate Thoughts

---

THE FILTER BUBBLE: ALGORITHM TO MANIPULATE THOUGHTS

Student Work

DESIGN
Hwang Da Eun
Kim Min Ji
Kang Yoo Sun
Gwak Min Yeong,
Anseong, South Korea

INSTRUCTOR
Kim Na Moo

SCHOOL
Hankyong National
University

PRINCIPAL TYPE
BoldD2Coding
Regular and Bold
소야뜰
Sandoll 고딕Neo1
Medium

DIMENSIONS
Various

CONCEPT
Google's and Facebook's algorithms show you the information they "think" you want to see. This might seem convenient, but it effectively traps you into a cultural and ideological bubble, eventually creating a biased person. This is known as "the filter bubble." This project arose from the question of how designers can solve social problems. An artificial intelligence algorithm called "Algorithm to Manipulate Thoughts" was created to manipulate human thoughts into the filter bubble. The purpose was to raise awareness of the danger of the internet's filter bubbles.

EYE CANDY

Student Work

DESIGN
Jay Jeon
Mark John
Mangayayam

URLS
jayjeon.com
itsmarkjohn.com

SCHOOL
Academy of Art
University,
San Francisco

PRINCIPAL TYPE
AT Osmose

CONCEPT
Eye Candy is a multi-format bookstore gallery designed to ultimately satisfy the visual appetite of artists, designers, and others in the field requiring creative thoughts. It is a collaboration with contemporary artists, designers, and writers to release a limited edition of books, typefaces, clothing, and objects. In addition to the bookstore, Eye Candy provides a space for collaborating artists to exhibit their works, a gallery for visual refreshment and consumption.

VIXEN DISPLAY TYPEFACE

Student Work

DESIGN
Simoul Premraj Alva,
Mumbai

URL
simoulalva.com

PROFESSOR
Sonia Da Rocha,
École Supérieure
d'Art et de Design
de Reims

SCHOOL
National Institute
of Design India

PRINCIPAL TYPE
Vixen Display

CONCEPT
Vixen is a display typeface created for large
print formats, album artwork, headlines,
titling, and anyone with a personality. Hidden
among voluptuous curves and high-contrast
forms is a subliminal sense of fluidity and
strength. It is not for the invisible.

2018 EVERY DAY GRAPHICS—DAILY CALENDAR

Student Work

DESIGN

Hye-ri Ahn
So-yeon Ahn
Hyo-im Ban
Da-hee Choi
In-young Choi
Ji-won Choi
Jin-a Choi
Min-young Choi
Seul Choi
Ji-hee Han
Chang-min Huh
Eun-sil Huh
Da-eun Hwang
Young-jin Jang
Tae-yeon Jo
Da-hee Jung
Min-a Jung
Bom-sil Jung

En-ji Jung
Ji-young Jung
Jun-young Jung
Yea-ji Jung
Yu-jin Jung
Tae-min Kan
Hae-min Kang
Hye-rin Kang
Min-ji Kang
Yu-seon Kang
Da-som Kim
Dong-im Kim
Eun-hye Kim
Hee-ji Kim
Min-hye Kim
Min-ji Kim
Min-ju Kim
Mo-ae Kim

Soo-bin Kim
So-dam Kim
Soo-jin Kim
Soo-jung Kim
So-young Kim
Yea-ji Kim
A-reum Kum
Min-young Kwak
Soo-Hyuk Kwon
Soo-Jin Kwon
Gyeom-dam Lee
Han-na Lee
Hye-yoon Lee
Jae-heon Lee
Jae-sun Lee
Ji-won Lee
Joo-Hyun Lee
Sin-hyung Lee

So-hyun Lee
Won-hyuk Mo
Hye-jin Oh
Chan-joo Park
Da-woon Park
Gi-Rin-a Park
Gyung-won Park
Han-sol Park
Sun-jin Park
Sung-eun Park
Soo-yeon Park
Young-jun Park
Joy Pyeon
Ji-won Shin
Tae-wan Uhm
Hye-jin Yoo
E-na Yoon,
Anseong, South Korea

CONCEPT

2018 Every Day Graphics is a daily calendar consisting of 365 graphics. Throughout all the pages, various styles of typographic work from seventy-one designers are displayed.

HFG OPEN DAY—JA/NEIN (YES/NO)

Student Work

DESIGN
Kijong Kim,
Offenbach am Main,
Germany

PROFESSOR
Sascha Lobe°

SCHOOL
Hochschule für
Gestaltung Offenbach

URL
kijongkim.com

PRINCIPAL TYPE
FF Murphy

DIMENSIONS
33.1 x 46.8 in.
(84.1 x 118.9 cm)

CONCEPT
In our lives we are surrounded by questions: "Do you want…?" "Are you…?" "Have you…?" "Do you like…?" "Can you…?" We constantly have to make decisions between two options: Yes or No (Ja/Nein). Likewise, we have to answer during open days: "Are you coming to open day?" "Was it good?"

THE LAST GIFT

Student Work

DESIGN
Janny Ji,
Baltimore, Maryland

URL
jannyji.com

PROFESSORS
Jason Gottlieb
Jennifer Cole Phillips

SCHOOL
Maryland Institute
College of Art

PRINCIPAL TYPE
Mrs Eaves

DIMENSIONS
Various

CONCEPT
Well-intentioned actions can cause harm, and harsh actions can
be served up as sweet as honey. Hidden deep within the lavish luxury
of a silk scarf and gold jewelry lie dark sentiments signaling the end
of a love affair.

LETTERS MAPPING THE SPACE

Student Work

DESIGN
Goeun Park,
Providence,
Rhode Island

URL
goeunpark.com

SCHOOL
Rhode Island
School of Design

PRINCIPAL TYPE
Founders Grotesk

DIMENSIONS
7.5 x 10 in.
(19.1 x 25.4 cm)

CONCEPT
This is a type specimen book that illustrates how letters can map and capture the dimensionality of space. Letters from A to Z are projected onto the ceiling, stairs, corners, and pipes of a stairway. Since each letter represents a part of the stairway, when the letters are written as a sentence, the sentence visualizes the space.

TO WHOM IT MAY CONCERN

Student Work

DESIGN
Tatiana Gómez
Bo-Won Keum
Angela Lorenzo
Goeun Park
Wei-Hao Wang
June Yoon,
Providence,
Rhode Island

SCHOOL
Rhode Island
School of Design

PRINCIPAL TYPE
Century Schoolbook
Titling Gothic

DIMENSIONS
5.5 x 8.5 in.
(13.97 x 20.32 cm)

CONCEPT
This publication for the 2017 RISD MFA Graphic Design Biennial offers a critical perspective on the role of design in the current political climate. There are two booklets: a catalog of work, and a reader of relevant political, artistic, and intellectual resources. Each booklet is printed in black and white and staple-bound. The two booklets are collected together with a black rubber band.

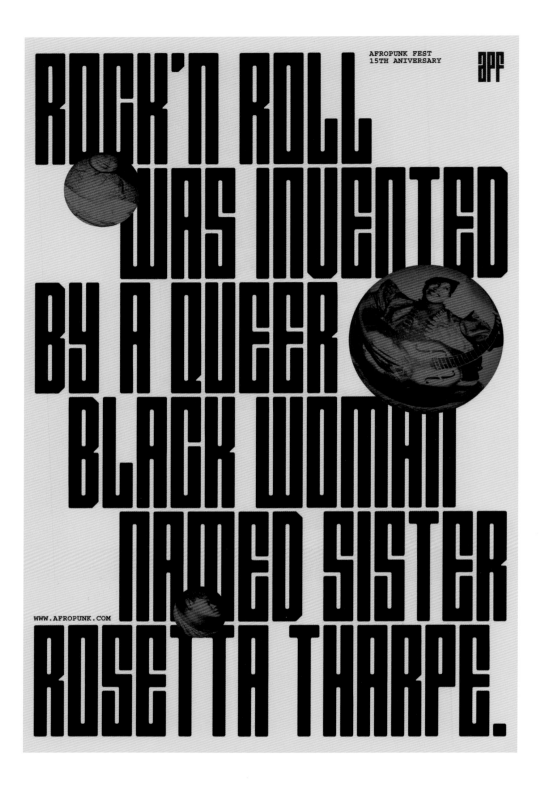

AFROPUNK FESTIVAL

Student Work

DESIGN
Yuma Naito,
Pasadena, California

URL
yumanaito.com

INSTRUCTOR
Brad Bartlett

SCHOOL
Art Center
College of Design

PRINCIPAL TYPE
APF Display
Cooper BT
Courier New

DIMENSIONS
24 x 36 in.
(61 x 91.4 cm)

CONCEPT
Focusing on individuals and the positive energy of community and
music, AFROPUNK Festival introduced its new visual language in
a playful way. A custom typeface, APF Display, was designed for the
logotype and the whole identity system. The first poster series with
the custom font was designed to communicate who they are as a
festival and as a human rights movement. And the second posters,
with onomatopoeia, tell stories in a typographic way about what
people will feel and experience at the event.

이 글자꼴 시스템은 한글과 라틴의 음성 소리로 연결되는 실험적 문자 시스템이다. 한틴 A는 로마자 표기법을 따라 한글의 문자와 가장 가까운 음성을 가진 라틴문자와 조합했다. 또한 한틴 B는 외래어 표기법에 기초해 라틴문자를 근접한 음성을 가진 한글 글자와 조합했다. 가장 비슷한 소리로 조합된 두 개의 글자는, 그 비례를 유지하며 겹쳐서 쓰는 문자로 제작되었다.

This typeface is composed by connecting the phonetic sounds of Hangul and Latin letters. HANTIN A matches the Hangul alphabet with the closest phonetic sound of the Latin alphabet, based on the Hangul Romanisation. In terms of HANTIN B, the Latin alphabet is met with the corresponding sound of the Hangul alphabet, according to the loanword orthography. While preserving the same typography proportion, HANTIN letters are made by overlaying corresponding phonetic letters.

HANTIN: A HYBRID MODULAR TYPEFACE DESIGN FOR MULTILINGUAL TYPOGRAPHY

Student Work

DESIGN
Da Chung,
Seoul

URL
dachung.kr

STUDIO
studio dachung

SCHOOL
London College
of Communication

PRINCIPAL TYPE
HANTIN

DIMENSIONS
7.2 x 19.1 in.
(18.2 x 25.7 cm)

CONCEPT
HANTIN is a hybrid modular typeface that combines Hangul (Korean) and Latin letterforms and writing systems. This typeface allows a reader to understand Latin phonetic sounds without needing to study English beforehand. Conversely, the typeface also allows a reader to understand Korean phonetic sounds without the need to study Korean.

SUPAFLAT

Student Work

DESIGN
Duy Dao,
Hanoi

URL
duydao.net

SCHOOL
Art Center
College of Design

INSTRUCTOR
Brad Bartlett

PRINCIPAL TYPE
DD Supa Display

DIMENSIONS
Various

CONCEPT
This is a branding design concept for Takashi Murakami's *Supaflat* exhibition. The project features DD Supa Display, a custom typeface created for the event. DD Supa Display was inspired by the rise of technology in Japan in the early 2000s, which also had a heavy impact on shaping this new art genre.

BRUTAL

Student Work

DESIGN
Tais Ghelli Bishop

INSTRUCTOR
Brad Bartlett

TEACHING ASSISTANT
Jon Nishida

SCHOOL
Art Center
College of Design

PRINCIPAL TYPE
BRUTAL
Folio

CONCEPT
This is an identity design for an exhibition on brutalist architecture in Brazil. The design of modular typography speaks to the brutalist architectural forms, while the boldness of the colors serves to establish a second layer of visual tension. This language travels across media, from print to web, and ultimately merges back into space through a typographic spatial installation.

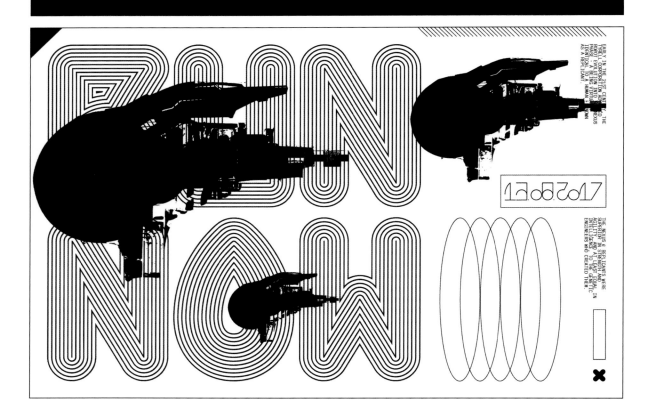

DD ALMOND DISPLAY

Student Work

DESIGNER
Duy Dao,
Hanoi

URL
duydao.net

SCHOOL
Art Center
College of Design

PRINCIPAL TYPE
DD Almond Display

CONCEPT
DD Almond Display is a custom typeface developed for the almond
milk brand AMILK. The typeface was designed based on the shape of
an almond.

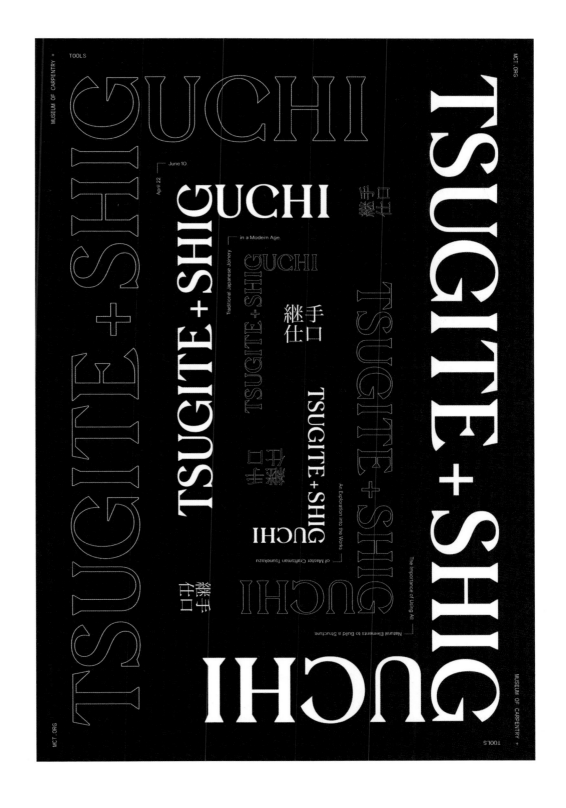

**MUSEUM OF CARPENTRY
+ TOO REBRAND**

Student Work

DESIGN
Clint Disharoon

URL
clintdisharoon.com

INSTRUCTOR
Brad Bartlett

SCHOOL
Art Center
College of Design

PRINCIPAL TYPE
Basis Grotesque Pro
Regular Basis
Grotesque Pro Mono
Morion Regular

DIMENSIONS
24 x 36 in.
(61 x 91.4 cm)

CONCEPT
The process of designing this identity began by investigating the
medium of wood from every possible perspective. I photographed
several species of wood under a microscope to create lush textures.
I built clear acrylic joinery, reflected light through them, and
photographed them to mimic traditional Japanese markings. These
explorations and more were embedded into the entire design process.
The structural elements and process of creating traditional Japanese
joinery influenced all of my typographic decisions.

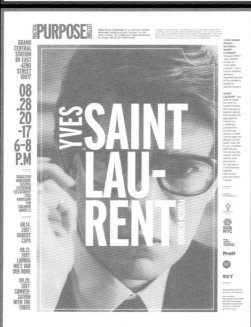

PRACTICAL PURPOSE
LECTURE SERIES POSTER

Student Work

DESIGN
Shanming Sally Guo°,
New York

INSTRUCTOR
Scott Buschkuhl

SCHOOL
School of Visual Arts°,
New York

URL
sguo.work

PRINCIPAL TYPE
Interstate
Compressed

DIMENSIONS
18 x 24 in.
(45.7 x 61 cm)

CONCEPT
This is a four-part poster design for a hypothetical lecture series
inviting world-class talents from the past. The artists chosen were
all pioneers in their fields connected by an emphasis on function and
practicality in their works. Based on these qualities, I named the
lecture series "Practical Purpose" and created a typographic system
to reflect them.

same with women. He had preferred to paint his bathers unmasked as well as naked, to give them faces that were merely extensions of their charming bodies and not deceptive symbols of a non-existent spirituality. It seemed to him more realistic, truer to the fundamental facts. He felt his good humour returning as he talked, and, as it came back, his dislike for Mary Betterton seemed to wane.

Huxley

is a revival of an early 20th-century American book face & Eric Doctor's first-term project in the Extended Program at Type@Cooper. It is based on the text of a 1928 Random House Modern Library Edition of «Point Counter Point» purchased at the Alabaster Bookshop on Fourth Ave. in New York City. Huxley is not a literal interpretation, but rather uses the original face's skeleton and proportions as a point of departure, restoring detail lost to ink spread but maintaining the warmth of the letterpressed page.

Brave New World
THE DOORS OF PERCEPTION
Point Counter Point
AFTER MANY A SUMMER DIES THE SWAN

AaBbCcDdEeFffGgHhIiJjKkLlMmNnOoPpQqRrSsTtUuVvWw
XxYyZzÆæŒœÞþÐðßßÀàÁáÂâÃãÄäÅåÇçÈèÉéÊêËëĘĘÌìÍíÎîÏïÑñ
ÒòÓóÔôÕõÖöØøÙùÚúÛûÜüÝýŸÿĀāĂăĄąĆćĊċČčĎďĐdĒēĔĕĖė
ĘęĚěĝĜğĠġĢģȝĦħĪīĭĬįĮıĶķĸĹĺĻļĽĿŀŁłŃńŅņŇňŊŋŌōŎŏŐőŔŕ
ŖŗŘřŚśŜŝŞşŠšŤťŦŧŨũŪūŬŭŮůŰűŲųŴŵŶŷŸŹźŻż ŽžſăĭŏŭÅåÆæÓó
ȘşŢţə ˆˇˋˊ˙ ˜ʻ'´˝ ˝Åµµṅ ẀẁẂẃẄẅẑ Ỳỳ–—\'",""„†‡•…'"‹›/ ™ +−×÷<=>≈≠
±≤≥ffffifffbfffhfjfkı́'-©®Ⓟ"#$€¢%‰&'()*,-0123456789:;?!¡¿¡¿@{|}~¨«¬¯°./

....

HUXLEY BOOK

Student Work

DESIGN
Eric Doctor°,
Brooklyn, New York

URL
ericdoctor.com

TWITTER
@therevdoctor

INSTRUCTOR
Hannes Famira

SCHOOL
Type@Cooper

CONCEPT
Huxley, a revival of an early-twentieth-century American book face, was my first-term project in Type@Cooper's extended program. It is based on the text from a 1928 Random House Modern Library edition of *Point Counter Point* by Aldous Huxley, found in Alabaster Bookshop in New York. It is not a literal interpretation, but uses the original face's skeleton and proportions as a point of departure, restoring details lost to ink spread and maintaining the warmth of the letterpressed page.

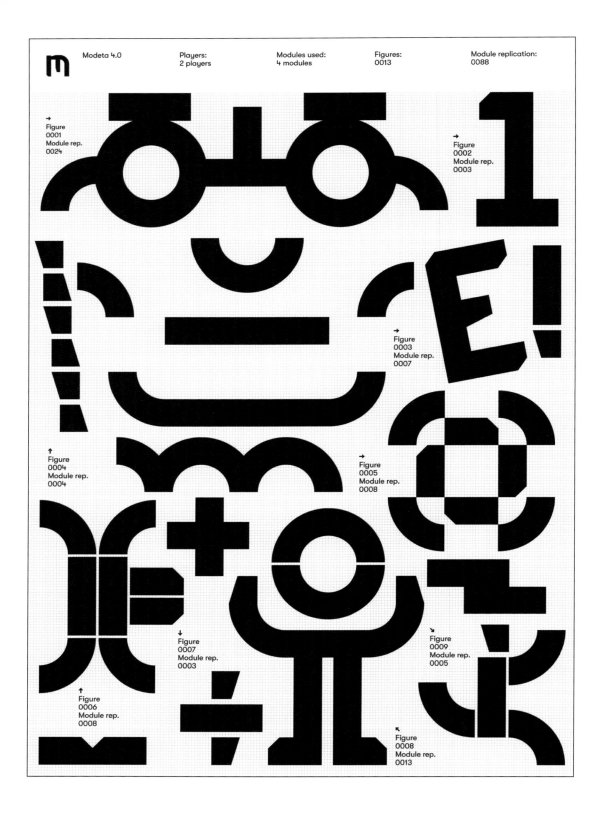

Modeta 4.0 Players:
2 players
Modules used:
4 modules
Figures:
0013
Module replication:
0088

MODETA 4.0

Student Work

DESIGN
Sebastian Anastasiei,
Bucharest

PROFESSOR
Radu Manelici

SCHOOL
Bucharest National
University of Arts

PRINCIPAL TYPE
GT Walsheim

DIMENSIONS
19.7 x 27.8 in.
(50 x 70.7 cm)

CONCEPT
Modeta 4.0 is a drawing game consisting of four physical modules and sheets of custom grid paper. The set can be used to generate letterforms, icons, or illustrations. The posters on display feature outcomes from experiments in playing the game. I created this project as part of my graduation portfolio in 2017.

ABCDEFGHI JKLMNOPQR STUVWXYZ 0123456789

SPARE RIBS HAR GOW SUI MAI CHA SIU BAO CHICKEN FOOT HO FEN LO MEIN WONTON CHANG FEN HONG KONG MILK TEA GLUTONOUS RICE BALLS TONG SUI MANGO PUDDING

XOKITCHEN

XO KITCHEN
148 HESTER ST, NEW YORK, NY, 10013
MON–SUN 8AM–11PM
TEL: 212-965-8645

HAR GOW $3.95
XOKITCHEN
148 HESTER STREET   TEL: 212-965-8645   MON–SUN 8AM–11PM

XO KITCHEN IDENTITY

Student Work

DESIGNER
Shanming Sally Guo°,
New York

INSTRUCTORS
Joseph Han
Natasha Jen

URL
sguo.work

SCHOOL
School of Visual Arts°,
New York

PRINCIPAL TYPE
XO Bold

CONCEPT
XO Kitchen is a restaurant in New York's Chinatown that serves traditional Cantonese-style dishes in a no-frills setting. The new identity and custom typeface were inspired by the calligraphy of iconic Hong Kong street signs.

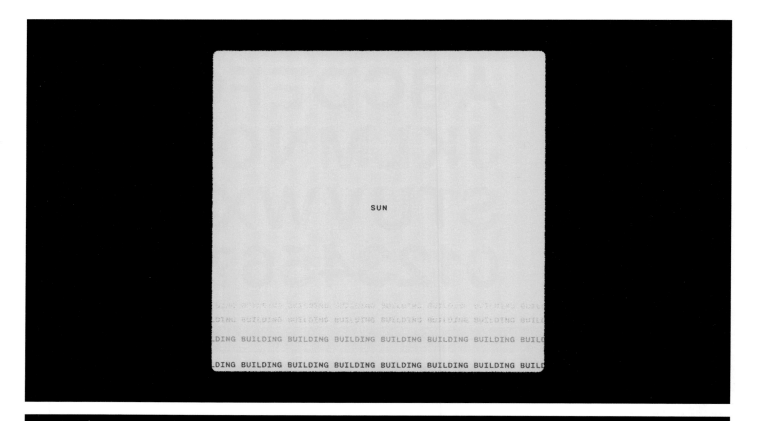

WORDS

Student Work

DESIGN
Enle Li
Liz Xiong,
New York

MUSIC
The Green Kingdom

SCHOOL
School of Visual Arts°,
New York

PRINCIPAL TYPE
Rational TW

CONCEPT
In this personal project, we explored the expression of words and
their creation of the visual world around us. The video focuses on the
fundamentals of natural laws and the laws of nature themselves.

MEET

Posters

ART DIRECTION
Moree Wu
Sijia Zhang,
New York

URL
moodofshape.studio

AGENCY
Mood of Shape

PRINCIPAL TYPE
MEEEEEEEET

DIMENSIONS
46 x 33 in.
(116.8 x 83.8 cm)

CONCEPT
Meet is a Korean barbecue restaurant targeting young people. To express the vivid brand image and promote the various meats, we abstracted eight kinds of meats to geometric graphics one by one and visualized the experience of grilling meat into six patterns. We collocated them to have the main visual elements for a poster series, which provided the emotional experience of vividness and hotness to consumers. There are ten pieces in this series.

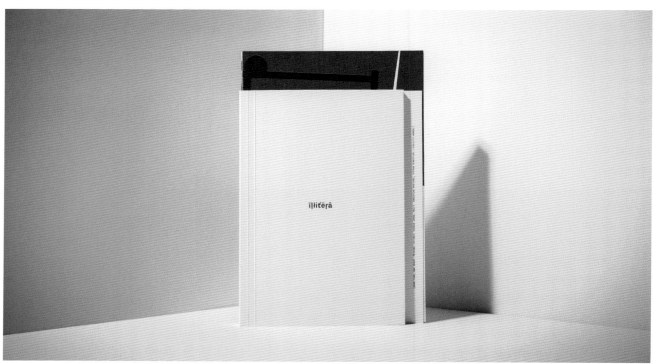

ILLITERA

Student Work

DESIGN AND CREATIVE DIRECTION
Nicolas Bernklau
Tobias Müller,
Stuttgart

URLS
illitera.de
nicolasbernklau.de
tobiasmueller.design

PROFESSOR
Dr. Klaus Birk

SCHOOL
Baden-Württemberg
Cooperative State
University Ravensburg,
Faculty Media Design

PRINCIPAL TYPE
Various

DIMENSIONS
Various

CONCEPT
No other group of people is as far away from typography as illiterates. To bridge the gap between type design and illiteracy we interviewed experts from these fields. We found illiterates and conducted artistic typography workshops to create letters together in a playful way. By shaping beautiful letters, we help the illiterates lose their fear of type and gain a sense of achievement. The touchpoints of the two worlds are the typefaces. Initiated in workshops, developed by us, and implemented in typographic posters by designers worldwide—finally all brought together in this book.

Richard Milhous Nixon

This typeface family was born from the inherent need for a consistent, legible, and official typeface for the United States Government. Spurred by the turbulent recent political events, it leans into a darker, authoritative spirit through its overall sharp texture, reductive nature and serif structure.

I owe special thanks to several people who made it all possible for me to complete this book in the face of my other responsibilities. Ivana Trump, my wonderful wife, and my three children were understanding about the many weekends I spent working on the book. The great Si Newhouse first came to me and convinced me to do a book despite my initial reluctance.

The silver platter. The sculpted ball of cottage cheese, flavored by slices of pineapple, perhaps canned. The glass of milk. This is the lunch that Richard Nixon ate on August 8, 1974, before he went on national television to announce his resignation from the Presidency of the United States.

ABCDEFGHIJKLM
NOPQRSTUVWXYZ
abcdefghijklmn
opqrstuvwxyz
1234567890!?&$@[{|}]*

*ABCDEFGHIJKLM
NOPQRSTUVWXYZ
abcdefghijklmn
opqrstuvwxyz
1234567890!?&$@[{|}]**

**ABCDEFGHIJKLM
NOPQRSTUVWXYZ
abcdefghijklmn
opqrstuvwxyz
1234567890!?&$@[{|}]***

How much arm-twisting is going on re: vis-à-vis the healthcare bill? The Vice President has had several of the conservative groups over today. All the conservative groups announced that they will actually be scoring.

The President is by far the most competitive person I have ever met. Officially, I've seen this guy throw a dead spiral through a tire. I've seen him at Madison Square Garden with a topcoat on. He's standing in the key and he's hitting foul shots and swishing them, okay? He sinks 30-foot putts. Obviously, the President is a winner.

Anthony Scaramucci called me to unload about all of the White House leakers, Reince Priebus, Steve Bannon. He started threatening to fire the entire White House communication staff. The swamp will not defeat him.

*They're trying to resist me, but it's not going to work. I've done nothing wrong on my financial disclosures, so they're going to have to go & *!? themselves. Within two hours he deleted the weet and posted a new one denying that he targeted the chief of staff. Wrong! Scaramucci then made a plea to viewers. "Let me tell you something, I am a straight shooter."*

Jared Kushner did very well yesterday proving no collusion with any of the Russians. Witch Hunt. Next up, 11 year old Barron Trump! Thank you @foxandfriends for the great timeline of the Obama failures!

A woman I don't know and, to the best of my knowledge, never met, is on the FRONT PAGE of the Fake News Washington Post saying I kissed her (for two minutes yet) in the lobby of Trump Tower 12 years ago. Never happened! Who would do this in a public space...doesn't fit Mainstream Media narrative.

NIXON TYPEFACE FAMILY

Student Work

DESIGN
Lauren King,
New York

URL
laurenqueen.com

CREATIVE DIRECTORS
Danilo Lubars
Greg Hahn

TWITTER
@lkokay

INSTRUCTOR
Hannes Famira

SCHOOL
Type@Cooper

PRINCIPAL TYPE
Nixon Regular
Nixon Italic
Nixon Heavy

CONCEPT
The Nixon typeface family was born from the inherent need for a consistent, legible, and official typeface for the U.S. government. Spurred by recent turbulent political events, it leans into its darker, authoritative spirit through its serif structure, reductive nature, and overall sharp texture.

POLISH AVANT-GARDE*
TYPOGRAPHY OF THE '20S AND '30S

Student Work

DESIGN
Magdalena Karcz,
Gdynia, Poland

PHOTOGRAPHY
Aleksander
Drożdżewski

URL
100typo.pl

PROFESSOR
Sławomir Kosmynka

SCHOOL
Strzeminsky
Academy of Fine Arts,
Łódź, Poland

PRINCIPAL TYPE
Paneuropa
Paneuropa Nova

DIMENSIONS
7.5 x 8.3 in.
(19 x 21 cm)

CONCEPT
The book was inspired by the hundredth anniversary of the Polish avant-garde movement. My goal was to recall the legacy of Polish typography and print design. I made use of techniques and tools used by artists a hundred years ago, e.g., photomontages or a digitalized version of the old Paneuropa typeface. Some elements, including chapter pages and the book cover, were composed by manual typesetting. I reduced the use of colors to black and magenta, the latter being "the new red," the signal color of the present times. I wanted to highlight certain aspects of presented works such as typography, composition, and layout.

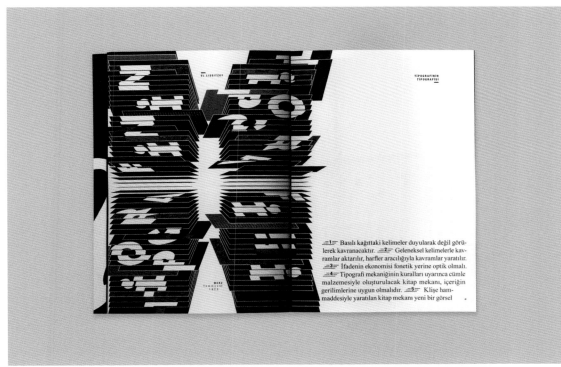

TYPOGRAPHIC WRITINGS

Student Work

DESIGN
Yasemin Çakır,
Istanbul

URL
yasemincakir.com

TWITTER
@yaseminckr

PROFESSOR
Umut Südüak

SCHOOL
Mimar Sinan
Fine Arts University

PRINCIPAL TYPE
Helvetica
Times New Roman

DIMENSIONS
6.5 x 9.5 in.
(16.5 x 24 cm)

CONCEPT
This book is a collection of articles and interviews from the *Yazılar* (Texts), published by the Turkish Graphic Designers Association. *Yazılar* is a four-page bulletin, published monthly, that includes local and foreign articles about graphic design. The book itself contains ten individual chapters, four interviews, and six articles. For each section, typographic illustrations were created to support the content.

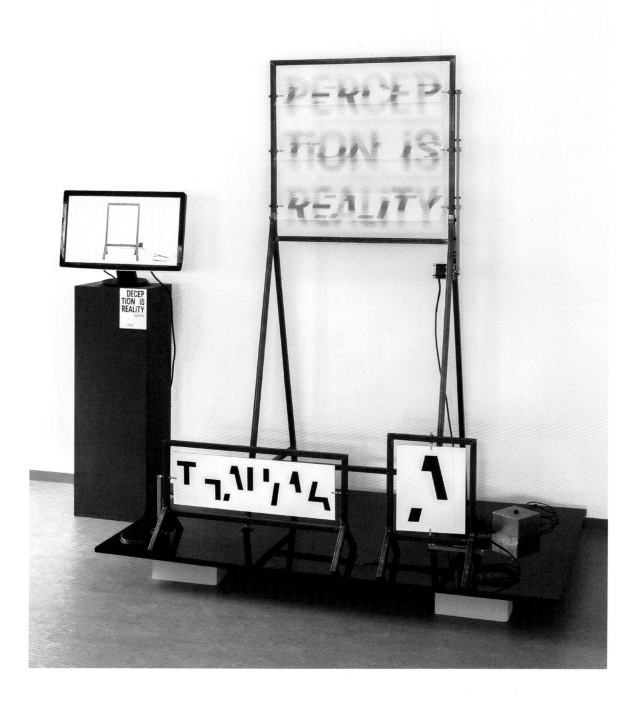

TYPOTROP

Student Work

DESIGN
Lena Windisch,
Streitberg, Germany

PROFESSOR
Andrea Tinnes

ASSISTANT TO PROFESSOR
Anja Kaiser

SCHOOL
University of Art
and Design Burg
Giebichenstein Halle

PRINCIPAL TYPE
Thauma

DIMENSIONS
Various

CONCEPT
This project focuses on the borders of our perception and the legibility of type. The underlying idea goes back to the optical illusion of the thaumatrope, which is based on the slowness of our sense of sight. The result is Thauma, a font split into two layers and printed on the front and back of plates. The letters are perceptible only through the rotation of the panels. This has the effect of making us question if we can trust in the unconscious thinking processes of our brains—or if we are deceived and don't recognize the truth.

MONEY DRAWSTRING HOODIE

Apparel

DESIGN
Jed Heuer,
Brooklyn, New York

URL
jeffersonheuer.com

PRINCIPAL TYPE
Hand-drawn

DIMENSIONS
36 x 24 in.
(91 x 61 cm)

CONCEPT
This is a hoodie that makes a dollar sign. Because, drawstrings.

TYPE FACE DESIGN 2018

TYPE CHAIR'S STATEMENT

I was honored to be asked to chair this year's Typeface Design Competition—arguably our industry's most rigorous and prestigious. That reputation comes from the strength and high standards of our seventy-one-year-old club of type lovers, and it was important to me to maintain the integrity of what it means to win in this global competition.

Typeface design is, in many ways, a field that's ever-widening. So the responsibility to best assess the work our industry produces each year requires more and more consideration. A topic often discussed this year has been how we refer to the variety of typefaces and scripts out there. When we consider how we categorize type, we are also considering its importance to its culture, its people, and the type designers themselves.

To that end, the responsibility we have to best reflect the standards and diversity of our field rests largely on the jury of judges. Ultimately, I chose four women with a formidable amount of collective experience, expertise, and enthusiasm. With 180 entries to assess, we needed judges who were authorities in the crafting, development, and use of type ... and not just Latin typefaces but also global writing systems.

Our criteria were: craft, aesthetic, relevance, and innovation. With these cornerstones, the four judges (Sahar Afshar, Verena Gerlach, YuJune Park, and Dyana Weissman), and crucial support from Maxim Zhukov and Gary Munch, the day resulted in eighteen strong winners. Half of the winning entries were global/non-Latin typefaces, a wonderful realization. This demonstrates the small but global community that type design truly is, and it's a refreshing thought that our field will continue to thrive from the new voices and perspectives we embrace.

ELIZABETH CAREY SMITH

ELIZABETH CAREY SMITH

CHAIR / TYPE DESIGN

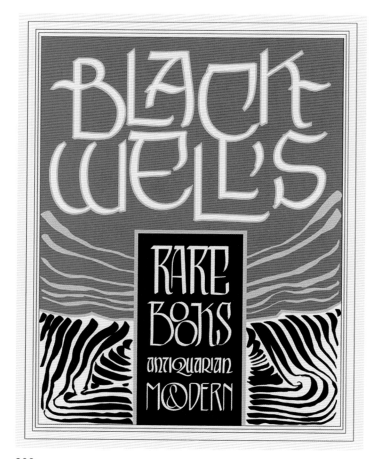

Elizabeth Carey Smith is a typographer in New York City who specializes in design and creative direction for type foundries, branding, fashion, and the arts. She earned her BFA from the College for Creative Studies in Detroit and completed the extended program of Type@Cooper in Typeface Design. Elizabeth is Vice President of the Type Directors Club, and she speaks and writes regularly for conferences, publications, and platforms around the world.

website: elizabethcareysmith.com

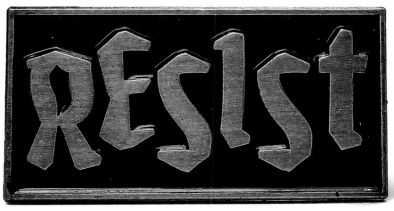

MEET THE JUDGES

SAHAR AFSHAR

Sahar Afshar is a type designer and researcher from Iran. Her interest in typography during her years as a student at the University of Tehran led her to the University of Reading, from which she holds an MA by Research in Typography & Graphic Communication. Since graduation, she has been working on the design, consultation and quality assurance of Arabic typefaces, as well as researching the printing history of Arabic and Indic scripts. She is currently based in the UK, and is a doctoral candidate at Birmingham City University, where she also works as a research assistant to the Centre for Printing History and Culture.

ارغوان شاخه همخون جدا مانده من

از بهاران خبرم نیست

امیر هوشنگ ابتهاج در رشت متولد شد. پدرش آقاخان ابتهاج از مردان سرشناس رشت و مدنی رئیس بیمارستان پورسینای این شهر بود. برادران ابتهاج عموهای او بودند. هوشنگ ابتهاج دوره تحصیلات دبستان را در رشت و دبیرستان را در تهران گذراند و در همین دوران اولین دفتر شعر خود را به نام نخستین نغمه‌ها منتشر کرد. ابتهاج در جوانی دلباخته دختری ارمنی به نام گالیا شد که در رشت ساکن بود و این عشق دوران جوانی دست مایه اشعار عاشقانه‌ای شد که در آن ایام سرود. بعدها که ابتهاج غرق خونریزی و جنگ و بحران شد. ابتهاج شعری به نام کاروان دیرست گالیا با اشاره به همان رابطه عاشقانه‌اش در گیردار مسائل سیاسی سرود. ابتهاج مدتی به عنوان مدیر کل شرکت دولتی سیمان تهران به کار اشتغال داشت

در دیدار با سارا

ATHELAS ARABIC

The messenger who arrived from the land of my friend

آن پیک نامور که رسید از دیار دوست

Brought a charm, fragrant, and in the hand of my friend

آورد حرز جان ز خط مشکبار دوست

Wonderfully displayed her beauty and her glory
خوش مردمد نشان جلال و جمال یار
With the tales of noble and regal stand of my friend
خوش می‌کند حکایت عز و وقار دوست
My heart took in the good news, though coy and shy
دل دادمش به مژده و خجلت همی‌برم

Elegant book printing in your screen

جنوح جماعي جديد لعشرات الحيتان في نيوزيلندا

نحن و القمر جيران

ELEGANT BOOK PRINTING — NOW IN ARABIC

زبان یک سیستم قراردادی منظم از الفبا یا نشانه‌های کلامی یا نوشتاری یا مود که به یک گروه اجتماعی با فرهنگی خاص برای نمایش و فهم ارتباطات و اندیشه‌ها به کار برده می‌شود. دانش مطالعه و بررسی زبان زبان‌شناسی نامیده می‌شود. زبان‌ها با گویندگان به نام خانواده‌های زبانی مرتبط هستند. خانواده زبان‌ها ریشه ...

In 1998, Verena Gerlach founded her studio for graphic design, type design, and typography in Berlin. Since 2006, she has been working as a freelance book designer for art book publishers like Hatje Cantz and Kerber, as well as for the international art world. She started lecturing in type design and typography in 2003, and she now gives lectures and workshops around the globe. Besides designing corporate fonts for global companies, she also is working on the typographic production for contemporary artists. In 2013, Verena published her book Karbid: From Lettering to Type Design. Verena has worked as freelance type designer for Monotype since 2016.

Selection of released typefaces:
FF City Street Types
FF Chambers Sans
FF Karbid Pro
FF Sizmo

website: fraugerlach.de

YUJUNE PARK

YuJune Park is the Associate Director and an Assistant Professor of Communication Design at Parsons School of Design and the co-founder of Synoptic Office. She served as the Program Director from 2014 to 2017. Her work has been recognized by the AIGA, the I.D. Annual Design Review, the Art Directors Club Awards, iDN, It's Nice That, Etapes, the Museum of Architecture and Design in Ljubljana, and the Ningbo Museum of Art. She holds an MFA in Graphic Design from Yale University and a BFA in Furniture Design from the Rhode Island School of Design. YuJune has worked for and collaborated with several studios, including Base Design, Graphic Thought Facility, and Pentagram, for a variety of clients including the Museum of Modern Art, Milk Studios, the Davis Museum, and the Metropolitan Museum of Art. In addition to teaching, YuJune speaks widely on design education and typography, most recently at Typographics, Northside Festival, and AIGA/NY.

website: synopticoffice.com
instagram: @synopticoffice
twitter: @ygparkgso

The WALDORF-ASTORIA
inspired by the lettering
of the facade of
301 PARK AVENUE
NEW YORK, NEW YORK
alternate sans serif capitals &
figures for ADA compliance

Dyana Weissman is the Senior Custom Designer at Type Network. For more than fifteen years, she has worked with international studios and brands, including Adidas, john st., Loyal Kaspar, *Marie Claire* magazine, Korn Design, Pentagram, Interbrand, *The Financial Times*, and *TIME* magazine. Dyana studied graphic design at Rhode Island School of Design, where her interest in typeface design was cultivated. When she has time, or is spurred enough, she writes for Typographica.org and Alphabettes.org. She has presented her work at ATypI, TypeCon, and at universities across the country. When she isn't doing all that, she is taking photos, gardening, or hiking somewhere in the world.

FERNET BRANCA
Dr. William's Pink Pills for Pale People
Midwives
Mortar and pestle ground fresh
HEXAMETHYLENETETRAMINE
Patented Flaxseed Panacea
Nostrums made from the fruit of the baobob tree
SNAKE OIL LINIMENT
SWAMP ROOT FOR WHAT AILS YE
OPODELDOC
Bonnore's Electromagnetic Bathing Fluid
Relieves instanteously
Curatives and potions

website: kernsandcairns.com

TYPEFACES JUDGES' CHOICES

URDU	PERSIAN	ARABIC

اک دن کسی منکھی سے یہ کہنے لگا مکڑا
حجاب چہرہ جان میشود غبار تنم
هذا الذی تعرف البطحاء و طأتة

اس راہ سے ہوتا ہے گزر روز تمہارا
خوشا دمی کہ از آن چہرہ پردہ برکنم
و البیت یعرفہ و الحل و الحرم

لیکن مری منکیا کی نہ جاگی کبھی قسمت
چنین قفس نہ سزای جو من خوش الحانیست
هذا ابن خیرہ عباد اللہ کلھم

بھولے سے کبھی تم نے میاں یاؤں نہ رکھا
روم بکلشن رضوان کہ مرغ آن چمنم
هذا التقی النقی الطاهر العلم

غیروں سے سنے میلے تو کوئی بات نہیں ہے
عیان نشد کہ چرا آمدم کجا رفتم
هذا الذی أحمد المختار والدہ

اپنوں سے مگر جاہیے یوں کھنچ کے نہ رہنا
دریغ و درد کہ غافل ز کار خویشتنم
صلی علیہ الہی ما جری القلم

آؤ جو مرے گھر میں تو عزت ہے یہ میری
چگونہ طوف کنم در فضای عالم قدس
لو یعلم الرکن من قد جاءہ

وہ سامنے سیڑھی ہے جو منظور رہو آنا
کہ در سراچۂ ترکیب تختہ بند تنم
یلثمہ لخرہ یلثم منہ ما وطئ القدم

URDU WITH LIGATURES

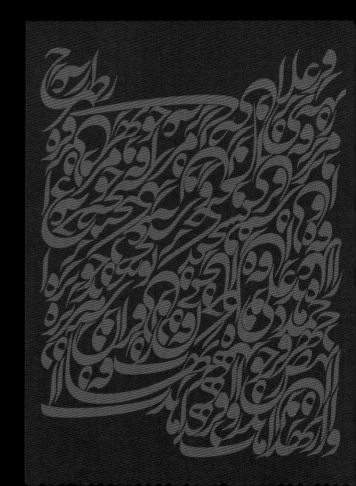

MARK POSITIONING

Sahar Afshar

The challenges of designing
a calligraphic Arabic typeface
are immense and many. On top
of the expected undertaking of
designing various alternatives
for contextual connections and
numerous ligatures to overcome
the limitations of current
technology, there exists the
added demand for consistency
and precision perfectly balanced
with thoughtful nuances;
there is no space or tolerance
for imprecision in proportions,
stroke widths, and balance
in Arabic calligraphy. Add to
all this a cascading baseline,
space-dependent diacritic sizes,
and required extensions across
several characters and
connections, and the technical
complications alone warrant
a floral tribute to Moslehi, who
has set the bar high with Mirza.

But his design goes above
and beyond this to stand out
from the rest. Mirza is a weave
of jarring strands; immense
control in the smoothest flow
of one letter to the next, the
proximity of hairline stroke to
dense knot, and elegant curves
against unswerving—but never
straight—lines. Even at its core,
it embraces a mix of history
and the poetic; Mirza Gholam-
Reza Esfahani's calligraphic
hand and the deliberate
construction of each letterform
is reflected in letters that, in
any given word, seem as though
they were never separate,
but always sharing the same
spine. Mirza never feels typed;
instead, it represents a
calligraphic tradition, and
presents as hand-drawn:
It imagines the future while
remembering the past.

TYPEFACE DESIGN
Amir Mahdi Moslehi,
Tehran, Iran

TWITTER
@AMMoslehi

STUDIO
Bagh-e Tafarroj
Studio

CLIENT
Maryam Soft

CONCEPT
Mirza is a contemporary Nastaliq typeface based on the hand of
Mirza Gholam-Reza Esfahani—one of the most celebrated Persian
calligraphers of the Qajar era. This typeface is the result of an
extensive study of the best specimens of Mirza Gholam-Reza's
work during the last decade of his life.

Mirza is a display typeface that fully supports Arabic, Persian,
and Urdu languages. The Nastaliq figures in this typeface are
designed based on the traditional technique seen in Qajar seals.

АБВГДЕЁЖЗИ
ЙКЛМНОПРС
ТУФХЦЧШЩЪ
ЫЬЭЮЯ

ABCDEFGHIJ
KLMNOPQRST
UVWXYZ

0123456789 %&@$€₴₽

Dyana Weissman

Visually appealing. Technically skilled. Broadly usable. As judges, we kept these criteria in mind when making our selections. A conceptual typeface rarely meets all of these benchmarks; at least one usually falls by the wayside. But ALS Lamon hits them all, taking a simple concept (at least on the surface), and turning it into a lighthearted, well-drawn, easily readable typeface.

What makes it even more remarkable is it achieves its goal in both Cyrillic and Latin, bringing amusement to readers from all around the globe. Fellow judge Verena Gerlach was delighted with the charming pig found in the Ё/ё. My in-laws, stern cultural observers who immigrated to the United States from Russia in the 1990s, validated its cleverness in the Cyrillic.

The idea of nesting a lowercase form in an uppercase form sounds straightforward enough. But as with most conceptual projects, this is easier said than done. It is evident that each letter of Lamon is carefully considered. And the dynamics are fascinating: A shape becomes a contour, as in the Q/q. A form becomes a counterform, as in the Б/б. The G/g is just marvelous.

Looking closely, one sees that the upper- and lowercase letters are not merely stacked; they dance a lively Tchaikovsky waltz with each other. They are complex, smart, and enchanting. The typeface accomplishes so much with seemingly so little. Its excellence stands out in so many ways. For me, there was never any question that ALS Lamon should be a winner.

LAMON

TYPEFACE DESIGN
Dmitry Lamonov, Moscow

ART DIRECTION
Artemy Lebedev

PROJECT MANAGER
Svetlana Kost

URL
artlebedev.com

DESIGN STUDIO
Art. Lebedev Studio

CONCEPT
Lamon is a soft-natured display typeface. Lamon's outlined glyphs are made of both uppercase and lowercase letters with the smaller letters hiding inside the bigger ones. The face's smooth lines give street signs, packaging, and decorative materials a friendly lightness, while the unexpected contrast involves the viewer in an interesting optical game.

ENCRYPTED UNDER TWO DIFFERENT KEYS

Sans Condensed Thin

OS–Extension

Serif Bold Italic

cryptographic complexity

Sans SemiBold

Modulate

Serif ExtraLight

Wireless personal area networks*

Sans Condensed Medium Italic

transflection

Mono Light

1562 kg/m³, solid at 1 atm and −78.5 °C

Serif Medium

LOCAL REGISTRY

Complete character set Sans Condensed

Latin lowercase

aabcdefggghijklmnopqrstuvwxy
zàáâãäåāăąçćĉċčdďđèéêëēĕėęěĝ
ğġgĥħìíîïĩīĭįıĳĵķĺļľŀłmnñńņňŉ
ŋòóôõöøōŏőœŕŗřśŝşšßtţťŧùúûüũūŭ
ůűųẁẃŵẅýÿŷźżž

Latin uppercase

AÀÁÂÃÄÅĀĂĄBCÇĆĈĊČDĎĐEÈÉÊËĒĔĖĘĚ
ÆÆÇĆĈĊČDÐĐEÈÉÊËĒĔĖĘĚ
ÈÉ∂ĜĞĠGĤĦÌÍÎÏĨĪĬĮİĲĴĶL
ĹĻĽĿŁMNÑŃŅŇŊ
ÒÓÔÕÖØŌŎŐŒŔŖŘSŚŜŞŠßTŢŤ
ÞÙÚÛÜŨŪŬŮŰŲẀẂŴẄ
ẀẂŴẄÝŸŶŹŻŽ

Ligatures
fi fl

Numerals

00123456789 0123456789 0123456789
⅓⅔¼¾⅛⅜⅝⅞

Arrows

∨✕←↑↓→↖↗↘↙↩↪
↰↱↲↳↴↵↺↻⇄⇅

Punctuation & symbols

&@·--—_.…:,;'''""‚„‹›«»¡!¿?()[]{}/\%‰|¦§¶©®™ªº°†‡#^~+−±×÷=≈≠<>
≤≥·•◊¬√∫∞∂№Ω؟¢₫¢£$€₣₤¥₦₩₭₮₯₱₲₽₹₵₸₺₼µ∆∏∑Ω∏

Sans Condensed Regular

Sans Condensed Light

№38

Sans Condensed ExtraLight

X

Sans Condensed Bold

Sans Condensed Medium

S

Sans Condensed Thin

H

Sans Condensed Text

G

Sans Light

WRAPPED AROUND A METALLIC CORE

Serif Bold + Bold Italic

Technology can be viewed as an activity that forms or changes culture.[14] Additionally, technology remains the *application* of math, science, and the arts for the benefit of life as it is known. A modern[16] example is the rise of *communication* technology, which has lessened barriers to human interaction and has helped spawn *new subcultures;* the rise of cyberculture has at its basis the *development of the Internet & the computer.*

Sans Medium

The magnetic field inside an infinitely long solenoid is homogeneous and its strength neither depends on the distance from the axis, nor on the solenoid's cross-sectional area.

An infinite solenoid is a solenoid with infinite length but finite diameter

Continuous means that the solenoid is not formed by discrete finite-width coils but by infinitely many infinitely-thin coils with no space between them; in this abstraction, the solenoid is often viewed as a cylindrical sheet of conductive material.

Mono Light

total: 938.742.095

THE PERFORMANCE

$ in billions except per share amounts

For the year ended December 31:	2012
Operating earnings per share	$ 15.25
Revenue	$ 104.50
Operating net income	$ 17.60
Free cash flow	$ 18.20
Returned to shareholders	$ 15.80

Serif Bold + Serif Text Italic +
Serif Bold + Sans Medium

Sans Condensed SemiBold +
Sans Condensed SemiBold Italic

We achieved record operating earnings per share, record free cash *flow & record* profit margins, with revenues that were flat at constant currency.*

Operating earnings per share were up 13%, putting us well on track to our 2015 Road Map objective of at least $20 of *operating earnings* per share [—year: 2012]

Sans Bold Italic

magnetic flux

Serif SemiBold

K̶890.31

Sans Regular

Dưới đây là một số điểm nổi bật của Tuyên bố

Serif Thin Italic

sağlanması gibi çeşitli

Sans Condensed Medium

[(45⅞ + 602⅜)³]⁸

Serif Light

Indéchiffrable!

Mono Text

Todos los cifrados polialfabéticos basados en el cifrado César

Serif SemiBold Italic

Größ/mäßig?

Verena Gerlach

This is a multifunctional type family I could imagine using in quite diverse fields. From coding via web and book design over to large displays—everything seems possible with the different variants of this typeface.

Through all weights and variants, the font seems to be very consistent.

Starting with the sans and its clean Grotesque appearance, one quickly begins to notice all the vivid and beautiful details. Although it has quite angled interior counters (taken from the original IBM logotype, but smoothed down), the round curves of the exterior strokes are a nice contrast.

The two-story a and g are quoting a humanist idea, without losing the overall modern (and modernist) characteristics of Plex Grotesque. It causes a balance between rational and human but not humanist.

In general, this seems to be a not geographically locatable typeface—that is, it combines optical features of many different regions of traditional type design.

I very much like the eccentric Plex Mono, which demonstrates the balance between technical and emotional/vivid at its best, especially in the (real) Italic. Just check out the fractions!

The neoclassical but also a little technical Plex Serif is beautiful with its round drops and dots. This serif variant is not too strong in contrast, with a modern, quite high x-height. It is very suitable for longer texts.

I am excited to find the right occasion to try out the complete Plex superfamily myself.

....

IBM PLEX

TYPEFACE DESIGN
Mike Abbink°
Paul van der Laan
Pieter van Rosmalen,
New York
The Hague
Eindhoven,
The Netherlands

CREATIVE DIRECTION
Mike Abbink

TYPE DIRECTION
Paul van der Laan
Pieter van Rosmalen

URL
ibm.com/plex

DESIGN AGENCY
IBM Brand Experience
& Design
Bold Monday

**MEMBERS OF THE
TYPE FAMILY**
IBM Plex™ Sans, Mono,
Condensed, and Serif

CONCEPT
IBM Plex™ is the new corporate typeface for IBM worldwide and an open-source project developed by the IBM Brand Experience & Design (BX&D) team. Plex is an international typeface family designed to capture IBM's brand spirit and history, and to illustrate the unique relationship between mankind and machine—a principal theme for IBM since the turn of the century. The result is a neutral yet friendly grotesque-style typeface that balances design with the engineered details that make Plex distinctly IBM. The family includes a Sans, Sans Condensed, Mono, and Serif and has excellent legibility in print, web, and mobile interfaces. Plex's three designs work well independently, and even better together. Use the Sans as a contemporary compadre, the Serif for editorial storytelling, or the Mono to show code snippets. The unexpectedly expressive nature of the italics gives you even more options for your designs.

思源宋体
思源宋體
源ノ明朝
본명조

Source Han Serif

Adobe 和 Google 合作研發的思源宋體是一個開放原始碼的 Pan-CJK 字型系列，可以透過 Typekit 提供桌上型電腦使用，也可以從 GitHub

SemiBold 24/42 pt TC

で、さらに GitHub からも入手できます。評価の高い Source Serif ファミリーのラテン文字、ギリシャ文字、キリル文字も含まれます。ファミリーのそれぞれのウェイトにつき（OpenType 形式が対応可能な最大数）65,535 のグリフ（字体）が、ファミリー全体で、およそ 50 万のグリフをカバーします。この新書体に課せ

Regular 22/38 pt JP

Adobe는 Google과의 협력을 통해 새로운 오픈 소스 한중일 통합 서체 모음인 본명조 (Source Han Serif)를 출시하게 되었습니다. 이 서체 모음은 데스

SemiBold 34/51 pt K

Bold 200 pt JP

스크탑용 Typekit을 통해 다운로드 될 수 있으며 GitHub에서도 받을 수 있습니다. 7가지 굵기로 제공되는 본명조는 하나의 서체를 통해 한국어, 일본어, 중국어 번체 및 중국어 간체를 모두 지원합니다. 또한 널리 사용되는 Source Serif 서체 모음의 라틴어, 그리스어 및 키릴 자모 글리프가 포함되어 있습니다. 앞에서 언급한 바와 같이 이 서체

Regular 14/21.5 pt K

しっかりと時代のニーズに応える、

Source Han Serif は、アドビと Google が協力して開発したオープンソースの Pan-CJK 書体ファミリーです。デスクトップでの利用には Typekit から入手可能

Medium 35/47 pt JP

しいものでした。前記の幅広い範囲の言語をカバーし、それら言語を用いる地域ごとのグリフのバリエーションにも対応する必要がありました（ひとつの漢字に対して、4つの地域別のバリエーションが必要となる場合があります）。従来のように紙に印刷するだけでなく、現在多く利用されるタブレット

Regular 16/24.5 pt JP

Bold 230 pt SC

明朝体 Pan-CJK フォントを実現。

SemiBold 39 pt JP

思源宋体是 Adobe 与 Google 合作开发的一款开源 Pan-CJK 字体家族，可以通过 Typekit 提供桌面系统使用，也可以从 GitHub 下载页面获得。思源宋体字体家族拥有七种字重，每种字重都全面支持日文、韩文、繁体中文和简体中文。它还包括来自我们颇受欢迎的 Source Sans 字体家族的拉丁文、希腊文和西里尔文字形。总的来说，字体家族里的每个字重都包含

Light 12/18.5 pt SC

檔案。思源宋體字型系列具有七種粗細，每種粗細都可為日文、韓文、繁體中文和簡體

Bold 24/35 pt TC

Bold 300 pt TC

やモバイルデバイスで表示する場合の読みやすさを向上させることが重要課題でした。東京を拠点とするフォント開発チームのシニアデザイナーである西塚涼子は、新しい書体ファミリーの基本デザインを作成しました。西塚涼子によるデザインは、シンプルで線幅の太さがかなり均質な直線で構成される、比較的現代的な様式です。その結果、タブレットやスマートフォンなどの小型デバイスでも読みやすくなります。そのシンプルさにもかかわらず、伝統的

Regular 12/18.5 pt JP

オープンソースの書体ファミリー。

Heavy 38 pt JP 字間詰め

ExtraLight
Light
Regular
Medium

Japanese 日本語
源ノ明朝

韓国語 Korean
본명조

JP　蘭陵の美酒はチューリップの香り、玉の椀に盛られて琥珀の光を放つ。

K　울금향 그윽한 난릉의 좋은 술을 옥잔에 따르니 호박빛이 아롱지다.

SC　兰陵美酒郁金香，玉碗盛来琥珀光。但使主人能醉客，不知何处是他乡。

TC　蘭陵美酒鬱金香，玉碗盛來琥珀光。但使主人能醉客，不知何處是他鄉。

思源宋体
Simplified Chinese 中国語簡体字

思源宋體
中国語繁体字 Traditional Chinese

SemiBold
Bold
Heavy
*

YuJune Park

In keeping with its name, Source Han exhibits the prototypical traits of a CJK (Chinese, Japanese, Korean) typeface. Ambitious, direct, and drawn with no nonsense, the typeface impressively maintains its legibility across its weights and sizes.

The Japanese, in particular, is elegantly drawn and works well with the Korean, Traditional Chinese, and Simplified Chinese.

Source Han is a sophisticated CKJ typeface and can accommodate a broad range of applications, on screen and off. It is notable for the sheer scope of its character set—thousands of characters optically balanced within each individual language and together as a whole.

TYPEFACE DESIGN
Ryoko Nishizuka (principal designer kana & ideographs) Frank Grießhammer (Latin, Greek, and Cyrillic) Wenlong Zhang (bopomofo) Soohyun Park Yejin We Donghoon Han (hangul elements, letters, and symbols)

URL
typekit.com/foundries/adobe

TWITTER
@AdobeType

CLIENTS
Adobe Systems, Inc. Google

MEMBERS OF THE TYPE FAMILY
Seven weights:
ExtraLight
Light
Regular
Medium
SemiBold
Bold
Heavy

Four languages:
Simplified Chinese, Traditional Chinese (Taiwan), Japanese, Korean

Released by Google under the name Noto Serif CJK in the same seven weights

CONCEPT
Source Han Serif is the companion serif-style Pan-CJK typeface family to Source Han Sans, and it is offered in seven slightly different weights and in several OpenType/CFF-based deployment configurations to accommodate various system requirements or, in some cases, limitations. Pan-CJK fonts, such as those provided in the Source Han typeface families, are intended to support and render the most important characters for Simplified Chinese, Traditional Chinese, Japanese, and Korean.

This is Noort

A **cartographic** typeface with **editorial** *inclinations*

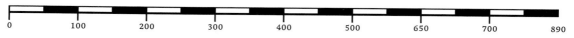

¿COORDENADAS DEL TRÓPICO DE CAPRICORNIO & CANCER?

NOORT

TYPEFACE DESIGN
Juan Bruce Paine,
Región Metropolitana,
Chile

TYPE FOUNDRY
TypeTogether

URL
type-together.com

TWITTER
@TypeTogether

**MEMBERS OF THE
TYPE FAMILY**
Regular
Italic
Book
Book Italic
Semibold
Semibold Italic
Bold
Bold Italic
Extrabold
Extrabold Italic
Display Black
Display Icons

CONCEPT
Noort is an analog serif family inspired by calligraphy from
seventeenth-century Dutch maps. Although the Italic kept most of this
flavor with its rough-and-fast approach, at some point in the process
the main idea shifted to creating a body typeface in which the Roman
and the Italic became best friends. Traits such as serifs straddling
every stroke, low contrast modulation, large x-height, and ample
spacing make Noort suited for 8–9 points. As a result, through a crisp
but stable texture in its paragraphs, Noort has skills that allow it to
deal optimally with complex typographical environments and thrive in
editorial typesetting.

Die Albatrosse sind eine Familie von
Seevögeln aus der Ordnung der Röhrennasen

Cabernet Sauvignon
One of the world's most widely recognized red wine grape varieties
Santa Cruz Mountains

The Zagros mountain range begins in northwestern Iran and roughly corresponds to Iran's western border and it spans the whole length of the western and southwestern Iranian plateau

ORIGEN

TYPEFACE DESIGN
Alex Camacho,
London

URL
alexcamachostudio.com
origenfont.com

INSTAGRAM
@alexcamachostudio

STUDIO
Alex Camacho Studio

MEMBERS OF THE
TYPE FAMILY
Regular
Light
Bold
Capitals

Teddy

TEDDY REGULAR

UPPERCASE STANDARD GLYPHS

A B C D E F G H I J K L M N O P Q R S T U V W X Y Z
À Á Â Ã Ä Å Æ Ç Ć Ĉ Ċ Č Đ È É Ê Ë Ē Ĕ Ė Ę Ě Ĝ Ğ Ġ Ĥ Ì Í Î Ï
Ĩ Ī Ĭ Į I J Ĵ Ķ Ĺ Ļ Ľ Ŀ Ł Ñ Ń Ņ Ň Ò Ó Ô Õ Ö Ō Ŏ Ő Œ Ŕ Ŗ Ř Ś Ŝ Ş Š
Ţ Ť Ŧ Ù Ú Û Ũ Ū Ŭ Ů Ű Ų Ŵ Ẁ Ẃ Ẅ Ý Ŷ Ÿ Ź Ż Ž Þ

LOWERCASE STANDARD GLYPHS

a b c d e f g h i j k l m n o p q r s t u v w x y z
à á â ã ä å ā ă ą æ ç ć ĉ ċ č ď đ è é ê ë ē ĕ ė ę ě fi fl ĝ ğ ġ ĝ ĥ ħ ì í î
ï ĩ ī ĭ į ı ij ĵ ð ķ ĺ ļ ľ ŀ ł ñ ń ņ ŋ ǹ ò ó ô õ ö ō ŏ ő œ ù ú û ü ũ ū ŭ ů ű ų ß
ţ ť ŧ ũ ū ü ů ű ų ú û ũ ŵ ẁ ẃ ẅ ÿ ĝ ğ ġ ÿ ź ż ž þ

SMALL CAPS

A B C D E F G H I J K L M N O P Q R S T U V W X Y Z
À Á Â Ã Ä Å Ā Ą Æ Ç Ć Ĉ Ċ Č Đ È É Ê Ë Ē Ĕ Ė Ę Ě Ĝ Ğ Ġ Ĝ Ĥ Ì Í Î Ï Ī Ĭ Į I J
Ĵ Ķ Ĺ Ļ Ľ Ŀ Ł Ñ Ń Ņ Ň Ò Ó Ô Õ Ö Ō Ŏ Ő Œ Ŕ Ŗ Ř Ś Ŝ Ş Š Ș S S Ţ Ť Ŧ Ù Ú Û
Ü Ũ Ū Ŭ Ů Ű Ų Ŵ Ẁ Ẃ Ẅ Ŷ Ý Ÿ Ź Ż Ž Þ

NUMERALS PUNCTUATION, SYMBOLS, ETC.

1234567890 1234567890 1234567890
¡ ! ¿ ? ‽ (|) { · } [¦] \ / / † ‡ . , … : ; - – _ * ' ' , " " „ "
‹ › « » & @ § ¶ © ® ™ ◊ µ π ∂ √ ∫ ƒ ª º ¢ $ ¢ ¥ ₤ ₡ ₱ ₩ ¤ §
@ † ‡ % ‰ ¶ ¹ ² ³ ⅛ ½ ⅜ < = > × + ≠ ± ≤ ≥ ≈ ÷ ∞ ☞ ☜ ↓ ↑ ↖ ↗

LIGATURES & LETTERPAIRS & CONTEXTUAL ALTERNATES

& bb dd ff ffi gg ggy jj ij xx ygg zz 1st 2nd 3rd
db dh dk dl k ffi ffl fr ffi fi fr fţ ft î ss co pp s v w ò ó ô ŏ
ś ŝ š ggy hh ii jj kk pp qq ʼʼ tf tfr tt uu vv ww lk xx zz etc.

TEDDY CLOUD AND OPEN

TEDDY CLOUD AND REGULAR

Héviz
São Gonçalo
VÄSTERÅS
Delémont
GDAŃSK
Helsingør
Žilina, Piešťany

TEDDY

TYPEFACE DESIGN
Minjoo Ham,
Berlin

TYPE DIRECTION
Jan Middendorp

TYPE ADVICE
Florian Hardwig
Dan Reynolds

PUBLISHER
Fust & Friends,
foundry and
typographic hothouse
(Berlin)

URL
fustandfriends.com

TWITTER
@fustandfriends

Pelago Cyrillic

АБВГЃДДЕЖЗИЙКЛЛМНОПРСТУФХЦЧШЩЪЫЬ ЭЮЯЁЁ́Ђ Ѓ Є S Ї Ј Љ Љ Њ Й Ћ
Ќ Ў Ц Ѣ Ѳ V Ѐ I Ѓ Җ Қ Ң Ү Ұ Х Ч Һ Ə Й Ѳ Ў • абвгддежзийкллмнопрстуфхцчшщъыь
эюябёђѓ є s i ї j љ љ њ ћ ќ ў ц ѣ ѳ v ѐ й ѓ җ қ ң ү ұ х ч һ i ə й ѳ ў • АБВГЃДДЕЖЗИЙКЛЛМН
ОПРСТУФХЦЧШЩЪЫЬ ЭЮЯЁ Ё́ Ђ Ѓ Є S Ї Ј Љ Љ Њ Ћ Ќ Й Ў Ц Ѣ Ѳ V Ѓ Җ Қ Ң Ү Ұ Х Ч Һ I Ə Й Ѳ Ў

Какая грусть! Конец аллеи...

Какая грусть! Конец аллеи
Опять с утра исчез в пыли,
Опять серебряные змеи
Через сугробы поползли.

На небе ни клочка лазури,
В степи все гладко, все бело,
Один лишь ворон против бури
Крылами машет тяжело.

И на душе не рассветает,
В ней тот же холод, что кругом,
Лениво дума засыпает
Над умирающим трудом.

А все надежда в сердце тлеет,
Что, может быть, хоть невзначай,
Опять душа помолодеет,
Опять родной увидит край,

Где бури пролетают мимо,
Где дума страстная чиста,—
И посвященным только зримо
Цветет весна и красота.

[Начало 1862]

Искусство эпохи Возрождения

Light ◆ *Light Italic* ◆ Light Text ◆ *Light Text Italic* ◆ Regular ◆ *Italic*
Medium ◆ *Medium Italic* ◆ **Semibold** ◆ *Semibold Italic* ◆ **Bold** ◆ ***Bold Italic***

PELAGO

TYPEFACE DESIGN
Robert Slimbach,
San Jose, California

URL
typekit.com
foundries/adobe

TWITTER
@AdobeType

FOUNDRY
Adobe Systems

MEMBERS OF THE TYPE FAMILY
Pelago Regular
Pelago Light
Pelago Light Italic
Pelago Light Text
Pelago Light Text Italic
Pelago Italic
Pelago Medium
Pelago Medium Italic

Pelago Semibold
Pelago Semibold Italic
Pelago Bold
Pelago Bold Italic

CONCEPT
Pelago is a semiformal sans serif type family with a crisp, contemporary appearance and an understated elegance. At display sizes Pelago exhibits subtly swelling stroke endings, animated letter counter shapes, and a moderate degree of stroke modulation—qualities derived from both humanist handwriting and Roman inscriptional lettering. At smaller type sizes these expressive accents recede, revealing a clear and readable text face that doesn't suffer from the structural rigidity found in conventional sans serif designs..

A GENTLEMAN

never talks about his tailor

Markdown

☞ **reading about life** ☜

Confident & Smart

★ **KNOPFLEISTE** ★

CONTRADTED SLAP WITH A BOWLER HAT

new ideas

vll wagyü → *vll wagyü*

A smart man only believes half of what he hears, a wise man knows which half.

HARRISON SERIF PRO

TYPEFACE DESIGN DIRECTION
Jakob Runge, Munich

TYPEFACE DESIGN
Lisa Fischbach, Hamburg

FONT PRODUCTION
Christoph Koeberlin, Berlin

FOUNDRY
TypeMates

URL
typemates.com

TWITTER
@TypeMatesFonts

MEMBERS OF THE TYPE FAMILY
Harrison Serif Pro
Hair Italic
Thin
Thin Italic
ExtraLight
Extra Light Italic
Light
Light Italic
Regular

Regular Italic
Medium
Medium Italic
Bold
Bold Italic
Black
Black Italic
Ultra
Ultra Italic

CONCEPT
Harrison Serif Pro is a sturdy yet contrasted slab serif that combines a rational and efficient approach with a warm voice. A typeface of nuances, the slightly carved and occasionally extended serifs evoke the friendly side of Harrison Serif and contrast with the straightforward nature of the typeface's squarish curves, open counters, and horizontal emphasis. The almost mechanical vertical terminals, open counters, and modest capitals combine with Harrison's generous x-height to ensure the typeface holds up on screen. Given this serif typeface's improved ClearType hinting and sturdy physique, no medium is a worry for it.

απокυπσαστε

συνυποστηκα

αναχαιζοντας

ξεσκοτισαστε

καταπθονται

ξανασζονταν

καταρεζεστε

εξαπαθηκαν

απокρυφισς

δεκαεξαιδου

ακοστνοντας

προσδιοζαμε

ειδοποιηκατε

καζαντισνους

απоηντουσαν

επιτετραμνου

Read Greek Condensed

READ GREEK CONDENSED

TYPEFACE DESIGN
Elliott Amblard
Théo Guillard,
Paris

TYPEFACE DESIGN
DIRECTION
Jérémie Hornus

FOUNDRY
Black[Foundry]

URL
black-foundry.com

TWITTER
@blackfoundry

CLIENT
Groupe Renault

MEMBERS OF THE
TYPE FAMILY

Read Greek
Condensed Light
Light Italic
Regular
Italic
Medium
Medium Italic
Bold
Bold Italic

CONCEPT
For the past several years, Groupe Renault has been creating synergies across brands while pursuing a premium design strategy, making their cars more iconic and desirable. As a part of this strategy, they realized that they needed an extensive font family to bring together the Renault, Alpine, and Dacia brands and perform across all platforms and all writing systems. That's why we created the Read family and developed Read in varied writing systems. Humanist at heart, Read works seamlessly onboard and off-board, on physical and digital elements, on screen and in print.

Lovely high contrast sans

From Light to Black

ENERGETIC CURVATURE

Flaring stems for a certain warmth to it

LUXURIOUS

Exclusive and Exquisite

DECIDEDLY WEIRD BUT ORDINARY

§ 8a Abs.12 Art.3 bis 5: Schriftgesetzblatt

December 31ˢᵗ 1987

KURSIVE SIND WIEDER EN VOGUE

Grounded Roman / Dramatic italics

KONING

TYPEFACE DESIGN
Luc(as) de Groot
Martina Flor
Jan Fromm
Phillipp Neumeyer
Daria Petrova,
Berlin

FOUNDRY
LucasFonts

URL
lucasfonts.com

TWITTER
@FontFabrik

**MEMBERS OF THE
TYPE FAMILY**

Koning Text:
Light
Light Italic
SemiLight
SemiLight Italic
Regular
Regular Italic
SemiBold
SemiBold Italic
Bold
Bold Italic
ExtraBold
ExtraBold Italic
Heavy
Heavy Italic
Black
Black Italic

Koning Display:
UltraLight
UltraLight Italic
ExtraLight
ExtraLight Italic
Light
Light Italic
SemiLight
SemiLight Italic
Regular
Regular Italic
SemiBold
SemiBold Italic
Bold, Bold Italic
ExtraBold
ExtraBold Italic
Heavy
Heavy Italic
Black
Black Italic

CONCEPT
Koning originated as a high-contrast version of the Corpid family, to satisfy a newspaper customer who wanted just a bit more difference between the thin and thick strokes. The high contrast required a new shape language, and, over time, a new name. Koning Display, with ten weights, has the highest contrast; Koning Text, with eight weights, has a medium contrast, which makes it work well in small sizes. Koning is Dutch for "king." A king represents elegance and prestige while also being in touch with his people—just like this typeface, with its display and text parts.

بِسْمِ اللهِ الرَّحْمٰنِ الرَّحِيمِ

به نام خداکه رحمتش بی‌اندازه است و مهربانی‌اش همیشگی

حٰمٓ ﴿١﴾ تَنْزِيلٌ مِنَ الرَّحْمٰنِ الرَّحِيمِ ﴿٢﴾ كِتٰبٌ فُصِّلَتْ ءَايٰتُهُۥ قُرْءٰنًا عَرَبِيًّا لِقَوْمٍ

حاء، میم(۱)[این کتابی است که]از سوی خداوند رحمان و رحیم فرستاده شده[است](۲)کتابی است که آیاتش به روشنی بیان شده، و برای مردمی که دانایند به زبانی

يَعْلَمُونَ ﴿٣﴾ بَشِيرًا وَنَذِيرًا فَأَعْرَضَ أَكْثَرُهُمْ فَهُمْ لَا يَسْمَعُونَ ﴿٤﴾ وَقَالُوا قُلُوبُنَا

گویا و روشن است(۳)درحالی‌که بشارت‌رسان و هشداردهنده است، ولی بیشتر مردم(که درغفلت‌اند از این دریای معارف)رویگردانند، و[از این رو با گوش قبول]

فِىٓ أَكِنَّةٍ مِمَّا تَدْعُونَآ إِلَيْهِ وَفِىٓ ءَاذَانِنَا وَقْرٌ وَمِنْ بَيْنِنَا وَبَيْنِكَ حِجَابٌ فَاعْمَلْ

نمی‌شنوند(۴)گفتند: دل‌های ما از[درک]حقایقی که ما را به آن دعوت می‌کنی درحجاب‌های سختی است، و درگوش‌هایمان سنگینی است، و میان ما و تو حائلی

إِنَّنَا عٰمِلُونَ ﴿٥﴾ قُلْ إِنَّمَآ أَنَا بَشَرٌ مِثْلُكُمْ يُوحَىٰٓ إِلَىَّ أَنَّمَآ إِلٰهُكُمْ إِلٰهٌ وٰاحِدٌ

درکار است، پس تو به کارخود بپرداز ما هم به کارخود می‌پردازیم[تا معلوم شود پیروزی نصیب کیست](۵)بگو: من[از نظر ظاهر آفرینش]بشری مانند شمایم، [نه

فَاسْتَقِيمُوٓا إِلَيْهِ وَاسْتَغْفِرُوهُ ۗ وَوَيْلٌ لِلْمُشْرِكِينَ ﴿٦﴾ الَّذِينَ لَا يُؤْتُونَ الزَّكَوٰةَ

از جنس دیگر]که که آیاتِ کتابم و سخنم را درک نکنید،]به من وحی می‌شود: که معبود شما فقط خداوند یکتاست، پس مستقیم[و بدون انحراف]به سوی او روی آورید!

وَهُمْ بِالْءَاخِرَةِ هُمْ كٰفِرُونَ ﴿٧﴾ إِنَّ الَّذِينَ ءَامَنُوا وَعَمِلُوا الصّٰلِحٰتِ لَهُمْ أَجْرٌ غَيْرُ

و از وی آمرزش بخواهید! وای برمشرکان[از عذاب دنیا و آخرت](۶)همان آنان که[به نیازمندان و بیچارگان]زکات نمی‌دهند، و منکرآخرت‌اند(۷)یقیناً مؤمنان که کارهای

مَمْنُونٍ ﴿٨﴾ ۞ قُلْ أَئِنَّكُمْ لَتَكْفُرُونَ بِالَّذِى خَلَقَ الْأَرْضَ فِى يَوْمَيْنِ وَتَجْعَلُونَ

شایسته انجام داده‌اند، برای آنان پاداشی پایان‌ناپذیر است(۸)بگو: آیا شما به کسی که زمین را در دو روزآفرید کفرمی‌ورزید، و برای او همتایانی[که اختیارچیزی راندارند]

لَهُۥٓ أَندَادًا ۚ ذٰلِكَ رَبُّ الْعٰلَمِينَ ﴿٩﴾ وَجَعَلَ فِيهَا رَوٰاسِىَ مِن فَوْقِهَا وَبٰرَكَ فِيهَا

قرارمی‌دهید؟! [فقط]پروردگارجهانیان[آفرینندهٔ زمین]است(۹)روی زمین کوه‌هایی استوار[و لنگرآسا]پدید آورد، و درآن خیرفراوانی قرارداد، و مواد خوراکی آن را

وَقَدَّرَ فِيهَآ أَقْوٰاتَهَا فِىٓ أَرْبَعَةِ أَيَّامٍ سَوَآءً لِلسَّآئِلِينَ ﴿١٠﴾ ثُمَّ اسْتَوَىٰٓ إِلَى السَّمَآءِ

[برای روزی خوارانش]به مدت چهارفصل اندازه‌گیری کرد،که برای[همهٔ]خواهندگان[برابر نیازشان]یکسان است(۱۰)آن‌گاه به[آفریدن]آسمان پرداخت درحالی که

وَهِىَ دُخَانٌ فَقَالَ لَهَا وَلِلْأَرْضِ ائْتِيَا طَوْعًا أَوْ كَرْهًا قَالَتَآ أَتَيْنَا طَآئِعِينَ ﴿١١﴾

[مادهٔ اولیه‌اش]به‌صورت[توده‌هایی از]دود بود، پس به آن و به زمین فرمان داد: خواه یا ناخواه[به وجود]آیید! آن دو گفتند: مطیعانه[به سوی عرصهٔ وجود]آمدیم(۱۱)

VAZEH

TYPEFACE DESIGN
Reza Bakhtiarifard
Omid Emamian,
Tehran

TWITTER
@rbakhtiarifar
@omidemamian

CLIENT
Ofogh Rooydad

MEMBERS OF THE
TYPE FAMILY

Vazeh Regular
Semibold
Bold

CONCEPT
The script of the Quran should look lovely and sincere, be easy to
read without form complexity, and prevent any problem that affects
quick understanding of the words. It's important for it to preserve
the formalization and glory of the word of God. Vazeh is designed to
promote the Quran on screens for the young generation, for whom
digital tools are an inseparable part of their life. Hence, clarity and
simplicity, important principles of design, became even more important
in this typeface. Transfer and comprehension of the Quran has become
fast and easy, thanks to the right design and accurate placement
of diacritics and signs.

فرمهای جامع اطلاعات

فرمهای جامع اطلاعات

ء اآآأأإإلأآ ااا ب بـب ب پ پـپ پ تـتـت ت ثـثـث ث جـجـج ج چـچـچ چ حـحـح ح خـخـخ خ
دد ذ ذ رر ز ز ژ ژ سـسـس س شـشـش ش صـصـص ص ضـضـض ض طـطـط ط ظـظـظ ظ
عـعـع ع غـغـغ غ فـفـف ف قـقـق ق کـکـک ک كـكـك ك گـگـگ گ گ گ گ گ گ
ل ل ل ل مـمـم م نـنـن ن و و و ؤ ؤ هـهـه ه ة ة ة ة یـیـی ی ئـئـئ ئ يـي ي ي ی ی
لا لا لآ لآ لأ لأ لإ لإ الله بی پی تی ثی خی یی ئی سی سی شی شی صی صی ضی ضی بی سی
شی شی صی صی ضی ضی بی پی تی ثی خی یی ئی بر پر تر ثر خر نر بز پز تز ثز خز نز
سر سر سز سز سژ سژ شر شر شز شز شژ شژ صر صر صز صز صژ صژ ضر ضر ضز ضز ضژ ضژ
بن پن تن ثن ین ین ئن ریال

[ ] ( ) (( )) ( ) "( ) '" , , . % ... % . % * ! ؟ : ، . ، : . ۰۱۲۳۴۵۶۷۸۹ ۰۱۲۳۴۵۶۷۸۹
۱۲۳ ¶ _ — — – – | | ° ∞ ≤ ≥ < > ¬ ≈ ≠ = ÷ × ± − + # " " ' ' ... \ / { }

RAY

TYPEFACE DESIGN
Reza Bakhtiarifard
Omid Emamian,
Tehran

TWITTER
@rbakhtiarifard
@omidemamian

**MEMBERS OF THE
TYPE FAMILY**

Ray Thin
Regular
Black

CONCEPT
Ray was designed as a teamwork job to go through an experience
of a collaborative task without any clients. The goal was to design
a heavyweight typeface for general usage with a commercial and
advertisement tendency. Our design process was contrary to
the common method, which helped us discover many new points.
Accordingly, the first weight was Black, then the Regular weight
derived from Black version. Ray is a typeface with a strong skeleton,
short ascender and descender, serious intonation, and flat surface
with sharp corners. It is a modern inspiration from the Naskh script
with new proportions.

Elementar

«Àękag(¥)25{ß}?&@»

Calligraphy and handwritting are slowly becoming a rare skill to have. Less and less people write by hand to take of their thoughts. This makes all fonts that have a warm connection to writting so popular nowadays.

Artigo Display

ARTIGO DISPLAY

TYPEFACE DESIGN
Joana Maria
Correia da Silva,
Porto, Portugal

FOUNDRY
Nova Type Foundry

URL
novatypefoundry.com

TWITTER
@joanatype

CONCEPT
This project was designed as the odd sister to the Artigo typeface. It was a side project that explored in more detail the handwritten aspects of the italics. It is more expressive and heavy with a bit of a blackletter feeling. The purpose was to bring texture and fun to the page while also remaining legible and retaining all the typographic features that a text requires.

Fascinated

❧ François Guyot, son of Jean Guyot and Jeanne Conbin, came from Paris, where his brother-in-law, Alexandre Beaujon likewise was a letterfounder. On 22 August 1539 he was enrolled as a citizen of Antwerp. ☙

Rally in London

SCIENTISTS ARE FIGHTING BACK

Trial in Belgium

President Anastasiades defeats leftist challenger

GUYOT

TYPEFACE DESIGN
Ramiro Espinoza,
The Hague

FOUNDRY
Retype Foundry

URL
re-type.com

TWITTER
@retypefoundry

CONCEPT
Guyot is a type family inspired by the work of the punchcutter François Guyot, who lived and worked in Antwerp during the sixteenth century. Researching French and Flemish punchcutters, Espinoza soon realized that the work of the most important masters of the period had already been digitized. However, he found the work of lesser-known punchcutters like Guyot, though perhaps not of the same superior quality as the others, equally compelling. Espinoza decided early on that his Guyot was not going to be a facsimile typeface, but rather a modern interpretation aimed at the editorial market.

Oi!

TYPEFACE DESIGN
Kostas Bartsokas,
Hamburg

URL
kostasbartsokas.
com/oi-you-mate/

TWITTER
@kostasbartsokas

CONCEPT

Oi! is an ultra-fat display typeface that has its roots in grotesque slab serifs, most specifically the style that sprang up with the release of Caslon's Ionic in 1844 and Clarendon by Fann Street Foundry in 1845. It is a free-spirited twisted interpretation of the Clarendonesques. With an unapologetic tendency for public shouting, it is a whimsical, loudmouth attention-seeker. Oi! supports Latin and Greek and comes in two styles: Oi! You!, the regular style, and its accompanying Oi! Mate!, a shadowed style that adds a third dimension to its playfulness.

A

Kinetic is an exceptionally well-crafted font

○ Typograph.Her

PANORÁMICA

affiche

Attraktion!

Visionäre

R

Kinetic is an artful interpretation of a geometric balancing act

○ AIGA Eye on Design

Kinetic is original and convincing

○ Gerard Unger

ICONS 👍

e.g. = ǥ

g

&

→ arrows ←

Kinetic is a very handsome sans geared towards the art world

○ Badson

T

Kinetic would be a hell of a nice typeface to own

○ Represent

MOMA

KINETIC

TYPEFACE DESIGN
Noel Pretorius
María Ramos,
Stockholm
and
Santiago de Compostela,
Spain

FOUNDRY
NM type

URL
kinetictypeface.com

TWITTER
@nm_type

CLIENT
NM type

CONCEPT
Kinetic is a geometric sans serif type family that draws on the simplicity and playfulness of Alexander Calder's art. Typefaces in this genre tend to look sharp and constructed. Kinetic adopts a different approach by creating a more organic text appearance. The slightly curved endings and the roundness of the shapes give a softer feel. The playful proportions, the large apertures, and the long ascenders define a distinctive typeface made for a light text texture. It is a unique design that renders well on screen and looks good in printed text.

Greta Text A Contemporary Typeface for Newspapers, Magazines and Books | Books

גרטה-טקסט גופן עכשווי לעיתונות, למגזינים ולספרים

غريتا
Greta
גרטה
ГРЕТА

גרטה **גרבו**

GARBO ó או

מרלן **דיטריך**

DIETRICH

חייהן
Sus Vidas
אהבתן
Sus Amores

אסטרלאדוס №1 ESTRELLADOS

ויקטור הראל

משאל העם הקטלאני רק מחריף את השסע בספרד. גם אם יופרד המחוז מהממשל המרכזי, האיחוד לא ימהר לקבלו כמדינה עצמאית והתוכניות הכלכליות שרוקם הש־לטון עלולות להתפוצץ לו בפנים.

שום דבר לא עוצר בעד ממשלת קטלוניה ותנועת הבדלנות בריצת ה"אמוק" שלהם לעבר שאיפתם לעצמאותם המלאה.

הפיגועים הקטלוניים ברחבות בברצלונה רק לפני שישה שבועות כאילו נשכחו, וכך גם האחדות הר־געית שחיברה את קטלוניה לשאר המדינה. ראשי קטלוניה אינם נר־תעים מהחלטות בית המשפט הע־ליון הספרדי, אינם ששים לכבד את החוק ואינם מתרשמים כראוי מה־נחישות של ראש הממשלה מריאנו רחוי למנוע "כמעט" בכל מחיר את היפרדותה של קטלוניה. רחוי פשוט לא יכול אחרת: בשוליים של המא־בק הנוכחי מביטים וממתינים הב־סקים, חלק מאזרחי גאליסיה ומי יודע מי עוד יבקש עצמאות.

משאל העם אתמול רק מעמיק את הקרע בתוך קטלוניה עצמה וב־חברה הספרדית בכלל. העימותים, בין אזרחים לבין שוטרים שהובאו מחוץ לקטלוניה (נוכח הפסיביות שגילו ה"מוסוס", השוטרים המקו־מיים בקטלוניה) הן מחזות שמעו־ררות חלחלה בציבוריות הספרדית. חלחלה וחלום בלהות מימים עברו שכבר כולם חשבו שהם קבורים עמוק באדמה. האחריות לכך נופלת ברובה על כתפיהם של נשיא קטלו־ניה קרלס פוג'דמון וממשלתו.

הסודנית
עם המקל עזבה
הם נרדפו ברחובות על ידי אנשים מוסתים, הילד הקטן לא ישן בלילות, הסבתא חדלה לדבר. בני המשפחהשהשכבר ראו זוועות קשות מאלה בדרפור, חשבו שזה הסוף, כבר אין לאן לברוח.

מוחמד וותד, עמוד 15

מתוך / הנדסת אקלים
שלומי חתוכה

חָתוּ יְמֵי מַחֲלָה וּשְׁנֵי הַרְבֵּה
כִּי תֻּכַּף יֵאָסְרוּ לַחְלֹם.
בַּשֶּׁלֶב הַבָּא יֵרְצְחוּ
אֶת כָּל מִי שֶׁיֵּשׁ לוֹ מַשְׁחָפִים
אוֹ הַשְׁמָפָה שׁוֹנָה עַל הַפֶּתֶם.
אַחַר כָּךְ יוֹצִיאוּ לְהוֹרֵג
אֶת מִי שֶׁיְּסָרֵב לַהֲרֹג
וְלִפְנֵי הַסּוֹף יִתְלוּ אֶת מִי שֶׁיְּנַסֶּה לִבְרֹר ...

GRETA TEXT HEBREW

TYPEFACE DESIGN
Hebrew:
Michal Sahar,
Tel Aviv
Latin:
Peter Bil'ak,
The Hague

FOUNDRY
Typotheque

CONCEPT
Greta Text is a contemporary typeface family designed for the demands of newspaper printing. It consists of four primary text weights (each in three grades) and is optimized for use at small sizes. Since the typeface was created to function in the extreme conditions of newspaper production, it is also ideal for other modern typographic situations, such as print and electronic editions of magazines or books. Besides Hebrew, Greta supports Latin, Greek, Cyrillic, and Arabic. The Latin/Greek/Cyrillic pair received the Type Directors Club Certificate of Excellence in Type Design in 2007, Arabic in 2012, and now Hebrew in 2018.

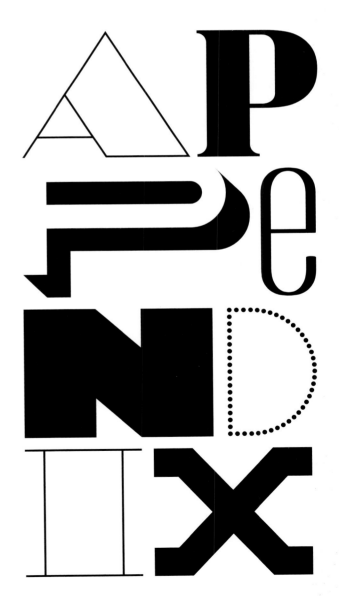

About the TDC

The Type Directors Club is the leading international organization whose purpose is to support excellence in typography, both in print and on screen.

Founded in 1946 by some of the industry's leading practitioners, the TDC's earliest membership included Aaron Burns, Will Burtin, Freeman Craw, Louis Dorfsman, Gene Federico, Edward M. Gottschall, Herb Lubalin, Edward Rondthaler, Bradbury Thompson, and Hermann Zapf. With this solid historical background, the TDC today represents and rewards the best of today's type design and type use.

The TDC holds two yearly type competitions: one for the use of type and the letterform in design and the other, typeface design. The winners are reproduced in our Typography Annual, published by Verlag Herman Schmidt and sold in the TDC Shop, as well as displayed in eight exhibits that travel worldwide. In addition to celebrating outstanding achievements, the typography competitions and resulting annuals serve as important historical records of typographic trends, and are an invaluable resource for both designers and scholars.

Officers 2017–2018

PRESIDENT
Doug Clouse,
The Graphics Office

VICE PRESIDENT
Paul Carlos
Pure+Applied

SECRETARY/TREASURER
Debbie Millman
Design Matters

CHAIRMAN OF THE BOARD
Matteo Bologna
Mucca Design

EXECUTIVE DIRECTOR
Carol Wahler

Directors-at-Large 2017–2018

Ana Gomez Bernaus
Anenocena

Dawn Hancock
Firebelly Design

Karl Heine
creativeplacement

Bobby Martin, Jr.,
*OCD | The Original
Champions of Design*

Joe Newton
Anderson Newton Design

Dan Rhatigan
Adobe TypeKit

Douglas Riccardi
Memo

Christopher Sergio
Penguin Random House

Elizabeth Carey Smith
The Letter Office

Nina Stössinger
Frere-Jones Type

Angela Voulangas
The Graphics Office

TDC Non-Latin
Advisory Board

NLAB is an informal group of
experts that provides guidance
and advice to the judges of the
TDC Type Design competitions
in assessing typeface designs
developed for non-Latin scripts
(Arabic, Cyrillic, Greek, Indic,
and others).

TDC Non-Latin Advisory
Board included:
Huda Smitshujzen AbiFarés
Misha Beletsky
Baruch Gorkin
Martin Heijra
Jana Igunma
Dimity Kirsanov
Gerry Leonidas
Ken Lunde
Klimis Mastoridis
Titus Nemeth
Fiona Ross
Prof. and Dr. Hyun-Guk Ryu
Graham Shaw
Manuel Shmavonyan
Danila Vorobiev

Type Directors
Club Presidents

Frank Powers, 1946, 1947
Milton Zudeck, 1948
Alfred Dickman, 1949
Joseph Weiler, 1950
James Secrest, 1951, 1952, 1953
Gustave Saelens, 1954, 1955
Arthur Lee, 1956, 1957
Martin Connell, 1958
James Secrest, 1959, 1960
Frank Powers, 1961, 1962
Milton Zudeck, 1963, 1964
Gene Ettenberg, 1965, 1966
Edward Gottschall, 1967, 1968
Saadyah Maximon, 1969
Louis Lepis, 1970, 1971
Gerard O'Neill, 1972, 1973
Zoltan Kiss, 1974, 1975
Roy Zucca, 1976, 1977
William Streever, 1978, 1979
Bonnie Hazelton, 1980, 1981
Jack George Tauss, 1982, 1983
Klaus F. Schmidt, 1984, 1985
John Luke, 1986, 1987
Jack Odette, 1988, 1989
Ed Benguiat, 1990, 1991
Allan Haley, 1992, 1993
B. Martin Pedersen, 1994, 1995
Mara Kurtz, 1996, 1997
Mark Solsburg, 1998, 1999
Daniel Pelavin, 2000, 2001
James Montalbano, 2002, 2003
Gary Munch, 2004, 2005
Alex W. White, 2006, 2007
Charles Nix, 2008, 2009
Diego Vainesman, 2010, 2011
Graham Clifford, 2012, 2013
Matteo Bologna, 2014, 2015
Doug Clouse 2016, 2017

TDC Medal
Recipients

Hermann Zapf, 1967
R. Hunter Middleton, 1968
Frank Powers, 1971
Dr. Robert Leslie, 1972
Edward Rondthaler, 1975
Arnold Bank, 1979
Georg Trump, 1982
Paul Standard, 1983
Herb Lubalin, 1984
Paul Rand, 1984
Aaron Burns, 1985
Bradbury Thompson, 1986
Adrian Frutiger, 1987
Freeman Craw, 1988
Ed Benguiat, 1989
Gene Federico, 1991
Lou Dorfsman, 1995
Matthew Carter, 1997
Rolling Stone magazine, 1997
Colin Brignall, 2000
Günter Gerhard Lange, 2000
Martin Solomon, 2003
Paula Scher, 2006
Mike Parker, 2011
Erik Spiekermann, 2011
Gerrit Noordzij, 2013
David Berlow, 2014
Louise Fili 2015
Émigré 2016
Gerard Unger 2017

2018 Scholarships
and Student Awards

2018 TDC SCHOLARSHIP RECIPIENTS
Lea Cawthorne,
Fashion Institute of Technology
Hua Chen,
Pratt Institute
Eva Gabrielsen,
The Cooper Union
Jiyeon Kim,
School of Visual Arts°
Nohemy Ramos,
Art Center College of Design
Kenneth Vanoverbeke,
PXL-MAD (Media, Arts & Design)
Yasemin Varlik,
Parsons School of Design

TDC BEATRICE WARDE SCHOLARSHIP 2018
Anna Skoczeń,
Jan Matejko Academy of Fine Arts,
Kracow, Poland.

2018 STUDENT AWARD WINNERS

STUDENT BEST IN SHOW ($1,000)
Yuliana Gorkorov°,
Folkwang University of the Arts,
Essen, Germany
SECOND PLACE ($500)
İdil Gücüyener and Anna Kabanina,
ELISAVA Barcelona School of Design
and Engineering
THIRD PLACE ($300)
Anna Feng,
Parsons School of Design,
The New School

Special Citations to TDC Members

Edward Gottschall, 1955
Freeman Craw, 1968
James Secrest, 1974
Olaf Leu, 1984, 1990
William Streever, 1984
Klaus F. Schmidt, 1985
John Luke, 1987
Jack Odette, 1989

International Liaison Chairpersons

CHINA
Liu Zhao
China Central Academy
of Fine Arts, Beijing
Liuzhao_cafa@qq.com

ENGLAND
John Bateson
Bateson Studio
5 Astrop Mews
London W6 7HR
john@batesonstudio.com

FRANCE
Bastien Hermand
ECV, École Communication
Visuelle
1, rue du Dahomey
75011 PARIS
b.hermand@ecv.fr

GERMANY
Bertram Schmidt-Friderichs
Verlag Hermann Schmidt Mainz
GmbH & Co.
Gonsenheimer Strasse 56
55126 Mainz
bsf@typografie.de

INDONESIA
John Kudos
Studio Kudos
347 West 36 Street
Suite 902
New York, NY 10018
john@studiokudos.com

JAPAN
Zempaku Suzuki
Japan Typography Association
Sanukin Bldg., 5th Floor
1-7-10 Nihonbashi-honcho
Chuo-ku, Tokyo 104-0041
office@typo.or.jp

MEXICO
Prof. Felix Beltran
Apartado de Correos
M 10733 Mexico 06000
felixbeltran@infinitum.com.mx

POLAND
Ewa Satalecka
Polish Japanese Academy of
Information, Warsaw
ewasatalecla@pjwstk.edu.pl

RUSSIA
Maxim Zhukov
3636 Greystone Avenue
Apt. 4C
Bronx, NY 10463-2059
Zhukov@verizon.net

SOUTH AMERICA
Diego Vainesman
181 East 93 Street, Apt. 4E
New York, NY 10128
diego@40N47design.com

SOUTH KOREA
Samwon Paper Gallery
papergallery@naver.com

SPAIN
Jaume Pujagut, Bau,
Escola Superior de Disseny
Pujades 118
08005 Barcelona
christian@baued.es

TAIWAN
Ken Tsui Lee
National Taiwan University
of Science and Technology
No.43, Keelung Rd., Sec.4,
Da'an Dist., Taipei City 10607,
Taiwan (R.O.C.)
leekentsui@gmail.com

THAILAND
Kanteera Sanguantung
Cadson Demak Co., Ltd.
140 Kaulin Building
Thonglor 4 Sukhumvit 55
Klongton Nua, Wattana
Bangkok 10110
kanteera.cadsondemak@gmail.com

VIETNAM
Richard Moore
21 Bond Street
New York, NY 10012
RichardM@RmooreA.com

TYPE DIRECTORS CLUB
347 West 36 Street
Suite 603
New York, NY 10018
212-633-8943
FAX: 212-633-8944
E-mail: director@tdc.org
www.tdc.org

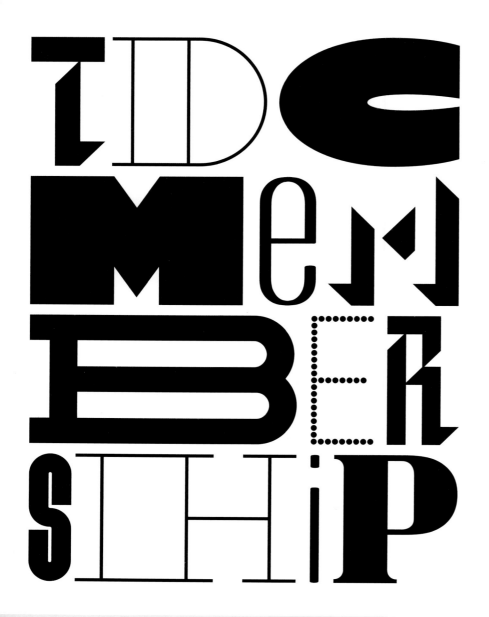

TDC MEMBERSHIP

Kit Hinrichs 2002
Jessica Hische 2010
Reid Hitt 2015
Serena Ho 2017lc
Jennifer Hoerig 2017
Maxwell Hofmann 2017s
Fritz Hofrichter 1980lll
Alyce Hoggan 1987
Victoria Holod 2018s
Karen Horton 2015
Kevin Horvath 1987
Paul Howell 2017
Debra Morton Hoyt 2016
Christian Hruschka 2005
Gene Hua 2017
John Hudson 2004
Aimee Hughes 2008
Keith C. Humphrey 2008
Ginelle Hustrulid 2014
Grant Hutchinson 2011
Christopher Hyde 2017
Elisabetta Iannucci 2017
Jacqueline Infante 2017
Todd Irwin 2016
Yuko Ishizaki 2009
Alexander Isley 2012
Ayaka Ito 2018
Borna Izadpanah 2016s
Donald Jackson 1978ll
Jessica Jaffe 2016
Torsten Jahnke 2002
Virginie Jamieson 2017s
Mark Jamra 1999
Etienne Jardel 2006
Alin Camara Jardim 2011
Song Jin 2017lc
Thomas Jockin 2016
Ben Johnson 2017
Dean Johnson 2017
Emmt Jones 2018
Patra Jongjitirat 2014lc
Giovanni Jubert 2004
Farah Kafei 2017lc
Earl Kallemeyn 2018
John Kallio 1996lll
Nour Kanafani 2015
Ellie Kantor 2018s
Boril Karaivanov 2014
Nana Kawakami 2017s
Richard Kegler 2017
David Kelley 2017
Margaret Kelly 2016
Paula Kelly 2010
Russell Kerr 2018s
Joyce Ketterer 2016
Ben Kiel 2014
Satohiro Kikutake 2002
Leslie Kim 2017s
So Yoon Kim 2018lc
Emily Kimbro 2018
Rick King 1993
Sean King 2007
Dmitriy Kirsanov 2013
Amanda Klein 2011
Arne Alexander Klett 2005
Brandon Knap 2018
Akira Kobayashi 1999
Kohki Kobori 2017s
Boris Kochan 2002
Markus Koll 2011
Irina Koryagina 2018
Thomas Kowallik 2010
Dmitry Krasny 2009
Markus Kraus 1997
Stephanie Kreber 2001
Ingo Krepinsky 2013
Bernhard J. Kress 1963lll
Gregor Krisztian 2005
Stefan Krömer 2013
Jan Kruse 2006
John Kudos 2010
Christian Kunnert 1997

Karin Kunori 2017
Dominik Kyeck 2002
Gerry L'Orange 1991lll
Ginger LaBella 2013
Raymond F. Laccetti 1987lll
Karolina Lach 2016
Nicole Lafave 2012
Caspar Lam 2017
Liliana Lambriev 2017
Karen LaMonica 2017
Meredith LaPerch 2017
Brian LaRossa 2011
Amanda Lawrence 2006
Antonio Mejia Lechuga 2018
Eugene Lee 2018s
Hyeona Lee 2017s
Jessica Lee 2016
Pum Lefebure 2006
Troy Leinster 2017
Simon Lemmerer 2016
David Lemon 1995lll
Brian Lemus 2015
Dennis Lenarduzzi 2017
Gerry Leonidas 2007
John Lepak 2017
Autumn Rose Lester 2018s
Mat Letellier 2010
Olaf Leu 1966lll
Aaron Levin 2015
Edward Levine 2017
Kent Lew 2016
Tom Lewek 2018
Siyang Li 2018
Yixue LI 2018s
Sofia Lignos 2017lc
Andrew Lim 2018
Jasper Lim 2017s
Jessica Lin 2017s
Michelle Lin 2017lc
Zenghui Lin 2018s
Armin Lindauer 2007
Sven Lindhorst-Emme 2015
Shadrack Lindo 2018
Domenic Lippa 2004
Caren Litherland 2017
Jason Little 2017x
Maria Little 2017
Wally Littman 1960lll
Richard Ljoenes 2014
Johanna Lobdell 2017
Sascha Lobe 2007
Ralf Lobeck 2007
Margeaux Loeb 2018
Uwe Loesch 1996
Oliver Lohrengel 2004
Utku Lomlu 2016
Xin Long 2017
Ana Lopez 2016ls
Sabrina Lopez 2016
Frank Lottermann 2016
Christopher Lozos 2005
Luke Lucas 2012
Claire Lukacs 2014
Gregg Lukasiewicz 1990
Abraham Lule 2017
Ken Lunde 2011
Annica Lydenberg 2016
Gary Lynch 2017
Kurt Lyons 2018
Bruno Maag 2013
Callum MacGregor 2009
Iain Macmillan 2018
Matt Maghan 2017
Avril Makula 2010
Fouad Mallouk 2017
Daniel Mangosing 2016s
Eduardo Manso 2016
Yi Mao 2017s
Anna Marcelo 2018s
Joe Marianek 2016
Shonna Marquis 2017
Bobby C. Martin Jr. 2011

Frank Martinez 2013
Jakob Maser 2006
Steve Matteson 2017
Scott Matz 2011
Ted Mauseth 2001
Andreas Maxbauer 1995lll
Elizabeth May 2017lc
Cheryl McBride 2009
Trevett McCandliss 2016
Jessica McCarty 2017
Robert McConnell 2017s
Mark McCormick 2010
Rod McDonald 1995
Lawrence McFarland 2017
Thomas McLauglin 2017
Kelly McMurray 2015
Marc A. Meadows 1996lll
Mark Medina 2017
Pablo Medina 2016
Robin Medina 2017lc
Uwe Melichar 2000
Jon Melton 2015
Adrien Menard 2016
Marco Meneghetti 2018s
Trevor Messersmith 2017
Lila Meyer 2018s
Monique Meyer 2018s
Abbott Miller 2010
Chad Miller 2018s
John Milligan 1978ll
Debbie Millman 2012
Michael Miranda 1984
Mary Moffett 2017
Manuel Molinari 2016s
Michael Mondragon 2017
Rachel Mondragon 2017
Sakol Mongkolkasetarin 1995
James Montalbano 1993
Mark Montalbano 2017s
Maria Montes 2017
Ian Montgomery 2017s
Sari Monzer 2017
Jessica Moon 2017
Richard Earl Moore 1982
Wendy Moran 2016s
Wael Morcos 2013
Minoru Morita 1975lll
Diana Mosher 2017
Richard Mosher 2018
Gillian Mothersill 2017
Lars Müller 1997
Joachim Müller-Lancé 1995
Gary Munch 1997
Camille Murphy 2013
Jerry King Musser 1988lll
Mumtaz Mustafa 2017lc
Kenta Nakano 2018
Christof Nardin 2017
Jamie Neely 2013
Titus Nemeth 2010
Mary Nesrala 2017s
Helmut Ness 1999
Christina Newhard 2016
Joe Newton 2009
Vincent Ng 2004
Charles Nix 2000
Stephen Nixon 2015lc
Dirk Nolte 2012
Gertrud Nolte 2001s
Matt Normand 2018
Heidi North 2018
Alexa Nosal 1987lll
Christopher Nova 2018s
Joshua Nychuk 2017
Jan Olof Nygren 2014
Gemma O'Brien 2014
Teresita Olson 2017s
Toshihiro Onimaru 2017
Lloyd Osborne 2017
Robert Overholtzer 1994lll
Aimee Overly 2017
Lisa Overton 2017

Michael Pacey 2001
Juan Carlos Pagan 2015
Maureen Panos 2016
Ryan Paonessa 2017
Amy Papaelias 2008
Niral Parekh 2015
Drew Park 2018
Vivien Park 2017s
YuJune Park 2017
Amy Parker 2016
Jim Parkinson 1994
Lillian Parry 2018lc
Michael Parson 2016
Donald Partyka 2009
Mauro Pastore 2006
Neil Patel 2011
Gudrun Pawelke 1996
Louis Pearlman 2018
Verónica Pedraza 2018
Isabel Urbina Peña 2018
Clara Peres 2017lc
Sonia Persad 2015
Lauren Peters-Collaer 2017
Max Phillips 2000
Stefano Picco 2010
Kate Pickworth 2017s
Ashley Pigford 2017
Estefania Pilatti 2018s
M.Joane Pillard 2017
Ruben Pineda 2017s
Carlos Pion 2018
Charlie Pitcher 2017
Massimo Pitis 2017
Beth Player-DiCicco 2018
Leon Lukas Plum 2015lc
Siri Poarangan 2015
J.H.M. Pohlen 2006
Maciej Polczynski 2016s
Niberca Polo 2016s
Albert-Jan Pool 2000
Yulia Popova 2017s
William Porch 2015
Jean François Porchez 2013
Carolyn Porter 2015
Jason Powers 2017
Nikita Prokhorov 2017
James Propp 1997
Cesar Puertas 2018
Maggie Putnam 2015
Nicholas Qyll 2003s
George Rabot 2018
Jochen Raedeker 2000
Jesse Ragan 2009
Gumpita Rahayu 2017
Erwin Raith 1967lll
Bjorn Ramberg 2016
Jason Ramirez 2016
Steven Rank 2011
Patti Ratchford 2012
Mona Rayachoti 2018s
Kyle Read 2016
Bryon Regej 2018
James Reyman 2005
Dan Rhatigan 2013
Douglas Riccardi 2010
Tamye Riggs 2016
Michael Riley 2016
Phillip Ritzenberg 1997
Jon Robbins 2016
Blake Robertson 2016
Ashley Roca 2017s
Nico Roca 2018
Cory Rockliff 2018
Thomas Rockwell 2014
Neil Rodman 2018
Antonio Rodriguez 2017s
Petra Sucic Roje 2017
Hanim Romainoor 2017
Salvador Romero 1993lll
Anna Ropalo 2017
Kurt Roscoe 1993
Camila Ruiz 2018lc

Nancy Harris Rouemy 2007
Erkki Ruuhinen 1986III
Leigh Ryan 2017s
Carol-Anne Ryce-Paul 2001
Michael Rylander 1993
Penny Sachdeva 2017s
Tala Safie 2017s
Jonathan Sagar 2018
Filiz Sahin 2018s
Mamoun Sakkal 2004
Thomas Sakowski 2016
Richard Salcer 2014
Ilja Sallacz 1999
Ina Saltz 1996
Timothy Samara 2018
Ksenya Samarskaya 2018
Rodrigo Sanchez 1996
Kristyan Sarkis 2018
Leticia Sarmento 2018s
Nathan Savage 2001
Alex Savakis 2017
Hanno Schabacker 2008
Joe Schafer 2017
Paula Scher 2010
Kat Schlich 2018lc
Hermann J. Schlieper 1987III
Holger Schmidhuber 1999
Hermann Schmidt 1983III
Klaus Schmidt 1959III
Bertram Schmidt-Friderichs 1989III
Thomas Schmitz 2009
Elmar Schnaare 2011
Guido Schneider 2003
Sibylle Schneider 2017
Werner Schneider 1987
Amanda Schoenemann 2017
Markus Schroeppel 2003
Eileen Hedy Schultz 1985
Eckehart Schumacher-
  Gebler 1985III
Robert Schumann 2007
Lisa Schwebke 2018
Peter Scott 2002
Yee Seul Jenny Sea 2018
Tre Seals 2017
Ringo R. Seeber 2016
Alessandro Segalini 2015
Brian Seidel 2016s
Erin Senior 2018
Christopher Sergio 2011
Thomas Serres 2004
Charmie Shah 2017lc
Michelle Shain 2012
Ellem Shapiro 2017
Mohammad Sharaf 2014s
Paul Shaw 1987
Benjamin Shaykin 2014
Lauren Sheldon 2017
Graham Shelton 2017
Nick Sherman 2009
David Shields 2007
Daniel Shires 2017s
Philip Shore Jr. 1992III
David Short 2014
Bernardo Siaotong 2016s
David Sieren 2017
Carolyn Siha 2017
Scott Simmons 1994
Mark Simonson 2012
Dominque Singer 2012
Charlotte Chan Siow 2017s
Diamuld Slattery 2017
Fred Smeijers 2016
Elizabeth Carey Smith 2010
Ralph Smith 2016
Tina Smith 2016
Ara Soghomonian 2017
Jan Solpera 1985III
Brian Sooy 1998
Christina Speed 2017
Erik Spiekermann 1988III
Erik Spooner 2017

Konstantin Staebler 2018
Will Staehle 2016
Adriane Stark 2017
Jamie Stark 2017
Steven Stathakis 2017
Rolf Staudt 1984III
Gwendolyn Steele 2015
Olaf Stein 1996
James Stepanek 2017
Charles Stewart 1992
Tara Stewart 2017s
Roland Stieger 2009
Michael Stinson 2014
Clifford Stoltze 2003
Sumner Stone 2011
Nina Stössinger 2015
DJ Stout 2010
William Strew 2018
Ilene Strizver 1988III
Hansjorg Stulle 1987III
Molly Stump 2015
Kelsey Sugg 2017s
Shantanu Suman 2017
Neil Summerour 2008
Dawang Sun 2018
Qian Sun 2017
Derek Sussner 2005
Zempaku Suzuki 1992
Don Swanson 2007
Mark Swimmer 2017s
Paul Sych 2009
Lila Symons 2010
Robin Tagliasacchi 2018
Yukichi Takada 1995
Yoshimaru Takahashi 1996III
Megan Tamaccio 2017
Katsumi Tamura 2003
Trisha Wen Yuan Tan 2011
Tasnima Tanzim 2017s
Jack Tauss 1975III
Pat Taylor 1985III
Pax Taylor 2018s
Shaun Taylor 2015
Michaela Taylor-Becker 2017s
Anthony J. Teano 1962III
Marcel Teine 2003
Eric Thoelke 2010
Doiglas Thomas 2018
Krongporn Thongongarj 2018lc
Jason Tiernan 2014
Eric Tilley 1995
Alexander Tochilovsky 2010
Laura Tolkow 1996
Alex Tomlinson 2017s
Andrea Trabucco-Campos 2016s
Tricia Treacy 2014
Jeremy Tribby 2017
Jakob Trollbäck 2004
Klaus Trommer 2012
Niklaus Troxler 2000
Ling Tsui 2011
Minao Tsukada 2000
Nina Tsur 2016s
Viviane Tubiana 2018
Manfred Tuerk 2000
Natascha Tümpel 2002
François Turcotte 1999
Anne Twomey 2005
Jef Tyler 2017
Andreas Uebele 2002
Diego Vainesman 1991
Oscar Valdez 2017
Patrick Vallée 1999
Jarik van Sluijs 2017
Arlo Vance 2014
Jeffrey Vanlerberghe 2005
Robert Vargas 2015
Richard Vassilatos 2017s
Rozina Vavetsi 2011
Mirko Velimirovic 2016
Valentina Vergara 2018lc
Hagen Verleger 2016s

Juan Villanueva 2013
Christa Vinciquerra 2017s
Danila Vorobiev 2013
Angela Voulangas 2009
Elliot Vredenburg 2017
Emma Wade 2017
Frank Wagner 1994
Oliver Wagner 2001
Allan R. Wahler 1998
Jurek Wajdowicz 1980III
Sergio Waksman 1996
Garth Walker 1992III
Henry Wang 2018s
Emily Wardwell 2017
Katsunori Watanabe 2001
Graham Weber 2016s
Harald Weber 1999
Ivan Webster 2017
Yaquan Wei 2017s
Kathryn Weinstein 2017
Melinda Welch 2017s
Laneen Wells 2017
Craig Welsh 2010
Mariano Werneck 2018
Sharon Werner 2017
Alex W. White 1993
Lutz Widmaier 2018
James Widman 2018
Christopher Wiehl 2003
Michael Wiemeyer 2013
Richard Wilde 1993
James Williams 1988III
Kersten Williams 2018s
Steve Williams 2005
Michelle Winberry 2018
Conny J. Winter 1985III
KC Witherell 2014
Delve Withrington 1997
David Wolske 2017
Chiu Yeung Wong 2017
Jason Wong 2015
Fred Woodward 1995
Annie Wu 2017
Qingyu Wu 2018s
Ping Xu 2017
Wendy Xu 2011
Hui Cheng Ou Yang 2018
Susan Yang 2015
Sylvia Yang 2018
Henry Sene Yee 2006
C.J. Yeh 2017
Munrie Yildiz 2018
Kayci Younger 2017lc
Garson Yu 2005
Yiheng Yu 2017
Noriko Yuasa 2015
Lynne Yun 2018
Xandra Zamora 2017
David Zauhar 2001
Zhao Zeng 2016lc
Oliver Zenger 2017
Evelyn Zhang 2017
Shuo Zhang 2018
Wenting Zhang 2017
Yunying Zhang 2018lc
Yueran Zhao 2018s
Ran Zheng 2017
Yijun Zhu 2016lc
Maxim Zhukov 1996III
Roy Zucca 1969III
Karolina Zuchowski 2017s

CORPORATE MEMBERS
Adobe TypeKit 2014
Bloomberg Businessweek 2017
École de Visuelle Communications 2011
ESPN The Magazine 2016
Grand Central Publishing 2005
OCD | Original Champions of Design 2016
Pentagram Design, New York 2014
School of Visual Arts, New York 2007
St. Martins Press 2017

GENERAL INDEX

TYPE INDEX

THE WORLD'S BEST TYPOGRAPHY

Copyright 2018 by the Type Directors Club
All rights reserved. No part of this book
may be used or reproduced in any manner
whatsoever without written permission
except in the case of brief quotations
embodied in critical articles and reviews.

First Edition
First published in 2018
by Verlag Hermann Schmidt
Gonsenheimer Str. 56
D-55126 Mainz
Phone +49 (0) 6131 / 50 60 0
Fax +49 (0) 6131 / 50 60 80
info@verlag-hermann-schmidt.de
www.typografie.de |
www.verlag-hermann-schmidt.de
facebook: Verlag Hermann Schmidt
twitter + instagram: VerlagHSchmidt

verlag hermann schmidt

Type Directors Club
Carol Wahler
347 West 36 Street
Suite 603
New York, NY 10018
Tel / 212.633.8943
E / director@tdc.org
W / tdc.org
Printed in Lithuania

ACKNOWLEDGEMENTS

The Type Directors Club gratefully
acknowledges the following for
their support and contributions to
the success of TDC64 and 21TDC:

DESIGN
Triboro, Brooklyn

PRODUCTION
Adam S. Wahler
A to A Studio Solutions, Ltd.

EDITING
Dave Baker
Super Copy Editors

JUDGING FACILITIES
Fordham University
Lincoln Center Campus

EXHIBITION FACILITIES
The Cooper Union

CHAIRPERSONS' AND JUDGES' PHOTOS
Catalina Kulczar-Marin

. . . .

TDC64 COMPETITION
(CALL FOR ENTRIES)

Online submission application and
development: adcSTUDIO

Design: Triboro, Brooklyn

Bespoke display typography for
The World's Best Typography, 2018
designed by Triboro.

The principal text typeface used
in *The World's Best Typography, 2018*
is Chivo designed and distributed by
Omnibus-Type

Triboro is the Brooklyn based design duo of Stefanie Weigler and David Heasty. The studio's global client base ranges from artists, to innovative start-ups, to some of the world's largest companies. Recent Triboro projects include a Nike logo for New York City; an experimental phone for Google, identities for the fashion brands Everlane and BLK DNM; restaurant identities for The Standard Hotel; collaborations with artists such as Ai Weiwei and Blonde Redhead; and publications for MoMA and GQ. Triboro has received numerous industry awards including being named one of the ADC Young Guns and "Print" magazine's 20 Under 30. In addition, the studio pursues experimental projects such as Triboro's Wrong Color Subway Map, now in the collection of MoMA.

website: triborodesign.com

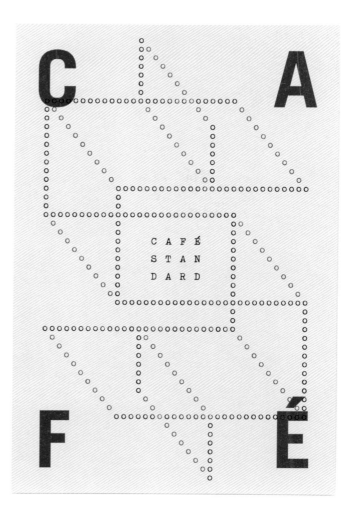

CAFÉ

CAFÉ
STAN
DARD

TYPE OVER HYPE

JO TG

IN THE CLUB

TDC DOT ORG

10876